Urban Lifelines

Cities are now on the front line of dangers associated with the climate crisis, health emergencies, uncontrolled artificial intelligence, escalating warfare, growing authoritarianism and capitalist profligacy. This is especially so for their unprotected populations who, in large numbers, now face a dire future of precarity as powerful elites seek to turn urban assets to their advantage in confronting an uncertain future. For the vast majority of people living in cities, the future is one of foreclosure – a future of dispossession and impoverishment that is lacking a horizon of hope.

What pathways remain open for cities to avert a future of foreclosure for people leading modest lives in modest neighbourhoods? To answer this question, this book looks to the popular practices and knowledges that exist within urban communities and neighbourhoods, finding within them elements that are potentially reparative and curative. Here the engagement with time is different, involving repertoires of horizontal relations, affinities of place and restive knowledge capable of making something out of nothing, of bending adversity towards other goals. Here, rich yet neglected ecologies of urban inhabitation – with all their wiles and improvisations – emerge as the ground of future-making. The book offers a body of concepts to encapsulate this threatened yet resistant urbanism, exemplifies its workings in the streets of Kinshasa, Lagos, Mexico City and Naples, and outlines an infrastructural and aesthetic politics to bring out its potential, thereby enabling another future to shine through urban foreclosure.

Ash Amin is Emeritus 1931 Professor of Geography at the University of Cambridge and Fellow of Christ's College.

AbdouMaliq Simone is Senior Professorial Fellow Emeritus at the Urban Institute, University of Sheffield.

Daniel E. Agbiboa is John and Ruth Hazel Associate Professor of the Social Sciences, and Associate Professor of African and African American Studies, at Harvard University.

Julie-Anne Boudreau is Senior Researcher at the Instituto de Geografía of the Universidad nacional autónoma de México (UNAM).

Filip De Boeck is Professor at the Department of Social and Cultural Anthropology at the University of Leuven.

Enrica Morlicchio is Professor of Economic Sociology at the Federico II University of Naples.

Urban Lifelines

Urban Lifelines

The Future Between Foreclosure and Foreshadowing

Daniel Agbiboa, Ash Amin,
Julie-Anne Boudreau, Filip De Boeck,
Enrica Morlicchio and
AbdouMaliq Simone

polity

First published in 2026 by Polity Press Ltd.

Polity Press Ltd.
65 Bridge Street
Cambridge CB2 1UR, UK

Polity Press Ltd.
111 River Street
Hoboken, NJ 07030, USA

ISBN-13: 978-1-5095-7567-1
ISBN-13: 978-1-5095-7568-8(pb)

A catalogue record for this book is available from the British Library.

Library of Congress Control Number: 2026936027

Typeset in 10.5 on 12 pt Sabon LT Std
Cheshire Typesetting Ltd, Cuddington, Cheshire
Printed and bound in Great Britain by Ashford Colour Ltd

For further information on Polity, visit our website:
politybooks.com

Contents

List of Figures

About the Authors

Daniel E. Agbiboa is the John and Ruth Hazel Associate Professor of the Social Sciences at Harvard University and a Fellow of the Canadian Institute for Advanced Research (CIFAR). He is the author of *People as Protection: Civilians Countering Terror in Northeast Nigeria* (University of Pennsylvania Press, 2026), *They Eat Our Sweat: Transport Labor, Corruption, and Everyday Survival in Urban Nigeria* (Oxford University Press, 2022) and *Mobility, Mobilization, and Counter/Insurgency: The Routes of Terror in an African Context* (University of Michigan Press, 2022).

Ash Amin is Emeritus 1931 Chair of Geography at the University of Cambridge. His books with Polity Press include *Cities: Re-imagining the Urban* (with Nigel Thrift, 2002), *Land of Strangers* (2012), *Seeing Like a City* (with Nigel Thrift, 2017) and *After-Nativism: Belonging in an Age of Intolerance* (2023).

Julie-Anne Boudreau is Senior Researcher at the Institute of Geography of the National Autonomous University of Mexico (UNAM). She was awarded the Sor Juana Inés de la Cruz prize in 2023 for her pioneer transdisciplinary work in Mexico, where she has been living since 2012. Her latest books are *City of Repair: A Street Epistemology of the Future City* (UC Press, forthcoming), *Mujeres*

Habitando la Ciudad. Transgresiones, Apropiaciones y Violencias (IGG-UNAM, 2022) and *Youth Urban Worlds: Aesthetic Political Action in Montreal* (Wiley, 2021).

Filip De Boeck is Professor of Anthropology at the University of Leuven. His books include *Kinshasa: Tales of the Invisible City* (with photographer Marie-Françoise Plissart, 2004) and *Suturing the City: Living Together in Congo's Urban Worlds* (with photographer Sammy Baloji, 2016). Baloji and De Boeck are currently finalizing *The Frontier Files*, a new book and exhibition project on the postcolonial history of Katanga, D.R. Congo.

Enrica Morlicchio is Full Professor of Economic Sociology at the Department of Social Sciences of the University of Naples Federico II. Her books include *Modern Guide on Urban Poverty* (co-edited with Enzo Mingione and David Benassi; Elgar, forthcoming) and *Poverty in Italy: Features and Drivers in a European Perspective* (Policy Press, 2020).

AbdouMaliq Simone is Senior Professorial Fellow Emeritus at the Urban Institute, University of Sheffield, co-director at the Beyond Inhabitation Lab, Polytechnic University of Turin, and Visiting Professor at the Federal University of Bahia. His most recent book is *The Surrounds: Urban Life Within and Beyond Capture* (Duke University Press, 2022).

Preface

This book is an attempt to manifest new practices of what Roberto Esposito has called 'communing' – a way of being with the world as it simultaneously gathers, expels, interweaves and separates. All are inextricable practices, some ascendant, some dormant, some visible, and others invisible. But all are present no matter how they are acknowledged. The book considers those points where territories, assemblages and institutions attempt to go beyond their familiar ways of operating to have some kind of traction in the larger worlds in which they operate and intersect. Such traction would seem to require a space of active translation where divergent actors, by attempting to convey what they stand for and what they do in a language available to another party, exceed the image of themselves that they attempt to translate.

This effort takes place in a time where the prevailing world order of the past half century is being dismantled – not in any systematic or judicious way, but in multiple and competing acts of coercion, amplifying anti-blackness, the expendability of entire populations, and indifference to law and human care. While there are many possible analyses of the current conjuncture – with inflated alarm and celebration across a widening chasm of political sentiment – all we have relied upon in terms of urban analysis and practice faces marked limitations, and whose incisiveness increasingly pales in the face of the instrumental use of turbulence and uncertainty as a predominant form of rule.

The authors of this book live in different countries across the world. In each, the increase in fear and anxiety is palpable; across institutions, people are hesitant to express their concerns, feelings and ideas. Public health programmes are collapsing, infrastructural projects are put on hold, urban services budgets contract, surveillance intensifies, and plunder – of people's resourcefulness – is rampant. Contemporary conditions exceed any simple application of existing urban theorization. While it is certainly possible to find some viable application in the legacies of existent conceptualization, what is seemingly unique about the present is a lack of preparedness for confronting urban futures, an inability of any institution to think effectively about planetary conundrums, and the exigency to engage in deliberations where the very process of imagination and invention is to be protected. This requires practices of sharing, cooperation and enquiry that must be rearticulated anew, and take precedence over deliberations that often veer towards academic posturing.

So, this book is an effort to use words to enliven the sensorium. For the contemporary sensorium is subject to, indeed is made subject by, an oscillation of power surges and outages, glitches and arrhythmias. It alternates from the faintest detections of sentiment to gross exaggerations of feeling, from indifference to the seemingly most alarming of occurrences to extreme passions over the slightest incidences. The inclinations to easy vengeance, the facile declarations of self-grandeur, the insistence on an equilibration of all events regardless of context or otherwise marked differences in valuation seem to dominate the behavioural field of everyday life. Everything becomes remarkable, worthy of documentation or dispute, while at the same time, tectonic shifts in both physical and social landscapes appear no more important than a casual weather report exchanged between strangers.

Take an incapacity to 'see'. On the one hand, there is a blindness occasioned by the dissipation of framing, or, more precisely, by a weakened capacity to 'figure'.

Figuring is often construed as a process of things 'closing in on themselves', of accentuating the distinction between figure and ground through which the outlines of a stable entity might be construed: stable in the sense that we might come to know what to expect of it, that is rendered in a form recognizable through multiple iterations, that holds 'its own' amidst conflicting expectations.

Yet figuring entails coming up with ways of envisioning the world in its multitudes, to invent a schema that enables a person to discern relationship with that which surrounds them, to compose a field of relationalities that enable both the individuations of otherwise undifferentiated matters and a grammar of connectivity among the subsequent entities. It is a thingness coming into the world whose forcefulness is prior to meaning, and which reinvents affect, sensation, thought and imagination. It enables individuals to engage and live through concrete images and events that intrude upon them, turning the seemingly determined course of history into an open possibility of common causes and complementarity. Otherwise, life's emplacement becomes too diffuse and boundless, like Tim Morton's notion of the hyper object – something too big to grasp, to orient oneself to, or to have a sense of what is going on. How then does one account for what is happening to oneself, to invent a narrative that enables a sense of continuity and a basis for decision?

In such circumstances the inclination is to depend on the banal markers of difference, where attributes and actions are reduced to oversimplified stereotypes; where no matter what an 'other' does or conveys they are always already seen as the projection of the observer's gaze. Subsequently occluded are all of the myriad of details that infuse everyday life with shifting and granular textures, which are the incitement to singular feelings and a heightened potential to instantiate oneself in the various cracks of time and space that open up when a person forgets to repeat a familiar action or accidentally walks down a new street or encounters something impossible to look away from.

Instead, action reverts to extraction and plunder – to take, to seize, to kill. To eliminate from the scene not only the elements used to support or elaborate life, but the potentials of inventive composition where heterogeneous backgrounds, practices and things are brought together to create something unprecedented or long thought vanquished. They – whatever 'they' might be in a particular instance – are thus not 'us'. It is an 'us' that comes to be nothing but the mode of defence towards an outside, which is never an outside since it is constantly mobilized to provide a range of 'services', from slave labour to embodying the dangerous excesses and uncertainties that cannot be thought to maintain the ability of a self to believe in its own individual existence.

Anti-blackness, now infused with a massive dosage of steroids issued as governmental agendas, rebounds as the predominant modality of sense-making, and thus the blindness that characterizes how we (do not) see. Take the ever-growing hysteria around migration as migrant bodies, reduced to rabid adherents to antediluvian religious passions, ineligible aspirants to viable livelihoods, or monsters intent upon ravaging white bodies. There is a generalized inability to see how the spreading out of the 'black world' – a more precise designation for the euphemistic 'global south' – indicates not only the ramifications of enduring colonial plunder but also a determination to make a viable life anywhere, with a conviction that one belongs anywhere, and that anywhere embodies the possibilities promised by any cultural cosmology or practice. Any location on the earth is deeply connected to any other, but also sufficiently separate that these relations must always be recomposed. Meanwhile, Europeans and Americans are for the most part just not able to see the diversities of migrant life and the ways in which the majority of urban areas have been and are being shaped by the albeit sometimes fraught capacities of migrants to not only eke out livelihoods but also to compose new territories and sensibilities. At the same time, they maintain relationships across fragmented terrain and great distances.

An increasingly larger proportion of the world is on the move. Running towards and away. Colliding, circumventing, the terrain is increasingly fractured everywhere, with a plethora of threats, friends who are enemies, and enemies who are friends. Indeed, enmity has become a pervasive form of insurance, of keeping friends and strangers on the backfoot, as if debilitating the manoeuvrability of others is a way of guaranteeing some limited space of personal operations.

Yet as music demonstrates, resplendent and sometimes jarring mixtures in an incessant practice of borrowing and improvisation are inevitable. They rattle, shake, grate, soothe, unsettle and enliven. Something infectious gets through; everything is contaminated, transgressed, haunted and carried away. How therefore do we see again, see that which falls in between indifference and exaggeration, faint signals and boisterous declarations? This book, then, is an attempt to restore the details and also offer ideas for nurturing the incipient potentials of all those persons and things reaching outwards in anticipation of touches that might, just might, make them feel like something else besides whatever they have been trained, condemned, coerced or seduced to be.

Acknowledgements

This book comes from sustained collaboration that would not have been possible without the sponsorship of the Canadian Institute for Advanced Research (CIFAR). The authors are Fellows of CIFAR's programme Humanity's Urban Future, working as a sub-group on how a future for cities might be imagined from the daily habits of their residents, now facing all manner of onslaught on their lives and livelihoods. Our work has greatly benefited from conversation with the Programme's other Fellows and advisers, and CIFAR's unstinting commitment to free thought and its generosity of time and resources.

Introduction

Kinshasa's residents, shut out from the city's resources and without the means to get by, are turning to holes in the street to rest, copulate and barter, and to graveyards, abandoned buildings and substances to find some form of escape. War, economic collapse and climate breakdown threaten further. In Mexico City, old revolutionary obligations to the poor are being tested by Trump's tariff assaults, the city's water crisis, uncontrolled gentrification and narcopower, leaving people marking time in faith, flight and improvisation. Outside Naples, the tolerant city that in seafaring and opposition to Northern Italian rule has always lived with difference, Europe's largest concentration of West Africans passes unrecognized, exploited in the fields and sex dens, and racially abused, while making their own culture and community to find joy. In Lagos, coastal communities once left alone in their informal settlements are being pushed out by elite waterfront developments in the name of climate mitigation, their homes torn down and their livelihoods from the sea taken away, but in having nowhere else to go, somehow they regroup, foraging further, building alliances, keeping faith.

In these four cities that feature in this book, populations are being remaindered by the combination of worsening existential circumstances, institutional and infrastructural negligence, and shameless colonization of the urban fabric by those with means and power. For them the future is barred in urban reappropriation, forcing new ways of enduring its foreboding threats. These shifts of displacement and reoccupancy, of meeting the future in different ways, are common across the urban landscape: varying in balance and intensity, but true to countless cities across the world. They need naming and their imbalances need correction. Urban dwellers in their billions are being assaulted by climate crises, capitalist profligacy, deepening inequality and impoverishment, health emergencies, uncontrolled artificial intelligence, and escalating warfare and authoritarianism. The threats are large, persistent and plural, increasingly difficult to anticipate and address, one following the other before any new normal can settle. In these conditions of permanent instability and exposure to hazard and risk, city dwellers confront a shifting horizon only constant in its threats. Broken is any old promise of the urban future as a reversal of past trials, urban settlement as a means to prosperity and wellbeing, time tamed by collective infrastructures and institutions and governance in the common interest. The watchwords of urban existence in the North are becoming copies of those long seen in the South: majority exposure to precarity, want, foreclosure, displacement. The lines of life are being cut by global escalations exhausting urban capacity, but there are also significant power asymmetries at work.

Urban capture has become a means by power to extend its reach in the unfolding turbulence. A predatory logic lies behind today's slum clearances, acts of gentrification, financialization and enclosure of land, privatization of public and welfare services, narratives of deserving and undeserving subjects, elite capture of institutions and infrastructures, technological surveillance of people, habitats and operating systems, and mergers of algorithmic, expert and governmental intelligence. At the apex of urban power have formed coalitions of corporations, developers, elites, planners and politicians colonizing urban value, normalizing the double-speak of self-serving returns as prudent urban management, and shutting out majorities from urban assets, infrastructures and circuits of social reproduction. The fate of those without means is to face the inhospitable future through the hit and miss of self-help, through a vain hope that a political economy of general wellbeing will make an appearance. Life in informal settlements, working-class neighbourhoods, rundown suburbs and faraway peripheries increasingly rests on local arrangements of reciprocity, informal connection, familiarity with place and a cobbled-together social infrastructure – just when global hazard and risk and urban predation are on the rise.

These very arrangements are being threatened by acts of slum clearance and gentrification sanitizing local informalities. What will remain of the balance between abjection and regrouping after these acts needs to be understood, especially if there is to be no enabling outside. There may be clues offered by the many remaindered neighbourhoods of cities in the South and the North, where the settled poor and new arrivals have long had to respond to denial and displacement. However forced, they seem to regroup by cobbling together shelter and infrastructure, making connections to improvise and seek, coming together in adversity, and responding to foreclosure without losing hope and initiative. The regrouping is always without guarantees, and fraught with duress, but persistent. The neighbourhoods and their social practices have a texture that meets looming threats of hazard and dispossession with some agency. What this is, how it might survive today's crisis-induced predations, how it bends the linearities of foreclosure, and how it may encourage a more reparative urbanism are the concerns of this book. Looking past a formal politics of equitable preparedness increasingly obstructed by today's impulses of authoritarian urban governance, the book turns to the molecular grain of remaindered spaces for signs of another way of addressing the inhospitable future.

To put the huge threats of contemporary urban foreclosure in conversation with the small acts of survival in remaindered spaces might seem strange, but these spaces and their ways are now ubiquitous. This is the outcome of power's reworking of the urban. The molecular is no longer the small, but instead a vast territory of popular organization turned into necessity to negotiate the future. Its dynamics of time and organization need better understanding for this scalarity, but also because there are few other vantage points of possibility. In the urban foreshadows there are ways, words and sensibilities of living the future through the given present that are analytically and politically significant. They work in and through cruel optimism and dashed hope, setbacks that perpetuate misery and desperation, the violence of strongmen and tricksters preying on vulnerability, broken infrastructures and institutions, the exhausting demand for improvisation that only yields so much. They warrant no false romance, yet offer their dispositions of artisanship, anticipation and foregoing for consideration. They offer the relations of surface – things in the here and now of inhabitation – whose incipience is made to count.

Of interest in these relations is a double blackness of removal and refusal, of subjugation to and circumvention of disjunctive time and of power's plans. Within this duality hovers the potential of another urbanism, another engagement with time that responds to the spectre of threat by altering it through the immediacies of the moment, the legacy of continuous adjustment to adversity, and lived ways of drawing in the horizon that mix apprehension and purpose. Time is rendered durational in its inhabitation, a perpetual dance of trying and failing, anticipating and adjusting, staying and fleeing, suffering and enduring, losing heart and finding joy. The intended temporality of foreclosure and radical newness is borne experientially in the improvisations of the moment, through skills passed down or accumulated in adversity, in connections made with others out of authority's control, and through a full spectrum of senses unflattened by brutalization. In the urban shadows, time as clearance meets lived time, and is altered by its 'untimeliness', in the way Giorgio Agamben (2009) writes of 'contemporariness' as a defiant already and not yet that moderates sequentiality. In the urban remainders, the future is met differently.

The intention of this book is to name and valorize the character of this contemporariness in spaces of remaindered life: to reconsider how such spaces – many and ubiquitous – enter into the future from the encounters with time in all its uncertainties, durational histories of subjugation, and improvisations in the now to tentatively reach for the future. It offers a set of new conceptual categories close to practices on the ground of edge existence never fully vanquished by the thrust of power, which make visible dualities of life denial and reassertion that remain systematically ignored, but wherein lie the traces of another, reparative urbanism that has no need for heroics of future-making by design, but which works up, expands and communes with extant practices of care formed in the permanence of denial and castigation. The book delves into the formative depths of remaindered urban spaces – into the edge between nothingness and somethingness where habitation practices of a particular kind exist, arising in momentary sutures of habitat, techne and sociality. In various forms of incompleteness and uncertainty arise dispositions towards the future based on reading the surface of the surrounds.

The primary task of the book is to offer a conceptual vocabulary and sensory aura of the precepts of urban habitation at the edge – largely left unconsidered, residualized or reductively treated in the literature on urban futures – by which another way of city making that is artisanal, reparative and collaborative can be given traction. We argue that in habitats of ruination, underplanning and opacity, where incompleteness of one sort or another is the condition of existence, the future forms in the cracks of the sidewalk, in the shadows of probability and plan, where circumstances make for knowledges of incipience – that is, the orientations of gathering and steering in the present that enable initiatives and experiments to make their mark in always unguaranteed ways. We call this an incipience of foreshadowing, a continual attempt to muster heterogeneous time, play the ambiguities of city life, stay constantly in movement to make territory and opportunity, perceive through the flesh lines of life, work through improbability by traversing geographies, making interfaces and communing with the unseen (pragmatically, sensually and virtually), and turn forced foregoing into an art of stillness, an indifference to perfection, plan, progress, and even to the intentions of power. In intimacies of place, never pristine technologies and lateral connections between familiar others are mobilized, states of suspension are negotiated, practices of switching and traversing are learnt to extend the surface of possibility, depths of the city's underbelly are scoured, and repertoires of refusal and parallel existence are produced.

In developing a language to grasp incipience in the urban foreshadows, our aim is not to diminish the weight and tests of suffering in remaindered spaces, but instead to acknowledge a livingness – a form of knowing without knowing – apprehending a future offering few signs through embodied repertoires of the kind listed above. This livingness – we want to argue – is a pre-cognitive form of knowing offering new directions of thinking and organizing urban futures. Ways are found through a popular epistemics honed in ontological opacity and disjunction harnessing people, infrastructures, street technologies and vernacular knowledges, one operating as a sensorium feeling its way through what may come next and how it must be met. Knowing is a tentative feel drawing on body memory, divination, magic and music, discrepant vocabularies and narratives, signs in the urban fabric, and haptic and aural skills – all extending the ecology of the mind. It is a mode of knowing through living quite at odds with the knowing of plans, expertise, scenarios and data scanning. It arises as a necessity to find ways through the epistemic foreclosures of growing urban command and control.

An important aim of this book, then, is to name and argue the case for this epistemics of livingness in duress. We call it – and propose – blackness as a method of negotiating the simultaneity of being both nothing and everything, a historic condition black people have long endured, and which now confronts swathes of poor – arrival and settled – communities as well as popular neighbourhoods being stripped of the right to the city and having to rely on crafts of inhabiting inhospitable ground. Our claim is that in this simultaneity, the resolutions of blackness are those of improbable knowing that is indifferent to perfection or annihilation, oscillates between diffidence and refusal to face fungibility, relies on the haptic, aural and sensorial for guidance, attunes to flashes of possibility, and inhabits the uncertainties of time and contingency as a kind of edge sensibility without expectation. We argue that this improbable knowing operates as a technicity of environmental adjustment, relying on reading surface mnemonics, working incomplete infrastructures, making calculations and developing agendas that are never singular or consolidated, and assembling what is at hand within an unconscious of owing or expecting nothing. It is a technicity of knowing in the dark with heterogeneous wiles and ways to bear but also defy ascribed fungibility.

Blackness, incipience, foreshadowing, contemporariness, and other keywords of inhabitation and knowing developed in this book are intended as an opening into urban worlds – remaindered spaces – that lie at the heart of an unfolding future of foreclosure. Our argument is that these worlds reveal the tragedies of popular disarmament and denial, but also the outline of another way with deep roots of making something in nothing through attuned inhabitation, surface scanning and associational alliances. In them lies the promise of making the urban future based on urban repair and black waywardness. With the right kind of synthesis, affective capture and political mobilization, they show that in the urban contemporary lie other ways of responding to the hazardous future: ways that might lack the power to meet the force of the predatory biopolitics riding today's polycrises, but not the signs – in the already here – of what a counterpush could look like. The ambition of the book is to propose the future from the remaindered urban, where time is made differently as endurant residue. It will come to matter more and more as digital, institutional and oligarchic incursions leave traces of possibility in spaces where power has deemed life to be surplus to requirement.

The first chapter names the trials of urban future-making by foreclosure – the various ways in which cities at risk are being reorganized by and for those with power and influence – and by foreshadowing – popular organization beyond probability and plan based on practices and knowledges of incipience. The chapter sets out concepts that help to explain how shadowed places enter into the future. Developing notions of incipience, surfacing and anticipation, it shows how the opacity and parsimony of the future are tackled through forms of alertness and care in the present riding urban ambiguity. These are forms of negotiating heterogeneous and uncertain time, dwelling in the ambiguities of city life, interfacing, narrating and steering in the present through improvisations and initiatives that leave their mark, and gathering available material and alliances to see what may come to pass. Illustrating these forms and their apprehensive logics, the chapter shows how the future – through these dispositions – forms in the flesh lines of inhabitation, is turned into enduring movement, and grounded in the present as heterogeneous time.

The next four chapters delve into different settings of urban duress, taking up the vocabulary set out and strengthening it with terms proposed from each context. Chapter 2 explores the ways in which the deathscapes of generalized violence in Congo's primary cities such as Kinshasa, through environmental degradation, extreme poverty, infrastructural and welfare failure, and abuses of power, are negotiated by the dispossessed. It describes how flights of fantasy, faith and magic, metaphors of hunting and foraging, cults of death and depravity, sensibilities of endurance and resistance, and practices of improvisation meet the finalities of foreclosure. They do so always on the back foot, yet recurrently. Adopting Congolese philosopher Valentin Yves Mudimbe's notion of *reprendre* ('to resume'), the chapter explores the nature of this returning and its engagement with the future, its timeframe of instantaneous capture and limit experience on the edge, that permits speculation on new forms of 'in-commoning' and living together emerging were Kinshasa to reconnect with the deep eco-time of the Congo River.

In chapter 3, the focus falls more decidedly on foreclosure's suffocations in Lagos, prompted by aggressive moves by developers and politicians to oust locals from waterfront slums for lucrative real estate speculations. The chapter describes the eviscerations of a new narrative of 'world citiness' and climate-change resilience involving the gentrification of vast swathes of waterfront areas resulting in the destruction of their informal settlements and fisher livelihoods. The old has been 'unfutured' and 'unpeopled' as though inconsequential. The chapter is a sober illustration of what can happen when the logic of clearance shuts down remaindered space, but it also finds traces of return, if not from the trampled ground, then from fishers finding new waters, residents renarrating displacement, journalists exposing the violence aided by legal cases, and youths elsewhere in the city and beyond condemning austerity. The faintest possibility of a coalition refuting an unpeopled future lingers.

Chapter 4 focuses on migrant unrecognition in an area north of Naples in Italy. Its operative term is 'suspension', a long state of inhabiting illegality, abuse and abjection, in which migrants have made time and space in fugitive survival. This making has been socially differentiated in Castel Volturno, a settlement on the coast above Naples marked by criminality, decline, illicit trade and hard agricultural work where West African migrants, displaced Neapolitans and an original population cohabit uneasily. In abandonment and segregation, the arrival communities have formed textured ecologies of inhabitation. The West African population has come through the early years of explicit racial violence and sexual slavery, and continues to be denied rights and stigmatized, but in time has been able to reap the benefits of cohabitation, shared faith and culture, and helping each other. Similarly, displaced Neapolitans living in the abandoned villas of Castel Volturno have dared to squat and pirate services, form community in illegality, and live in the nostalgia of happier days when NATO was still in the locality, but face erasure from unannounced evictions. Texture in suspension has brought fragile hope for Africans, but only cruel precarity for displaced Neapolitans.

Chapter 5 centres on extendability – the force of social imagination – in negotiating foreclosure. It does so through three examples in Mexico City of other-worlding helping to simulate movement and direction: an aesthetics of living with the dead to tap into an ancient energy; shifts in the built environment to benefit from digital nomadism; and uses of hallucinogenic mushrooms, cacao rituals and herbal medicine as a form of therapy. The chapter argues that the impossibility to plan, project or prepare for a future in a city where state capacity and resources just do not allow it renders the present opaque. Yet, this endless present is not a thick fog that makes movement impossible, because the other-worlding extends the horizon, making room for practical adjustment, multidimensional existence and social instincts of maintenance and repair. Extendability allows people to inhabit 'elsewhere', and merge the material, ghostly and memorialized to expand the stilled present. A livingness beyond the body, as Simondon might put it, has opened a pathway.

Chapter 6 discusses the connotations of seeing the future through the vocabularies of remaindered spaces. It reproposes urban time as an untimely and durational contemporariness that disrupts its projection as sequential, showing how residues, technicities, dispositions and stories linger even in spaces of abandonment. From this reinterpretation, the chapter considers the ways in which the forms and words of popular response to foreclosure identified in this book can be given traction. It outlines a politics of infrastructural enablement in remaindered spaces, parainstitutional organization (following Brian Massumi) to flexibly gather, connect and amplify within them anarchist energies, and aesthetic efforts to make public their repertoires of care and repair. The chapter argues this politics of the margins is anything but marginal as a new technopolitics of urban preparedness silences other forms of expertise and formal opposition.

The final chapter returns to the epistemics of foreshadowing: how things get to be known, and how this knowledge should be named. The political amplifications outlined in chapter 6 are not straightforward, as a matter of simply making the invisible seen and heard. There are also implications of method, concerning the distinctions of ground knowhow and its uses, and where these distinctions take conventions of urban analysis and writing. The final chapter describes the modulations of knowing in a historic condition of being nothing and something as blackness, a vernacular of non-arrival and navigation of the edge of fundamental ambiguity that requires knowledge, language and sentience to convert the deleterious into a way of being in the world. It presents the edge – the border between abjection and survival, the now and the near future, the deterred and still to be realized – as a redemptive space in which flight and fugitivity form in heterogeneous inclinations of refusal, sensoria of autonomy, narratives of journey, and extensions of knowledgeability into the mythic, ghostly and virtual. There are edge repertoires that words on paper seamlessly pieced together in conventional scholarly writing on urban futures fail to capture.

I
Foreshadowing the Future*

Instead of just thinking about urban futures, what might it mean to urbanize the future? Such a proposition would seem to reveal something ungraspable in both terms, 'urbanize' and 'future' – something about urbanization that goes beyond its usual purviews, and the same for the future as well. In its simplest sense, urbanizing the future would entail a continuous intersection and agglomeration of temporalities that go beyond simply stating that the city is a domain of many different times. It would upend linear trajectories, recursivity, temporal collapse and immanence to become a complex inter-relay of various measures, sensibilities and projections. It would entail a black practice that anticipates a wide range of dispositions and scenarios that are not just 'to come' but may already be present without the capacity to be recognized. Or, in another sense, that which must remain unrecognized, for now.

As for the future to be urbanized: this would assume something already available to be worked on; something worked on that could shift gears at any moment, refuse all probability or prophecy. Yet either way, in the recognizable culmination of all the work put into it or its sudden refusals of that work, new pathways for living are opened for those prolific and diverse gatherings of bodies and things that make up the urban. We call this process *incipience*, i.e.

* Drafted by AbdouMaliq Simone.

a process of gathering and steering a 'knowing before knowing' – before empirical verification, before semantic assuredness – across different geographies, situations and institutions that enable them to exceed the terms of their own self-recognition and present functions. The objective of the chapter here is not so much to foresee the possible contents of urban futures but rather to think through a range of tactical practices that enable initiatives, experiments and positionalities of such incipience to leave their mark; to urbanize the future. As Zeiderman and Dawson (2022) caution:

> We urge urbanists to question the teleological inevitability of the 'urban' and to remain open to future visions emanating from outside their purview – that is, from beyond the urban world, however defined. We believe this is especially necessary at a historical moment in which the urban future is radically uncertain, given ecological and epidemiological concerns of a global nature – concerns that force us to contend with the possibility that the city as we know it may be threatening the future survival of humanity. (p. 276)

In contrast to the contemporary preoccupation with ensuring sustainable futures in face of unprecedented planetary conditions, our concerns with the future here are directed towards the amplification of practices of care in the present. That no matter what happens, addressing the future becomes primarily a way of generating and abiding with tactics of nurturance – not as an exhibition of fundamental human values, but rather the deployment of a wily intelligence cognizant of the violence that underpins human progress and, as such, aimed at tricking our worst instincts and evading our often exhausted attachments to identity, house, profession or nation. This chapter will explore the various concepts and practices needed to deploy such intelligence.

The City as the Witch

First let's consider all the ways in which the urban tricks us into thinking of it in ways that perhaps it is not. How might such trickery be harnessed for other ends? Instead of a process of constant development – the city as a harbinger of good things to come – the city is the 'witch', as Pentecostals would likely call it. It is a force that has long cultivated almost inextricable attachments to an array of promises and social imaginaries, holding out the promise of multiple possible futures. Around any corner might be found the conditions of a new life. In a world of constant furtive glances, one glance held beyond the accepted protocol might open entirely unanticipated histories. Yet the capacity of the city to act as a promising machine – its dependence on fossil fuels, on deeper excursions into financial abstraction and financializing the virtual potentials of interoperable relations among innumerable variables, and the relegation of majority populations to more precarious forms of accumulation – renders it a 'witch'. Inhabitants are knowingly seduced, caught in a spellbinding desire for excess which, at times, includes destruction.

Contemporary black abolitionist movements rightly identify the 'city' – its logics of agglomeration, the subsumption of liveliness to systems of valuation, and its punitive approach to waywardness – as the embodiment of all that needs to be abolished. Their adamancy presents the conundrum: if we continue to live in the city, then destruction seems immanent; but if we abolish the city, then where do we live? Part of the trap lies in the terms of the question itself. 'Where' will we live, rather than 'how' will we live – as if the 'where' will take care of the 'how'. In fact, urban analyses of all kinds have found themselves stuck in such a conflation, thinking largely about locational advantages and spatial appropriateness. For example, selections of residential locations are often made based on assuming possibilities of self-regulation, a kind of cybernetic ideal of optimality that ensues less from what one does and more from where one is situated. This is the premise of the so-called 15-minute city.

In many cities, residence in specific neighbourhoods immediately disqualifies a person from consideration for employment or access to specific educational institutions. If someone is demeaned for coming from the 'other side of the tracks', this points to ways in which 'tracks' themselves are used to bound specific ways of living in distinction from others. Here, tracks function less as an infrastructure of connection and more as a gradation of value. On the other hand, the preoccupation with 'where' one is located tends to occlude the ways in which zones of purported 'normalcy' and quietude become bastions of domestic pathology. They elide the violence that is expended to guarantee their placid surface demeanours, just as stigmatized zones often implicitly inflate the stereotypical criminal behaviours for which they are known to provide a protective sheath to all those acts of care and generosity that sustain local life.

Locations obviate attention to the 'how' by being representations of needs – this place needs better infrastructure, or policing, or employment. Needs are often identified through statistical indices, the constitution of a population in aggregate. While such surveying is often useful, the pathways to an image of a median often obscure the intricate oscillations of gain and loss, of decisions and expenditures revised, of alternating periods of turbulence and calm that then 'average' themselves out in some representative number. Instead of place as some kind of preset formula, it is the interweaving of different 'hows' that composes space, and the built environment is a materialization of such interweaving. It is all the ways in which greeting, selling, gossiping, making, trading, tending, retreating, resting, eating, playing and administering make room for themselves amidst a multiplicity of claims and uses.

Concomitantly, the city has also been a locus of continuous repurposing: graveyards as places for sexual encounters, the street as a place of sales, the automobile as a place of inhabitation, the flat as a factory or space of commercial storage. Urban inhabitants often find themselves ensconced in places not of their own choosing. They then pursue idiosyncratic practices of momentarily settling in, inscribing a fold into landscapes that do not so much become private property but are inscriptions in an elongated and ongoing story being 'told' by a landscape. A landscape is thus a specific way of witnessing all that has and is taking place. This concerns the way in which urban built environments are partly a play of and on surfaces that can be ruptured and redirected but which remain unbounded. One thing leads to another across multiple story lines, in trajectories that the story of how specific built environments got the way they are can't fully account for. Just think of all of the chase movies across urban rooftops and streets.

Yet urbanization seems to persist with the production of 'destinations': each registering more synergistic relations, wider access to services and amenities; each curtailing the need to expose oneself to other territories and events in the larger urban context, while, at the same time, providing opportunities to be 'a part of the globalized world'. What is promised here is time freed to develop oneself in alignment with continuous enhancement of individual skill and the opportunity to live in conditions analogous to all of those other 'successful' inhabitants near and far. The irony about such destinations is that they could be anywhere, that the specificity of their location doesn't matter, for what is desired is this very appearance of being anywhere – where history doesn't count. For many, then, the ultimate location is an effacement of location: it is possible to live a 'global lifestyle' anywhere, if it is sufficiently sealed off from the troubling territories – those of the poor and working classes – that characterize the bulk of many cities.

While many of these 'anywheres' end up relying on highly localized practices and economies to ensure their ongoing viability, the kind and degree of their dependence are largely obscured in the ways in which their governance remains the purview of management companies that are themselves mired in thick opacity. Here, it is often difficult to identify the location of ownership as well as who is responsible for attending to what matters. In the troubling zones, things get done largely as a matter of negotiation and multiple tradeoffs, where important functions and responsibilities rarely have a fixed designated location but must be assumed in tandem with a shifting set of characters. Not everything can be addressed in the same way or with the same affordances, and so there are intermixtures of seizure, withdrawal, repair, decay, parasitism, generosity, transparency and secrecy to make an array of livelihoods, buildings and aspirations remain in tune with each other.

People will not do the same things, and even while their households and persons may be eminently locatable to neighbours and other figures, what they do to contribute to this attunement, in addition to keeping their heads above water, is not always easy to locate. So, the city acts as the witch in part because it overvalues the location of the body as the critical potentiality – click your heels twice Dorothy and you can be taken back to Kansas. Also, this witchcraft is like Zeno's paradox, i.e. there are some who see the arrow leaving its quiver but never arriving; and others who attend to the arrival without seeing the departure, so that the arrow is in an eternal freeze frame, always at rest, always in-between in motion. Affliction and possession in witchcraft are the results of in-between motions. For the magic is the connection of arrows to a source and a destination without bothering about the character of the middle traversed. The city, then, is both the curse and the cure, and the act of sorcery here is the conversion of one to the other without anything else seeming to have been altered.

The city seems to fulfil its part of the bargain by always showing something new, guaranteeing a successful profit on prophecy. But that new arrives already 'old' in many respects, cognizant of its temporariness, and so the speeds at which things are undone come to exceed those that would contribute something perhaps truly reparative. At the same time, the city piles up, like Benjamin's beleaguered angel, with more and more things and situations that need to be abolished, which hang on tenaciously to our antediluvian pretences to glory, no matter how decimated our circumstances might be. What do we do with the witch? Do we reveal it for what it is, i.e. a sleight of hand, an interminable card game? Or do we redirect its apparent magic for more judicious ends? And if so, how?

Removal

The answer to these questions has much to do with whose future is to be urbanized? Who will be left to entertain a future, as certain inhabitants across the world are being 'absented' from the process of future-making altogether? While it is perhaps of little use to compare today's often wholesale 'removal' of urban populations from the present with other eras, the disposability of inhabitants from the present is now extensive. This disposability takes many forms: from the actual genocide of entire peoples, the exhumation of ancient historical spirits that haunt inhabitants into a state of near terror, the undermining of the cultural frameworks through which a people were able to identify a sense of belonging and commonality, to the selective culling of particular kinds of persons deemed ineligible for life or public participation, and the zombification of persons through exposure to severe trauma and deprivation. There is also the curation of 'strange' persons, barely recognized as humans or so excessively transgressive as to be unrecognizable, through having to navigate intensely weird situations beyond the ken of available interpretations and reason. Here immiseration is less a by-product of prevailing practices of economic growth and more an instrument of debilitation and elimination, sometimes exceeding premature exposure to early death (Gilmore, 2007). It constitutes a substantiation of death within life, a lively death, with bodies which barely survive or survive resplendently as quasi-mystical forces, soldiers of the night, or renegades beyond redemption.

These dispositions are both the next stop and the refused stop of an expanding and youthful urban precariat faced with the absolute provisionality of livelihood, the escalating costs of urban living, the limits of woefully overburdened extended families, and the growing indifference and incapacities of states and other institutions to provide any sense of anchorage. In urban economies based on using available money to not only make more money but to monetize a fuller range of gestures and transactions – both in ordinary life and in the curation of extraordinary encounters – those without access to even the capacity to make minimal investments face little choice but to weaponize their desperation.

In Lagos, long renowned for its chaos, entrepreneurial drive, aggressive style and sheer intensity and size, recent years have witnessed inordinate displays of wealth, cultural creativity and middle-class consumption. This has ushered in intricate games of demonstrating access to money when there is little actually on the table, of cultivating cults of style, seduction and arrays of pyramid schemes, where access to specific locations – restaurants, clubs, bars, shopping malls, marinas, residential communities – connotes a 'seriousness' that can be parlayed into more concrete money-making opportunities. Social media become an extended platform of impression creation, instigations and lures where one exerts 'influence', and influence is instrumentalized into exposure and cash (Adeniyi-Ogunyankin, 2024). There is a constant sense of immediacy because configurations of influence and valorized style always move on: one must consolidate some kind of position, and 'cash out', because prolonged participation in this game tends towards an accelerated depreciation of energy and resources.

But for those who have no access to such a 'playing field', the desperate will line the main thoroughfares, quivering with anger, pleading not so much for money, but rather exhibiting themselves as 'the' crisis – a performance now often abetted by the availability of drugs and pharmaceuticals everywhere. From cities where the lessons of self-sufficiency in face of scarcity and imperial domination were perhaps the most generative, there are now too many instances of obliteration, such as Khartoum; total infrastructural failure, as in Kinshasa; the subcontracting of basic security to foreign mercenary contractors, such as in Bangui and Goma; state regimes underpinned by a volatile and fickle allegiance of urban poor youth, such as in Conakry, Ouagadougou, Bamako and Niamey; the wholesale transfer of poor and working-class residents from the urban core to new settlements in the periphery, such as in Cairo and Casablanca; and the persistent exodus of youthful populations headed, at least officially, to Europe, but who are 'strung out' at various locations along the way. There are scores of small cities across Africa that are literally off the map, holding steady populations but without any discernible prospects. Some were built as accompaniments to extraction, with the concomitant boom and bust. Others were sites of factories long gone, repositories of hopes that quickly vanished but which left inhabitants without resources or motivation to move on, and who find basic survival in finding minimal ways of tending to those also barely surviving.

Beyond Africa, there are cities whose administration is predicated on the wholesale incarceration of inhabitants involved in illicit economies, the extrajudicial killing of supposed deviants, the relegation of nascent migrants to 'sacrifice zones' of intense toxicity, climatic turbulence or violence, and the enrolment of largely youthful residents into various mafia and militias with high mortality rates. It could be argued that these dispositions constitute a form of 'inclusive exclusion' – where the bodies and lives of the immiserated become elements of an expansive game of financial deprivation. Here, states demonstrate their commitment to fiscal discipline and exercise their 'bare' sovereignty – by showing how they can successfully deal with an expendable population (Tadiar, 2022). All of these examples of removal accentuate a future that is increasingly nurtured as private property, the exclusive purview of a register of eligibility consigned to an authentic entrepreneurial self. Here the swelling of the US prison population is a cogent example:

> African American prison populations function within the prison-industrial complex not as labor but as raw material. Put differently, African American criminalization, which is legitimated through narratives of racialized, gendered, and sexualized deviance, is not only a way to relegate subjects to surplus labor pools but also a way to relegate to surplus existence. In the era of the supremacy of speculative

> capital, being surplus means being extinguishable. To be 'surplus' in this moment is to be valueless, unprotectable, vulnerable, and dead. It is to be racialized, gendered, and sexually nonnormative in ways simultaneously old and new. (Hong, 2015, p. 70)

Unlike forms of prophetic futures premised on reconciliation – e.g. the first shall be last, and the last first; no child left behind; or sustainability for all – the future increasingly appears indifferent to a process of reconciliation. The world is too complicated, too overpopulated, too hot and turbulent, too close to an edge to worry about notions of human equality. At a time when the concept of species-being is rehabilitated as a means of talking about threats to a common humanity, and where that humanity is viewed as the only viable agent of transformation, just what makes up the worthily human is being narrowed. At the same time, efficacy is not measured in terms of what an individual person might do on their own. Rather, it is the extent of their learned affiliations with, leverage over and directional command over technological affordances – artificial intelligence most particularly.

If the composition of the learning and delivery processes of such affordances has become the purview of a limited set of university-corporate entities, the expressions or proof of a viable humanity increasingly becomes a matter of exclusive and private domains. Not only are urban inhabitants being removed from the familiar constructs of the human community, but that community is also being substantially redefined to remove a range of participation by default. This double-edged removal – of subtracting persons from the present, and in doing so, reducing the capacity of the present to imagine and elaborate a multi-textured future – is a form of future-making reliant upon editing out the troubling details, the wild vernaculars, the residual solidarities, the irruptive affective expressions emanating from intuition and divination, and the experimental improvisations on hegemonic forms of value. Such subtraction reveals the violent underpinnings of any optimalization.

While certain humans may be able to secure their futures in motley collections of artificial environments, with strict limits placed on population size, while others detach themselves as fugitives in remote regions, the question remains whether any such removal is entirely successful in the terms imagined, let alone other ethical and political considerations. What are the traces left behind; what kinds of forces, ghosts, spirits come to haunt whatever transpires, especially in all those cultures where violent removals engender a population unable to move on, that are interminably stuck as residuals in the present, denied paradise or the status of ancestors? In places such as Mexico and Ecuador, governing the dead has become an expanding obsession incurring increasing levels of anxiety as to how remains are to be disposed of, exhibited, buried or incinerated.

At the same time, long histories of the *lumpen* have shown their importance as vectors of incitement, the occasion for spurring innovations, even as these are largely directed towards control and pacification. What happens when the trouble is no longer there, and how might the acknowledged troubles get so much worse? Here, the notion of a future has long become a resource for the expendable – where the past condition of possibility of the present can be queried and the present becomes the future, as such, which then reframes the future as sheer potentiality (Happe, 2024). In other words, somewhere in the present is a key to other kinds of histories that have ensued from a past, at work in figuring possible worlds, but which were occluded, curtailed or rendered empirically unavailable. Path dependencies then are always plural and uncertain.

By re-imaging stories of defiance and alternative worlds in black pasts, Happe emphasizes that what 'might have been' is conjoined with 'what will have been', as the present becomes the unfulfilled potentiality (future) of the past. Yet, more important here is that a demand can be made without any assessment of the prospect for success; it is what Happe (2024) calls a conversation with the unthinkable, which, in her example, characterizes contemporary prison abolition movements, undaunted by the unavailability of the social relations that would seemingly permit the end of prisons. What is viewed as practically possible in the present is not to deter from a fundamental demand for something to be other than it is. And so urbanizing the future means that the sheer intensification and spread of the demand is the only way to create a space where any informed impetus for social alternatives might be available.

To Fore-shadow

But demand is not enough for such urbanizing. There is also a need to usher in, to steer through whatever seeds can concretize the imagination of what is demanded. We call this *foreshadowing*. To foreshadow conventionally means to identify an incipience in the present of future dispositions. A child who is completely taken with Lego eventually becomes an architect – and so that early play foreshadows a later career. It is a way that the future announces itself in the present, or a way to retrospectively draw a line between the future now present and a present now past. Here, we want to highlight a different connotation of foreshadowing. Not one just of incipience, but the actual provision of 'shadows' as a protective cover for an incipience vulnerable to removal. This is a relationship with the future that less imagines what it will look like, less consciously sets out to work diligently and fully for a specific imagination of it, but rather tends to a range of 'seedlings' – real differences that emerge in the present – by providing a milieu through which they might unfurl over time, and become enduring and generative.

Foreshadowing is based on the presumption that one works with incipience as a matter of experimentation, that incipience is the very form of engagement between humans and non-human entities and processes. It is the stage through which things become available for experimentation and nurturance – not to shape precisely the trajectory of growth, but rather as the occasioning of attentiveness, care and the indeterminacies of becoming.

The task is not to define or control, but to coax, instigate, tease, cajole and conjure. Here the future is inextricable from these practices, whatever content ensues. For the future is not a destination but a process of engaging; it is a play of interlocutors, and open-ended call and response, and call again, where the future is called into existence by humans and others responding to a call, a call without clear origin or agenda.

As the future is not one thing – but rather a suite of virtuality, forward remembrances, self-fulfilling prophecies and inventive reiterations of various pasts – such tactics assume different forms and rhythms. Current emphases on developing more precise measures and data sets, and calculations of interoperability among variables to enhance the rigour of probabilities are certainly critical aspects of planning for futures. However, we focus here less on maximizing degrees of certainty, and rather 'stay with' uncertainty – not to attenuate it, but rather to mobilize it as an affordance, a way of bringing into existence inventive thought and action. Such thought and action thus refuse the linear trajectories of progress or decline, seeing the future not so much as a crystallization of definitive dispositions but an ambiguous, murky terrain connoting radically divergent feelings and possibilities. While it is certainly possible to have a comprehensive image of what urbanity will look like across forthcoming eras, our emphasis is how to see present urbanities through a pluriversal lens that holds open different implications for seeming inevitabilities (Amin and Thrift, 2017). This is not just a matter of choice, but also a requirement in terms of how emerging urban environments present themselves.

So, part of this orientation of foreshadowing stems from seeing just how ambiguous the urban present can be. It points simultaneously to very different kinds of possibilities that are inscribed into the built environment, with projects that seem to work 'too well' and those, perhaps right next door, that don't work at all. The point here is not just the heterogeneity of functions, land uses, investment portfolios, governance scenarios and residential compositions that all operate near each other. Rather, it is the reality that so many of these things are literally half-full, half-empty, and in such a way that without detailed genealogies of each individual project and the elaboration of possible 'algorithmic' relations among them it is nearly impossible to assess the efficacy of any setting. Where is it going; how do we assess the viability of how such settings are inhabited? If there is no empirical clarity, then we must nevertheless make decisions about what something is; and then how do we make such decisions?

Just like models for rates of infection and probable morbidity in epidemiology, the models of urban development also tend to err in favour of upward projections, the ability of each new development to handle potential demand, to avoid price inflation based on scarcity, and to manage possible multiplier effects that are envisioned as the outcome of the intensified urbanization of spaces. Part of the ability of developers to raise the necessary finance for projects is to represent them as bigger and better than they have a reasonable chance of becoming. In financing schemes that must cover debt accrued for past project development, the terms of new projects must be inflated accordingly, so that new projects are sometimes conceived as an instrument to more firmly consolidate the asset class of those past.

While normative scenario planning, combined with speculation and financial calculations, is clearly at work in the 'half full–half empty' character of the ways in which extended urban regions appear to develop, there is an experiential dimension that exceeds these factors. It is not that these different built environments are not built to last, even if this is the seeming disposition for many condos and commercial projects. Rather, it is that, implicitly, these environments are being made available to potential uses and futures beyond their purported expectations. Even if, for example, laundering money is the primary motivation for putting up an additional thousand shop houses in an area that already has a glut of them, the sheer fact that they come to exist opens possibilities for their eventual repurposing. Such may not happen now but nevertheless is a prospect that can be brokered in exchange for yet other possibilities somewhere else.

In Jakarta's periphery, in the city of Cikarang, just such a scenario took place when a South Korean consortium purchased 500 contiguous shop house units, converting them into thirty-seven small artisanal factories, thus circumventing existing industrial regulations and taxation systems. At the same time, it converted a barely functioning tyre manufacturing factory into storage facilities for other nearby industrial plants. The workers staffing the improvised factory system were mostly already working in small artisanal workshops informally built along irrigation canals running through industrial land that was still tended by peasant farmers.

Not only is a degree of undecidability built into the operations of industrial zones, sub-cities, new towns, workers' hostels and low-income suburban estates as to their viability but also as to the proportionality of what characteristics are at work in their construction and management. Not dissimilar to the situation of the territories housing the urban poor and working classes, it is exceedingly difficult to say for sure exactly what these environments are beyond their apparent use. Clearly various modes of financing are at work: government subsidies, tax breaks, foreign investments, laundered money, personal and collective savings of various kinds, debt, secured and unsecured loans, barter, diverted funds, futures and bonds. Yet it is often difficult to work out the proportionality of each of these elements within the confines of a single project, or more precisely, the ways in which discrete projects are intersected through various management structures.

In the industrial estates, industrial production is not just industrial production, just as farming is not just farming, recycling of waste is more than this, hostels housing migrants go beyond this function, and shop houses are rarely shop houses in these new dispensations. But to what degree and how remains largely occluded. Not because it is a secret to be hidden, but because the very genericity of the specific projects themselves is able to compress so many different types of uses and possibilities. It is not so much to ward off detection but to make any form of detection dysfunctional from the outset. For investigations will find what they set out to find, but what will be found won't be everything that exists. So, for environments that could be used in many kinds of ways, that exist in the present as infrastructures in waiting, even if some are deteriorating in the absence of active use, it is important to actively consider how they might be appropriated, activated.

If urban built environments seem more generic, then the generic breaks the possibility of detection being the method through which individuals and populations are subsumed into a system of proportionality – more or less healthy, more or less immune, more or less eligible, more or less valuable. Instead, the generic connotes a space or composition capable of holding within it things and processes that may be related to each other, or not. It is where what something is may be multiple, but it does not owe its existence to how it is positioned within a network of multiplicities, through which it is accorded statuses and potentialities. It is impossible to tell what the generic is; there is no way to affirm the value of a particular instance, but only in terms of indicating what *it is not* (Galloway, 2014). And so, the periphery is not the periphery, though it might now be everywhere.

Improbabilities

So, we see that albeit in the most normative forms of urban development, there can be improbable outcomes even when the most generic of imaginations are applied. So, what can we make of such improbabilities, especially in terms of urbanizing the future?

Urbanity is already elsewhere and otherwise than we normally consider it to be; indeed, one of the primary implications of urbanization itself is to undermine any specific rendition of its supposed coherence. In other words, the designation 'urban future' is in some ways an oxymoron, when we begin to think of the future as increasingly 'urbanized'. There is the sense that our understanding of the future increasingly entails an agglomeration and densification of multiple and highly differentiated ways of doing things. The 'urban' is also a predominant modality of the future, in the sense that urbanization processes, in the constant and accelerated intensification of relations among things, bodies and scales, become a future-making machine.

It is possible to apprehend this in the ways in which 'futures' in their financial connotation have come to underpin urban economies, such that the valuation and comprehensive use of spatial products, and the built environment in general, is not something assessable in the 'now', but will only find its culmination, its 'true sense', at some future point. Additionally, the largest proportion of the global economy, in terms of monetary valuation, is made up of contracts – bought and sold – that basically constitute speculations on all kinds of urban phenomena and base the production and distribution of resources according to a statistical averaging of the totality of such contracts at any given time.

Here the future is folded into the present, not as a means of domesticating uncertainties or pre-empting adverse prospects, but rather in exhausting, as Massumi (2021) puts it, virtuality – financializing all that could possibly happen. This massive extension of colonization thus precludes futurity and coincides with the ways in which the critique of linear progress – applied across the world – ends up sneaking progress in through the back door. Here, we want to refuse these foreclosures and restore the generativity of indeterminacy as a fundamental aspect of urbanization – the sense that with all the interactions of bodies, materials and practices taking place in urban contexts no form of computation can specify what exactly will take place, and, as such, as Yuk Hui (2016) puts it, new *improbabilities* are being introduced into the world. So, we want to stay with the improbable, the unlikely. If humanity is confronted with an impasse, a condition that seems intractable with deleterious consequences from which it is unable to reverse, then the orientation to this future should not be panic, or a heightened urgency to do something now. Rather, we would follow Linz and Secor's (2021) recommendation to relish the unexpected, the withdrawn, the strange bundling of things that don't go together, the capacity for improvisation, the wayward:

> Inhabiting the impasse means subsisting in uncomfortable dissonance, in the paradoxical copresence of irreconcilable affirmations. The impasse is the gap where the antinomy closes/opens/becomes – 'dialectics at a standstill' (Benjamin 1999, 463). By entering an impasse and holding it open, by guarding 'against every new closure, every new reconstitution' (Deleuze and Guattari 1986, 14), we blast open the potentiality of the now and create the conditions for a different way of being in the world. (Linz and Secor, 2021, p. 201)

Instead of thinking about the future as a 'thing' or a specific temporal designation, how might we consider it rather as a practice or orientation, and not only of humans to a larger surround, but as a mutual conversation or calling, a field of mutual lures and instigations, that which compels both volitional decisions to do something differently as well as involuntary injunctions and solicitations? There is something, for example, in the ways in which cities speak to us, not only as a reflection of what we have done in making them but as voices from elsewhere composed of all the unanticipated interactions of materials, uses and symbols that have been generated by such makings.

Here, the future may be a specific vantage point that enables us to listen to or 'read' the city in terms of such interactions – their heterogeneous patterns of fractals, grids, curvatures, abruptions, roundabouts, over- and underpasses, and cul-de-sacs that place built environments in particular kinds of touch with each other, and which themselves open or close different vistas of apprehension. Zooming in and out hones and detracts attention to specific details, as well as reminds us of all the processes that we are unable to detect at any scale. Navigating the possibilities of such perspectivism is itself then a practice of futurity, where the 'same' never remains just that, but reflects choices on how to see and live with.

Addie (2024) has recently written about the polyrhythmic composition of the city, its quotidian cyclical times that register improvisations among repetition, the constant reverberations of making at various scales and the ways that infrastructures are implicated and an integral aspect of such making: all the cascading of arrhythmic accumulations, the accelerations and slow-downs of circulation, the interruptions of projects and the cadences of circumventions, evasions, getting out of the way. Cities are replete with the looping of all kinds of ritualistic practices, the interchanges of the diurnal and nocturnal, and the often-invisible modulations of interfaces among different activities, agendas and their concomitant rhythms.

> Even as a specific infrastructure may set the rhythm for a particular service of provision (trains, water supply, and so on), these are dependent on other rhythmic activities and orders, thus constituting infrastructure and the city as polyrhythmic bundles of organic, social, and technological temporalities. Approaching urban infrastructure through a rhythmic framework enables us to bring a variety of seemingly discrete or oppositional temporal moments into dialogue: the mechanical and organic, repetition and difference, fast-paced rhythms and slow movement/violence. (Addie, 2024, p. 31)

In an even more basic sense, the future points to a process of continuous exertion, the work that inhabitants do with each other to both continuously compose a shared *milieu* – a context that provides a series of affordances necessary to the reproduction of their sociality – and adapt to it. Here urbanizing the future has much to do with the notion of *individuation* and how it relates to the formation of a collective intelligence – an intelligence that displays the capacity for 'knowing before knowing'. That is, realizing the variegated possibilities of the future within both the past and present.

As that urban milieu is only artificially bounded and thus presents inhabitants with a constant series of challenges, it raises the question of who inhabitants are for each other; what their responsibilities are to each other; how indebted they are to each other. As humans have no natural habitat, no inevitable ecological niche to which they belong (Virno, 2009), all milieus are necessarily self-constructed – Gilbert Simondon (2009a) uses the term 'metastable'. Within such self-construction, inhabitants must figure out ways of being with each other that enable expressions of individuation – whereby individual lives become themselves a specific kind of affordance and resource – and where such expressions support a shared collective project, which is fundamentally a 'collective mind', an extended cognition to which individuation provides additional capacity and reach.

Both collective mind and individuation are never static formulations. They must continuously be replenished; as each individuation, besides constituting an affordance, also generates a problem that must be addressed, because such individuation introduces into the world something that may be unexpected, unprecedented. Inhabitation and its experiences of stability, then, always anticipate the realignment of relationality, especially as each milieu is also affected by a virtual reserve of forces, ideas and practices that precede every individuation. Every relationship among multiple enactments of individuation, then, entails both an interconnectedness – of human and milieu, human and machine – and detachment. Each expression of an individuation – whether it be that of a policy direction articulated by an institution, or a piece of art, or the formation of a new household – is simultaneously connected to a wide range of other expressions but is also detached from them as well, or acts as a singular contribution to some problem or issue. Emphases on simply an essential relationality too often detract from individuation as separateness, the impossibility of conciliation. At the same time, as Karen Barad emphasized, these specific enactments of agency emerge from *within* a relationship, and not through the interaction of preconceived entities that endure unchanged through time (Barad, 2012).

Individuation is not a process referring to the character of individuals but the singularities that emanate from within the attempts to constitute a milieu of metastability through which it is possible to identify specific vectors of force and the provisional agential entities that express these forces. Seen from this vantage point, the urban environment is not so much made up of specific pre-existent institutions and sectors – housing, transportation, industry, etc. – but that these emerge from the intersection of various forces, circulations, materials and interchanges. This is particularly evident in some postcolonial cities, where inserting the imaginaries and forms of so-called modern urban governance resulted in an array of formal institutions and ministries unable to perform their designated functions, which indeed were then undertaken and at least partially fulfilled by an array of informal arrangements across the boundaries of such sectors and institutions.

Not dissimilarly, whereas it is possible to accord individual identities to all of those which make up a household, for example, the ability of the household to cohere momentarily as a force in the world has to do with engendering forms of expression, practice and interchange that draw from a field of divergent metabolisms, desires and inclinations. There is no ontological basis from which a specific household operates as a fixed entity; there is nothing that essentially separates out household members from a larger field of interactions. Yet, it nevertheless comes to perform its own boundedness in ways partly prescribed by codes that come from elsewhere, as well as its own vernaculars that perform an affective sense of intimacy in which the household is considered as its most appropriate form. The shifting interfaces of the household with an exterior world are always dynamic, refiguring the modalities of interconnectivity and separation.

Using Simondon's (2009a, 2009b) notion, a process of *interfacing* makes specific elements available to each other to make something, to exert new knowledge or capacity – a position predicated on the fact that not all elements will be available to each other. One sees this in the relative foreclosure of mutual understanding as a necessary condition for the communications between humans and machines, as they can be made available to each other while many of their respective operations remain occluded. What this says about futurity is that it is not a product of enhanced knowledge; it is not about mapping more precisely the interaction of a larger number of variable and potential causal loops. Rather, it is a choreography of separateness and interconnectivity, a process of attending to the ways in which both continuities and discontinuities become available to each other within a temporal milieu. Here technicity, rather than raising perplexing ontological questions as a driving concern for the near future, dispenses with them, little concerned about choreographing availability based on knowing exactly what something is (Simondon, 2011). Again, it is the importance of 'knowing before knowing'.

Here the future is what necessarily must come to reiterate the viability of a present. A key question today is who or what bears responsibility for this work; to what extent is it being outsourced to various computational and artificially intelligent procedures? In the past, if the work to be done had to find an appropriate modality of conveyance, this was assumed largely by the stories we told each other – the rendering of experience into stories. These stories are miniature reconciliations between the need and desire to be distinct, singular and bounded (as a species in common) and enmeshed in webs of intra-activity with other species (bio-symbiosis) – a constant working out of sameness and difference (Hayles, 2021).

Of course, technical instruments impact on those stories, and this is evident particularly in the stories we tell about the 'present', and our ability to live in exactly the moment in which something takes place. This is the case of the missing half second that transpires between the impact of sensory experience and our subsequent consciousness of it. Hayles (2014) has examined the implications of what she calls 'nonconscious cognition', not only in terms of setting up a platform for conscious deliberation but in exposing human action to a kind of targeted messaging that compels attentiveness prior to any conscious mediation. Hansen's (2015) conception of *worldly sensibilities* in turn refers to operations that expose bodies to forms of sensory experience, ways of experiencing the world that do not produce any kind of perception and that remain outside of consciousness. Here, technical operations generate atmospheres of affective influence that bypass the association of an individual or collective with a given milieu and impact directly on the sensibility of the overall environment, producing a subjectivity that is not bound to any subject – operations such as: *swarm intelligence*, *neural networks*, *cellular automata*, *machine consciousness* and *general adversarial networks*.

While such atmospheres can extend human sensitivity and activity, attention needs to be paid to the apparatuses that operationalize them. It is possible, for example, to see in the contemporary manifestations of artificial intelligence the reduction of storytelling and the very meaning of words to a range of objective functions that have been statistically formulated for the process of machine learning based on circumscribed data sets. Instead of semantic and narrative flexibility, there is a constriction of meaning to that which constitutes a mode of optimality and averaging. As a result, our stories and our world become exceedingly thin, devoid of the variations that constitute the world itself (Foster, 2023). This is a turn away from the improbabilities the stories attempt to bring into the world, perhaps undermining the motivation for stories altogether.

Descriptions of urban life also tend to focus on various agencies and structures and the play between them. Residents inhabit, navigate and shape the city; they do something to it and with it within the constraints imposed by the decisions and forces exerted by different collective actors – whether they are forms of production, institutions, transactions or ecological processes. Such action assumes the consolidation of ideas, energies, designs and intentions that are instantiated as and in an environment. Residents, various institutional actors and economic activities impose agendas, objectives, schedules, stages and anticipations.

But the profusion of initiatives in urban life produces an incessant volatility where it is often difficult for any actor to steer their objectives intact through the choppy waters of intersections, contestations and collisions occasioned by agendas trying to make their way through and with each other. Navigation here is a matter of drawing and feeling lines of connection between different horizons, vantage points, signals and adjustments; it is not a matter of reading a map and pointing yourself along the shortest trajectory (November et al., 2010). Rather it is the reliance upon a range of technical manoeuvres that bring dimensions of disparate and continuously shifting phenomena, domains and operations into an experiential connection associated with an imagining of a coherent, overarching scene or world.

Futures as Enduring Movement

We see, then, that urbanizing entails movement. Movements that can be oscillations back and forth; movements that can be leaps, increments, emergences. They all require technical facilitation. They can be impeded, blocked, diverted. It can sometimes go anywhere and nowhere. It is a release of energy that can travel along well-worn paths or generate new ones. These movements alternate in time; things slow down and speed up; others grind away in a steady rhythm, sometimes coming to a halt, or jolting forward. Others go round and round, and still others leap across seemingly impossible divides. In these ways the future is urbanized.

But one way in which movement is both expressed and contained can be found in the formation of territory. The impetus to consolidate space, to enclose it and to limit its operability has been a long-term urban political project (Elden, 2010). Contemporary mega-developments are largely claims on space, driven by the exigency to tie up space before others do so. It might have been alright if developers built a few shopping malls, but when the city is littered with several new ones every year, all the subsequent barely occupied space just isn't worth the space these projects take up, as well as the social costs rung up for getting hold of this space to begin with. But this excess has been taking place for a long time. It is somewhat understandable that colonist households wanted to put some space between themselves and the natives – regardless of whether they should have been in the cities they occupied in the first place. Similarly for regimes that want to hang on to power for whatever reason – either to complete the revolution, to bring development to the people, or to get as rich off the state as possible – it makes sense that they would put some distance between their zones of residence and administration and the more troublesome popular neighbourhoods or populations.

But territories have never been consolidated as a matter of an overarching form. Rather they emerge fractally from the continuous circulations of bodies enjoining, exchanging, collaborating with each other. Social differentiation of position is never spatially static but constituted and reaffirmed through acts of extensionality and dissipation, moving in and through space, and creating space through such movement. Points of exposure are maximized through proximities, which also reinforce differentiation as both by-products of and lures for circulation. For example, Jakarta has expanded its urban footprint exponentially over the past few decades. Not in an onward march to the peripheries, but rather through multiple, spiralling circulations backward and forward across different zones, landscapes and functions. There are 'contagions' and mimicry which rapidly populate and depopulate specific places; there are hedges on new developments that never materialize and where money and labour and material are moved to another part of town. Specific settlements are deeply implanted in specific places and thus have to be leap-frogged in order for new developments to take place.

Specific patterns of movement – dispersals to an exterior, the concentration of trajectories from peripheries, the branching of specific settlements – occur in tandem with specific modes of rule and knowledge production. Orientations and ideas of the future thus coincide with specific framings of movement, all of which are subject to mutations, divergence and transformation – as reflected in the history of many cities which transformed their very 'operating codes' in terms of styles of rule and distribution of resources. For there is something in the conjunction of both the built environment and the sensations and sensibilities that are possible that is amenable to tipping points and unanticipated synergies with other kinetic patterns that may only appear through small distortions in the circulatory systems (Nail, 2018).

Movement entails a heterogeneity of times, again as if an extensive temporal surface of navigatory circuits. Think again of all those chase movies. The heterogeneity of time is less that of a collective composition within specific places than a matter of highly stylized individual itineraries of movement across urban spaces in the pursuit of better opportunities and resources. As the embodiment of a public commonality, of people situated in specific places being enjoined in a larger orbit of belonging, the state often seems to no longer have the legal, political or financial means to produce a sense of belonging. If residents can piece together such a shared sense of identification with a city or region, it is increasingly via their navigation of it through continuous circulation – even if the state intervenes to shape the terms of this circulation.

For urban youth in the Global South, particularly, the ability to circulate becomes an overarching value. Even though short-term employment contracts are the norm, and even though the belief that once one attains a job it should be held onto at all costs, youth in cities such as Jakarta, Abidjan and Hyderabad normally change jobs every couple of months, using an infrastructure of cheap boarding houses and rooms for rent to expand their orbits across wider swathes of the urban region. More extensive circulation of individuals in search of better opportunities then, itself, constitutes an income opportunity for residents to convert space in their homes into short-term rentals. Neighbourhoods then exude an atmosphere of transiency, of people coming and going, which while on the one hand may destabilize local solidarities, also, on the other, provides a medium of connections to a larger surround (Simone, 2018).

If the simultaneous erasure of time's heterogeneity and its particularization through intensified spatial division appears to be a key characteristic of contemporary urbanization, the extension of urbanization into various hinterlands also underlines the simultaneous existence of many temporalities. Here, different ways of doing things, transacting, buying and selling, making and distributing, deliberating and deciding are *extended* to each other. Rather than a multiplicity of times being subsumed into a standardized version, across much of the South, discrepant temporalities tend to coexist, even if the terms of coexistence tend to disallow the capacity of any one of them to posit its own trajectories of implication. They move with each other, and sometimes against or indifferent to each other.

The time of bazaar, the festival, the factory, the neighbourhood, the coordinates of modernity, the time of extended family and kinship relations, the time of religious devotion, the time of diurnal and nocturnal markets, the time of administrative bureaucracies all coexist, not as individual tracts, not as the rhythms of autonomous worlds, but as pressure points that avail any operation to the exigencies and operational practices of the other. In a world of logistics, just-in-time production and constantly recalibrated commodity chains, the bazaar, that multifaceted commercial system that integrated individual merchants and trades, that provided credit to those unable to access formal banking mechanisms, that mobilized political sentiment, that charted specific geographies of articulation, that shifted resources across various kinds of social, geographic and religious ties, that established the price of things based on considerations that far exceeded those of supply and demand, and that shaped the structure and settlement of built environments, continues to thrive. It thrives not because of what it was, and the implications of its own logics and operations, but because those very logics and operations offer a resource to so-called modern economies and to advanced logistical operations when those economies and operations run into difficulty, when they confront choke points or blockage.

Increasingly, urban inhabitation shifts from spatial emplacement and territorial consolidation to the circuitries of everyday movement, where the *itineraries* of movement are the media of inhabitation as much as the home. In these oscillations between settlement and unsettlement, technical systems not only realize specific human desires and designs, but in their multiple intersections generate occasions of inhabitation for which there is no available conceptual language. Urban movement and a politics of inhabitation informed by the valuation of movement comes to represent, in part, a *refusal to be governed or to be settled* within specific regulatory frameworks.

While technical instruments can survey and control movement, they also can facilitate such a refusal, as inhabitation comes to operate simultaneously within and outside shifting registers of control. Instead of inhabitation being reduced simply to the sustenance of survival, of attending to an established repertoire of 'human needs' and affordance, it expresses itself as an ongoing political question about what kinds of life are worth living. The apparently apolitical dimensions of the technical are re-posed as contestations over how emerging modalities of 'affecting and being affected', of the composition of collective life, are to be used and valued.

Circulation – making people available to each other – is also significant because social life is spurred by imitation, and imitation consolidates a sense of collective effort (Barry and Thrift, 2007). Imitation drives the formations of sectors, economies of scale and social cohesion. Yet, it frequently gets out of hand. In one neighbourhood of Jakarta with which we are familiar, Jembatan Lima, working with patches of cloth and textile remainders is one of the main economic activities. It is something that has worked well for this area. But then again, almost everyone is trying to do it. They invest in machines, make space in their homes or create new spaces, and garner the necessary contacts. But then they can't find enough labour to keep up with demand or even get started. Each street is full of signs seeking different kinds of machine operators and semi-skilled labour. Some workshops are humming 24 hours a day, while others languish. Here imitation got carried away.

Endurance means something different than survival. A lot of emphasis has been placed upon how residents survive the city, particularly the large numbers of urban poor. Sometimes their survival efforts are realistically acknowledged – a great deal of resilience and street smarts are demonstrated under otherwise debilitating conditions. The celebratory, however, sometimes gets out of hand and the poor then become urban heroes, proof of the resilience of human ingenuity and spirit no matter what is thrown at it. There is nothing necessarily heroic about demonstrations of a willingness to rush to the bottom.

On the other hand, much disingenuousness is also conveyed in the bafflement about how the poor manage to survive, as if only a truncated view of middle-class efficacy constituted the terms of survival. One can hear almost a palpable sense of relief as massive statistical toolboxes are paraded listing high mortality and crime rates for the poor, as well as a host of psychological, medical and social problems. Especially when cities are dangerous – like Karachi, Rio or Caracas, for example – stereotypical notions of survival seem predicated on a capacity to remain almost invisible, for if one tries to be or have something of any significance it is bound to attract all kinds of unwanted attention, and the chances are that the person is not going to be around for very long.

How then do we gather up cities to think about matters of endurance, of what they might individually and collectively offer in considerations of the future? For to make something feel similar is not a matter of finding the terms through which one way of doing things or being is translated into another. Translation certainly exists as a necessary and constant activity of interchange; something that we do all the time. Endurance certainly relies upon the capacity of the diverse experiences and perspectives of different actors to be translatable. Yet, as one returns to Zeno's arrow, translation faces clear limits. Causes and effects have no built-in articulation; there is no plan that an observer sees in its entirety that originates in a single intention and then unfolds across the trajectory of space. This doesn't mean that there are no intentions; it doesn't mean that people do not set out to do harm or good. Rather, the intention doesn't guarantee a certain path, nor does the movement along a path necessarily mean that something either about the arrow or the intentions that were at work in sending it is interrupted. It simply means that it is difficult to translate the arrow leaving into the arrow arriving and that a bridge must be built between them. This means constructing a conceivable way to see these events as sufficiently similar so to conclude a relationship among them, or, just as well, to conclude a relationship between them and then work backward to see all the possible ways in which such a condition could be sustained.

Endurance as a pathway to and in the future is a by-product of bridge building – a way of concluding a trajectory of movement that makes things similar no matter what they might be. This similarity, then, is lived through as a means of continuance. Ways of life, territory and identities may indeed be defended needlessly to the bitter end. Outcries that something should survive at all costs are certainly not unfamiliar in all cities. But the capacity to endure – i.e. the capacity to construct lines of connection between seemingly discordant experiences or ways of doing things, and which are without confident translations – is perhaps more significant.

For today's conditions of *generic instability* point to the ways in which protracted histories of practice – through which the details of how the material and technical bases of cities have been articulated, disjoined, converted, juxtaposed and amalgamated in both parallel and intersecting vectors of force – perhaps are no longer capable of holding the city together. Nor at times do they seem capable of being rejigged and readapted to increasingly volatile atmospheres – climatic, financial, political. The specificities of materials, actors and technicities are not constellated into patterns or evidence of macro-structural manoeuvres. They figure their own *alliances*. Strange relations are being 'designed' anyway, and what is important is not to try and settle things down, but to move with them, and learn how to modestly, without grand expectations, turn or steer them into specific possibilities that often only accidentally present themselves. Again, this is what we mean by the foreshadowing of incipience.

For there is an aesthetics that renders any overarching organizational logic inoperable. We may walk through the streets as we always have, may be caught up in the same routines, and expect the same results of these redundant actions. But these are invested and enacted with a sense of always something beyond, right here and now, through which the familiar could veer off into new directions. This is an eerie form of an aesthetic arithmetic that suggests that whatever appears in front of us is always 'less than' and 'more than' at the same time. This in turn is, as Foucault (2005) reminds us, *life's priority*.

This is a matter of how any event, interaction or scenario works off all that precedes and follows it, how their very conditions of possibility are posed, not simply within the personalities, histories or situations of a given context, but in the time underway, in the urbanizing of time itself. This is the multiplicity of indetectable transversals of responding to the entirety of the world at a given moment, which makes itself present in an unprecedented specificity. Any event, scenario – no matter how insulated, specific, power-laden – takes place in the midst, in the simultaneity of multiple other events. Each exerts impacts beyond the locales and boundaries that would structure their relevance and the ways in which they would be conventionally attended to.

Instead of the search for 'order', in the rough and tumble everyday worlds of trying to make the most from what was available, of putting together people and things that didn't seem to really go together, inhabitants of majority urban worlds tended to be convinced to let many different scenarios play out, demonstrated a basic tolerance for ways of doing things that didn't necessarily correspond to their values or beliefs. There was something else besides, right next to the amplified attentions to identity, parochial interest and parasitism, and this something else was located, not within the ambit of human and social will, but in the materialization of the urban itself. It is a notion that resonates with Deleuze's figuration of a 'centre of determinacy'. All the traumas of the past, everything that has been tried so far, whether it works or not, all of the times where one has fallen down to pick oneself up again, do not prepare a person for what will take place now. All of that suffering won't be redeemed, but has thickened your skin, turned the surface of the body into a confusing map of contradictory itineraries.

Again, the key consideration here is to circumvent the anchoring of relationality in any predeterminate overarching sense of attachment and fantasies of everything tied together in some supra-positional subject or subsuming ecology, as stereotypically characterizes certain strands of Anthropocene thought. Our technical imagination is still firmly linked to the *additive*, to what new knowledge and tools can be brought to the table – when the more relevant challenge perhaps is how to bring things to an end; how to subtract from the world the obsession with maximizing, to subtract the search for status and recognition, and rather live as *unrecognized* and *inoperable*.

Claire Colebrook (2017) makes this clear in a radical detachment from the *furtherance* of life as an orienting principle to relationality:

> Why [in the Anthropocene] have we fetishized the differences of our own making, and why are we so sure that we know about the differences that make a difference, or the differences that are readable? It is only with the appropriation of **surplus** labor that a culture can develop the symbolic systems required for the organized sacrifice and subjection that marks religion and cultural sublimation, and that in turn enable the collective investment for mass warfare. The geological sublime is therefore the challenge of looking at the entire archive of the earth – including human script – as one might look at the marks left on buildings by the forces of weathering. How would we read ourselves if we were not to assume some ultimate readability or spirit beneath the materiality of text? (p. 15)

The question of foreshadowing, then, entails how to maintain a sense of detachment inseparable from the capacity of relations to produce spaciousness, where neither abstracted ideas of human commonality nor the exigency of human furtherance or even survival become the gravitational force of associating differences with each other. As Yuk Hui (2016) emphasizes, the question is how to introduce new improbabilities into the world, amenable neither to contract nor democratic accountability, but available to anyone *and* as incalculable territorializations of liveliness and collective gathering.

Conclusion

What we have attempted to do in this chapter is to explore the urbanizing of the future through the notion of foreshadowing to think about the future as incipience. While the word's conventional usage points to a capacity to retrospectively anticipate the dispositions of a past future through the character and signs of the present, we place emphasis on the 'shadowing' as a means of protecting the potentialities of incipience in face of rampant extraction in the interest of capitalist accumulation and the predominance of foreclosure as the modality of governance and rule. As the French-Congolese philosopher Nadia Yala Kisukidi (2021) states: How to conduct the affective conversion of the desire for spiritual death that has long been embodied by social theory – a theory that seeks to undo the *fleshiness* of history in favour of abstraction; how to learn from the 'library of torn pages', where bodies perhaps long for definition, but not within the terms through which they have been defined. This is where dispossession has been a process of stealing souls, undermining a multiplicity of subjectivities in favour of 'coherent selves', of turning selves into expendable and fungible flesh – what might be seen as the ultimate dispossession. For her, flesh can repossess itself: not in any authentic or free form – now long gone, no longer here – but rather as an extensiveness, a materialization of spirit.

For Kisukidi, in contrast to Hegelian tropes, spirit is the basis of endurance, the medium of communication between humans and all things, a process of tending to, caring for the capacity of becoming that in-forms all things. The future for her is the cessation of plunder, not as some hoped-for outcome, but a cessation that must take place now, without delay, without assessment of its realistic possibilities. It must simply come to an end with no consideration of its implications.

Conceptualized differently, incipience is a function of the edge that marks the intersection of a pluralization of time. For any context, any city is marked, as we have indicated before, by an urbanization of temporalities. There are seasonal times, geologic time, redemptive time, just-in-time, algorithmic processing times, ruptures and continuities, slow violences, rapid conversions, accelerations of innovation, the roadblocks that interrupt circulation and the bypasses that seek to curtail interruptions, the repetitive drudgeries of service labourers, the variegated times of delivery, the time of news cycles, the affective rhythms of pharmaceutically compromised metabolisms, the dance floor times of 160 bpm, the prolonged daily commutes for the majority of urban inhabitants, the boredom of a 'dromospheric generation', increases and decreases in life expectancies, the speculative times of securitization and derivation, the duration of leases – and we could go on.

While each has its own character and duration, they all sit with each other in uneasy tensions, and the preponderance of anxieties that characterize most urban residents' lives is a manifestation of the constant work needed to try and reconcile competing rhythms. In a beautiful essay Doreen Lee (2015) speaks to the conundrums faced by women commuters in Jakarta: quality time with the kids for one woman is the ability to make it home in time to kiss them goodnight, tell them she loves them just before they fall asleep. At the same *time*, the constant interruption of functional traffic flows turns the time of appointments into rough approximations. One will show up, but never on time, unsettling any capacity to precisely address the question, 'what time is it?' As in the Chamber Brothers famous hit of the 1960s: 'Now the time has come; time has come today', as if time was something to be awaited and only apparent in a state of immediacy – particularly in an era where perhaps the most common complaint is that 'there simply isn't enough time'.

The future may inspire all kinds of feelings: hopefulness, dread, anticipation, concern and indifference. But perhaps its more important function is to occasion and serve as a platform for a broad range of practices. From owing, deferring, speculating, planning, praying, predicting, protecting, avoiding, insuring and saving, the future is the locus of many different concrete practices that materialize the sense of time, that detract from living simply 'in the moment', that compel activities to 'mean something'. Across cities, the future is increasingly something that is 'here today, gone tomorrow' – a notion that fuels an exigency for inhabitants to be as opportunistic as possible, to grab whatever opportunity presents itself.

Rather than assess the long-term viability of investments, for example, urban built environments are subject to an ethos where 'developers' need to act quickly, because if they don't invest now, then someone else inevitably will, and thus any opportunity will be lost. Notions of eventuality now dominate the temporal sensibilities of much of urban development. A 'project' may not seem profitable or sensible now, but *eventually* some viable use will come to it – and so entire landscapes are dotted with the materialization of various eventualities. Yet, urban populations must live today, and in many instances occupy the materialization of such eventualities as temporary and undocumented inhabitants, rendering the future as an affordance in the now, occasionally reshaping what is there to fit with their own needs and sensibilities, knowing that in time they will have to relinquish what they occupy to discovery of other uses by more powerful actors.

Yet as these 'occupiers' are often fond of saying, 'in the *meanwhile*, we are here'. There is no strong intent to consolidate a place that will last. They know they will eventually have to move on. They do not plan for a future, or at least do not identify one specific trajectory along which their anticipated future will unfold. They hedge their bets. They spread out, keeping close to the 'edge' of things, distributing family members and friends to various sites across the city, covering the angles, playing the dozens. More than past, present and future, urban time is a time of the 'meanwhile', the interregnum, the middle of things, the interim, something in-between, something neither ephemeral nor enduring – this despite the ways in which space becomes increasingly crystallized, balkanized and niched. While Jane Guyer (2007) may have argued for the disappearance of the *near-future* – a time of preparedness, concrete imagination and planning – in favour of a more millenarian sense of time, the meanwhile combines the simple practice of marking time – a time that doesn't really mean anything specific – with a sense of incipience, something that need not come to pass, that need not constitute a generative past, but an opportunity to gauge and try things without compelling too much attention.

So, incipience emanates from these multiple times, which themselves are approximations, each finding a particular aesthetic form in which to announce themselves; each being also something other than they appear to be. The future, then, is not something that is yet to come, it is not the outgrowth of the dynamics of a present, it is not the marker of an eternal return, nor is it the infinite running of a generalized Turing machine. It is not the object of prophecy or the fate of a perpetual sadness at the futility of existence. Nor is it the manifestation of promises kept or broken. It is not a matter of probabilities and enhanced data sets; it is not the justification for sacrifices made now. It is not about sustainability or about a self-referential ensuring of an ongoing existence. Rather, incipience as foreshadowing is the invention of a language through which to communicate with and convey that incipience to a larger world: how to talk to and with it in ways that simultaneously permit an intensive engagement but also knowing when to leave it alone; how to reframe, reword, rework the tropes through which we understand our places in the world, using all the toolboxes of sly and uncanny manoeuvres at our disposal.

We will have to sit with the detritus of all our exhausted preoccupations, as well as our voluminous data sets, technicist romances and formulas of interoperability. Cities will be constantly administered IQ scores and personality tests to measure happiness. Consultancies and institutes delivering assessments, monitoring and probabilities will continue to run rampant, as possible futures will be offered like a Chinese Denny's menu. There may indeed be no future as we remember or imagine it, and the future will remain something that is basically over for a large percentage of the world's population. Despite this, a thousand flowers bloom in the most unexpected of terrain with artisanal gardeners re-honing what were thought to be long vanquished skills or simply trying their luck. The first order of business then is to tend to such incipience, to curtail premature judgement, enable the artisans to proceed with their work, and strategically figure out ways to provide access to what is needed. At the basis of human life is trickery. For we are the entities without clear niche or purpose; existence has tricked us, and we have tricked it, as we have also forgotten how much chance has played in our history, mistaking it for imperative and sovereign rights.

Part of this order of business is to halt plunder where we can, to envelop the potentially useful in the shadows without depriving it of light, and to foreground, where politically feasible, all the ways of living the urban that too often are dismissed as transgressive, dysfunctional, infeasible as specific modes of incipience, the generative grounds of a new language. For we must always ask ourselves: Are what appear to be manifestations of normality really *that*, or do they conceal some untoward acts of pretence or a masking of evil? Are what appear to be manifestations of dysfunctionality really *that*, or are they competence and wellbeing masking itself as protection against really becoming the image it exudes? Do what appear to be manifestations of extraordinary imagination or collective presence really go beyond comprehension, or can they be subject to an accountable genealogy, simply the extraordinary effects of essentially quotidian action and events, an unanticipated manifestation of the ordinary?

What languages might enable us to see *what might be*, right now, as the future of a reciprocal creation among all urban creatures? Within this multi-temporal and its relational ties, there may be space for the crushed, a matter of chance as the characteristic of emergence in complex systems – the recuperation of the 'real city'. It is about making virtuosity in the shadows, to somehow steer the fullness of the 'fore' in generative and fulfilling directions. The question then is how this is possible, and through what means, as we sort through existing technicities, moral orientations and forms of regulation; as we invent new ones.

2

To Resume *Reprendre*: Urban Futures in the Era of the Congolese Anthropocene*

Language and the City

Allow me to start on a personal note, a confession if you want. For some years now, I have been finding it increasingly difficult to write about urban worlds, *in casu* Kinshasa. There are many diverse reasons for this growing incapacity, but the most important one has to do with language. Robert Hughes, in *The Shock of the New*, his acclaimed history of modern art, wrote about the horrors of mechanized trench warfare during World War I in a way that strongly resonated with me in relation to Congo's capital:

> In the Somme valley the back of language broke. It could no longer carry its former meanings. World War I changed the life of words and images in art, radically and forever. It brought our culture into the age of mass-produced industrialized death. This, at first, was indescribable. (Hughes, 2013 [1981], p. 57)

Of course, Kinshasa is not the Somme valley and even though Congo has experienced more than its fair share of violence and warfare throughout its colonial and postcolonial history, the daily wars that must be waged

* Drafted by Filip De Boeck.

in the city in order to survive are often – though not always (see e.g. Kienge-Kienge Intudi and Liwerant, 2017; Liwerant and Kienge-Kienge Intudi, 2019 on gang violence in Kinshasa) – of a different order. They have, however, also deeply impacted the possibility to describe and make sense of the daily hardships of urban life. If city life within the context of Central Africa is often characterized by dangerous edginess and unpredictability, the language of the city is inevitably affected by this and becomes an unstable discursive borderland 'where contradictory discourses overlap, or where discrepant links of meaning-making converge' (Tsing, 1994, p. 279).

I was reminded of the Hughes quote when listening to a talk that Stefania Pandolfo gave at my department in Leuven in autumn 2024. Discussing the situation in Gaza she cited from Freud's 'Thoughts for the Times on War and Death' (1915):

> In the confusion of wartime in which we are caught up, relying as we must on one-sided information, standing too close to the great changes that have already taken place or are beginning to, and without a glimmering of the future that is being shaped, we ourselves are at a loss as to the significance of the impressions which bear down upon us and as to the value of the judgements which we form. We cannot but feel that no event has ever destroyed so much that is precious in the common possessions of humanity, confused so many of the clearest intelligences, or so thoroughly debased what is highest. Science herself has lost her passionless impartiality. (Freud, 1957 [1915], p. 275)

In the second part of his essay, Freud identifies a second factor to which he attributes 'our great sense of estrangement in this once lovely and congenial world', namely 'the disturbance that has taken place in the attitude we have hitherto adopted towards death' (Freud, 1957 [1915], p. 289).

If, according to Mbembe, one of the social scientist's most important *raisons d'être* is *witnessing* and narrating the profound changes and mounting upheavals that the (urban) world is undergoing, then the question inevitably arises what witnessing might mean when it has become, *dixit* Pandolfo, an *apocalyptic witnessing* of worlds where the boundaries between life and death have been profoundly disturbed and there no longer seems to be an adequate language to make sense of life itself. Again, Kinshasa is not the Somme or Gaza, even though in other parts of the country Congolese citizens have been witness to the production of death on a scale that equals and even surpasses that of Gaza's horrors. . . But in Kinshasa too, the deep rumblings around the implacability of death, and the effervescent and often delirious and violent manifestations shaping up around the city's infrastructural failures (most notably, perhaps, in and around the city's cemeteries, see De Boeck, 2016), have had a great impact on the city's capacity to enunciate its own condition. They have profoundly syncopated the urban language in the process, reducing or 'cutting away' the urban residents' capacity to reveal, demystify, clarify or explain the unsteady urban ground of their lives.

Time, Death and Retreat

All of this plays out within a specific temporality. In *Tram 83*, Congolese novelist Fiston Mwanza Mujila's masterful debut, which is set in the 'City-state' – an unnamed Congolese city that greatly resembles Kinshasa – the main protagonist, whose name is, not coincidentally, Requiem, asks of whoever he encounters: *Vous avez l'heure?*, 'do you have the time?' Indeed, what *is* the time of the 'urban now' in a city that increasingly seems to be caught in the temporal frame of a biblical end game? The whole of the city (and the country at large) seems to be stuck in an 'apocalyptic interlude' (De Boeck, 2005), a time that is experienced as a period of endless suffering, and of violence, war, natural disasters, floods and erosions, as well as uncontrollable epidemic outbreaks (after all, Kinshasa was one of the ground zeros of HIV). What is being foreshadowed here is the moment of the last judgement and an afterlife where only the chosen and deserving will be saved from the world's ending. Hence, to a large extent, the city's chronicity is already situated in a 'beyond the grave' (De Boeck, 1998), in an urban reality that is not only 'on edge' – in a 'nervous state' (Hunt, 2016), agitated and about to lose it or snap – or 'at the edge' – in a precarious position and state of effervescence from danger, risk and an all-pervasive material and spiritual insecurity – but frequently also already 'over the edge', in a state of seeming insanity and loss of control, marked by an increasing zombification of the living, while the dead are becoming more restless and lively by the day, wandering around in the city and refusing to become ancestors (and much remains to be said about the incapacitated production of ancestrality, and the ensuing erection of the Zombie as one of the main figures inhabiting the Central African urban setting, the presence of which is enhanced and rendered very tangible and real through the widespread use of Bombé, a new zombie-drug that started to hit Kinshasa's streets some years ago (see Musa Obadia et al., 2023).

Here, then, this bitch of a city indeed becomes a witch: it unleashes, feeds off and builds on the occult and nocturnal powers of an invisible but very palpably present second world. These powers continuously invade the 'reality' of the first, visible world, and as such they exert a tremendous impact upon daily urban life, even to such an extent that an escape from this overflowing otherworldly underneath no longer seems possible. Likewise, the possibility of a physical detachment or retreat from the city to recover from its exhausting demands, the violence of its competition for resources, and the suffocating weight of social proximities and claims from which one can only disengage oneself at great social cost, is not easily realized. Dreams of leaving the city to export oneself to different elsewheres and inscribe oneself into a diasporic existence on the continent or beyond are common and widespread. But they have also become increasingly difficult to achieve (see De Boeck, 2012). Similarly, the dream of a return to more rural worlds, usually imagined in the form of one's village of ancestral origin (which, for a growing number of urban residents, has become a very vague and hypothetical notion), is not easily achieved either, for the rural environments surrounding the city have themselves often become problematic, unsafe and eroded worlds that currently face a deep economic, but also political, social, moral and cultural crisis.

For most city dwellers it is, therefore, almost impossible to escape from the crushing weight of the city. Apart from a temporary retreat to the Pentecostal prayer camps in the maquis on the hilltops surrounding the city, where people gather to purify themselves of the sins of the city, the only other routes of flight available to them are in the toxifying pleasures offered by drugs (such as the aforementioned Bombé), alcohol (often in the form of cheap but very strong, locally brewed and bootlegged booze, also known as *nzela mokuse*, the 'shortcut' to becoming drunk as rapidly as possible for little or no money), and the temptations held by the 'holes' of the flesh, as described for example by a popular Kinshasa-based DJ, Mombochi, in a song that became a smash hit with Kinshasa's youth in 2023: 'Red inside, chocolate outside, surrounded by forest, you go down a little, there is a hole, you go down deeper into the hole, and deeper into the hole.'[1]

It is this viscerality that offers the most viable form of retreat, and relief, from the excessive pressures of the city: a descent into the underbelly, the cavities and the *kuzus* of Kinshasa. The *kuzu* is a relatively new but very widespread phenomenon that the local press loves to report on, in a highly moralizing but also voyeuristic fashion. In Kinshasa's street argot *kuzu* means 'discreet', 'effaced', 'hidden', and this word also became the name of the obscure sanctuaries, rapidly erected out of cardboard, plastic tarpaulins or sheets of corrugated iron along the roadside, where people retreat in order to plunge into the hole and engage in what is called *mougou* (sexual relations) in Kinshasa's argot.[2] *Kuzus* are found everywhere in the city, but mostly in various *terrains vagues* of popular neighbourhoods. The most famous for its *kuzu* infrastructure is Pakadjuma, a shantytown that has sprung up along the city's sole railway line and the *Poids Lourd*, a major traffic artery in Kingabwa, a municipality that lines the left bank of the Congo

River. In April 2025, Pakadjuma attracted international attention because it was identified as the epicentre of a severe national and global outbreak of the Mpox virus. In the slums of this neighbourhood, those who cannot offer to pay for a hotel room (and that is the majority in this pauperized city where most get by on less than a dollar a day) pay a small and affordable amount of money to engage in rapid, often anonymous and unprotected sex with lovers or other, random, bodies under cover of darkness. The *kuzu* thus serves as a *déservoir*: a spillway, a passage for instant release and immediate but short-lived satisfaction, an 'undoing of time' (Barad, 2018, p. 70) that is encapsulated in the temporality of the moment, the timeframe of instantaneous capture and consumption, of momentary conquest and dispersal.

This is the pervasive timeframe that forms the essential backdrop to the city and basically defines the rhythm of its urban life. In such a setting, thoughts of the future are an impossibility, almost an insult even. There is no time to waste on accumulative moves and plans beyond the immediacy of the instant. On the contrary: in order to exist in the city, one has to be what the inhabitants of Kinshasa call a *cascadeur*, a stuntman, fully inserted in and concentrated on the moment, living life dangerously, recklessly and to the full. As a famous Kinois saying has it: *Tia mutu, bakata!* – 'If you lay your head down, you run the risk that it will be cut off.' So, stand up and fearlessly face whatever comes your way in the urban here and now. This is how one survives in the city: by blazing a trail into the unknown, like a hunter who cuts a way for himself through the forest. And since the city is often compared by its inhabitants to this hunter's landscape, the forest, this is also how the city is made and how it expands. The person who sets out to construct a house on previously unoccupied land in the city's periphery, or on landfills at the riverbank, is referred to as *panda nzila*, the trailblazer, the builder of the city. In the Central African context, the art of hunting and of engendering new (political) worlds (*ukeleeng*) have always gone hand in hand. Elsewhere (De Boeck and Plissart, 2004, pp. 40ff.) I have analysed in more detail how, in the local imagination, the idea of the Forest has been mapped onto urban space, and how the accompanying figure of the Hunter as cultural hero and maker of worlds has infused the city, both metaphorically and practically, with its own moralities of accumulation, expenditure and redistribution, and its own specific pathways of individual and collective realization. I will return to this later.

'Living at/over the Edge'

To qualify an urban reality where the difference between the living and the dead, or the first world and the second world, has become very porous, and where the distinction between Eros and Thanatos is constantly blurred, the word *mouroir* comes to mind, not only as a place where the dying gather, but also in the sense once given to it by the much regretted Breyten Breytenbach (2009 [1984]): the *mouroir* as a contraction between *mourir* and *miroir*. Kinshasa, one could say, constantly fashions itself in the mirror of omnipresent death, and as such the city may be said to exist in the form of a 'limit experience' on the edge. As noted, this limit experience greatly impacts the discursive field of the city, but it also gives form to the very praxis of urban living itself. Here, I am using the concept of 'limit experience' in its Foucauldian sense: that of an experience which, in terms of its intensity and seeming impossibility, leads a person to life's edge by 'seeing to it that the subject is no longer itself, that it is brought to its annihilation or its demolition' (Foucault, as cited in Sluga, 2005, p. 224).

Elsewhere I have analysed how urbanites have recourse to divinatory protocols to convert this problematic limit experience that is responsible for 'wrenching the subject from itself', in order to counter this breaking away from oneself and bring one back to oneself by reconfiguring the social (and infrastructural) boundaries between oneself and the surrounding environment (De Boeck, 2015). This is what Silva (2011), in her work on basket divination in the incipient urban environment of Zambian refugee camps, describes when she states that divinatory technologies (about which we still do not know a great deal) allow objectified individuals, marked by a sense of existential powerlessness, uncertainty and diminution, to de-objectify themselves, as it were, by ritually generating and sympoietically 'birthing' an alternative order for the suffocating, bewitched world that one inhabits (Silva, 2011, p. 6; see also De Boeck and Devisch, 1994). Whatever the situation may be – whether illness, misfortune, witchcraft attacks, professional setbacks, troubled marriages, or the sheer weight of city life itself – the divinatory oracle identifies and reformulates the problem at hand by embedding it in a different, less closed, less suffocating but more constructive narrative that always suggests the possibility of agency, of acting upon the world and thereby transforming and reorienting the problematic limit experience of the city itself (and the diverse objects of the divinatory apparatus, the divining basket, do not constitute a closed class of 'traditional' objects such as figurines, and animal or vegetal substances. On the contrary, the diviner also incorporates the city itself into their basket, in the form of locks, parts of cell phones, car keys, etc.). Again, within the necropolitical context of such 'living at/over the edge', what futures, what futurities can one still speak of, then, in this postcolonial, postmortem, world?

The City as Graveyard of Official Futures

Overall, urban settings have become graveyards filled with various dead, non-viable, futures. The future of salvation as promised by the Christian eschatology, that has become all-pervasive ever since the opening up of the religious space that accompanied the democratization process in the early 1990s, when Zaire's Second Republic started to unravel, has not inaugurated a second coming, a salvation, or a resurrection. The 'Pentecostal Revolution' (Marshall, 2009) has not culminated in the creation of a City of God (even though attempts have been made in that direction, as Nkamba, the Holy City of the Kimbanguist church in the Congo Central Province, illustrates). All it has done is plunge the context of urban life in the Central African context into the enduring liminal temporality of a pandemonium world: a violent and never-ending struggle between the forces of good and evil, a cacotopia from which there seems to be no possible escape or salvation in this life.

Similarly, the future as envisaged by colonialist modernity, the capitalist promise of progress and prosperity, has died multiple deaths since its initial implementation in the early era of formal colonialism, even though the spectre of its teleology continues to inspire and haunt present infrastructural dreams, underpinned as they are by 'Africa Rising' and *émergence* narratives (see Veithen, 2024). In reality, more often than not, all they do is recycle non-inclusive and segregationist urban colonial policies, parasitizing the corpse of the city in the process (De Boeck, 2021). Other, more dissident and alternative Congolese dreams of insertion and inclusion into a more global urban future, such as those described by Pedro Monaville (2022), have also dissolved into nothingness. . .

And then there is the (re-)emergence of a deep eco-time that seeps back into the city, undoing another promethean promise of colonialist modernity: that of the city as a civilizing place in which Africa's untamed nature would finally be domesticated. Today, this deep ecological time-frame that regulates and rhythms the vast and complex aquatic world of Kinshasa's Malebo Pool has returned to the city with a vengeance.[3] The unbridled demographic growth of Central Africa's urban worlds has contributed to the further expansion of a 'Congocene', as De Groof (2020) calls the vastly damaged Anthropocenic landscapes in and around Congolese cities and in rural hinterlands that were already massively mutilated and polluted by the violently extractive and toxic nature of (post-)colonial palm oil plantations, timber exploitation and/or mining economies. As a result of this ecological decline, pluvial cycles and alluvial water levels are rapidly transforming into highly unpredictable forces, causing landslides and inundations that increasingly result in the loss of urban lives and infrastructures on an unprecedented scale.

Kinshasa, Bukavu and many other cities in the Democratic Republic of the Congo (DRC) are increasingly suffering the consequences of these changing weather cycles and are being converted into inundated landscapes of disaster and (often literal) darkness (see Bola et al., 2022). All of this is powerfully captured in *Tongo Saa* (*'The Break of Dawn'*), a recent documentary film by Nelson Makengo (2024) that offers a sensitive portrait of Kinshasa residents' struggle as they face the challenges of life in this harsh urban environment. We follow a young man, Davido, who kills time by working out and dreaming of a better future while literally trying to stay afloat amid the infrastructural and ecological violence that the city imposes upon him. Every rainy season, and for several years in a row now, there are thousands of people like Davido who either die or become homeless because of floods caused by the unprecedented rise of the Congo River's water levels, or because of sudden erosions caused by torrential rains that in no time wash away houses, roads and whole neighbourhoods.

How urban worlds are completely made over by water in this way was poignantly captured by Congolese photographer Arsène Mpiana in a recent exhibition, *Parcours de l'eau*, that opened in Kinshasa in 2024 (see Mpiana, 2025, and figure 2.1). In it, Mpiana also focused on an urban project that is called *La Cité du Fleuve* (see De Boeck, 2011).

At the time of its inception in 2008, the *Cité du Fleuve* housing project, a new city extension constructed on an artificial island in the Congo River, was presented as Kinshasa's new urban future. For the last four years in a row, however, this new city was totally flooded (figure 2.2), and the rising water completely destabilized the artificial island construction in the process. In this way, Kinshasa's presumed new urban future has literally been sinking back into the mud and water that constitute the city's timeless surrounds. The crumbling and undoing of these infrastructured neo-modernist futures strengthens the apocalyptic temporality that pervades the daily life of Central Africa's urbanites, while also enhancing it with

Figure 2.1 Flooding of the Pompage neighbourhood, municipality of Ngaliema, Kinshasa, 9 January 2024 (Photo: Arsène Mpiana).

the slow violence and the enduring toxic temporalities of waste and plastic pollution once the water retreats.

Reconceptualizing the Urban Archive: What New Grammars and Syntaxes for the Urban Ground?

Again, navigating *Entre les eaux* (Mudimbe, 1973) of all these failed promises, what future can still be conjured up? What remains to be told but the unspeakable? And how to speak about it then? Nelson Makengo and Arsène Mpiana engage with image, film and photo, to give body to their own form of apocalyptic witnessing, but what instruments do we, as urban theorists, still have at our disposal to document and reflect upon these transitions? What words can we still use that have not themselves run cold from rigor mortis, or that have not been touched, marked and deformed by *l'odeur du père*, 'the stench of the father' (Mudimbe, 1982) and by the extractive forms of (neo) colonial knowledge production that are accumulated in what Mudimbe has famously called the Colonial Library: a library that continues to exert its strong influence on the development of procedures of acquisition, distribution and reclamation of land (control of physical space);

Figure 2.2 Flooding of the *Cité du Fleuve* site in the Kingabwa neighbourhood, municipality of Limete, Kinshasa, 16 January 2024 (Photo: Arsène Mpiana).

on the management, integration and implementation of autochthonous histories into new and externally imposed modes of production; and on the mental colonization and domestication of local worlds and cosmologies.

What kinds of words can we put up as an alternative to the epistemic violence contained in Prospero's books, now that the toxic teleological ideologies of linear progress and development they propose have so clearly and visibly failed? What kind of alternative futures can we conjure by opening up the suffocating straitjacket of the Colonial Library? And how could this apply to (Central African) urban worlds?

Here, perhaps, while being a curse, the return of deep eco-time into the heart of the city might also offer a cure and a possible opening, for it confronts us with the pressing urgency to come up with more inclusive and encompassing grammars to rethink the urban ground beyond the human.

In the 'Earthly community' speech that Achille Mbembe delivered upon receiving the 2024 Holberg Prize (Mbembe, 2024) I was struck by the following passages, which offer ways of 'detoxifying' the Colonial Library:

> As the age of Europe gradually comes to closure, many increasingly feel the need to reopen the archives of the world at large (Glissant's *le Tout Monde*), mindful of the fact that only a 'planetary library' might provide us with the resources we need to confront the planetary challenges we now face while enacting a new figure of the *in-common*.
>
> Furthermore, and contrary to what has been long thought, in Africa, we are faced with traditions that made a constant and articulate use of images and objects, objects as images and vice-versa. This does not mean that 'orality' was not important. Words and speech, in ceremonial as in non-ceremonial contexts, constantly or simultaneously called upon or instigated sounds and images. This is the reason why in African traditions and cultures, memory was based on both images and artefacts as well as on words. Images and objects did not only orient visual inference. They entertained an extremely close relationship to thought.

In other words, what Mbembe is calling for here is the need to look for other forms of exercising thought (and action), by moving beyond conventional concepts of language and text – indeed a precondition to refigure and reconfigure the archive itself in order to conceive of the possibility of a *living-together*, an 'in-commoning', in a different, more appropriate 'language' that has rid itself of toxic colonial connotations. What he proposes is to look into other forms of 'archiving', consisting of more ambient technologies of knowledge, world-making and affective mapping of social worlds and beyond (including human and non-human entities). These take shape in complex local systems of embedded knowledge production including, but also transcending, discursive and logocentric forms of knowledge production, and as such they overcome the classic opposition between *techne* and *episteme*, or more fundamentally between orality and the written. Again, one might incorporate here the various ways in which divinatory technological apparatuses were designed (and continue to circulate and be used) in large parts of Central Africa as particular and complex embodied forms of demiurgy, of poesis and collective world-making, through an entranced state of affectual feeling beyond the strictly discursive into the complexities of the (urban) world. But one could also think of the performance of *kasala* ritual poetry, for example, and how, through the specific rhythms of its spoken word – a form perhaps best described as proto slam poetry – body and world give birth to each other, the word becomes a womb that births existence, and the world is conjured up and pasts 're-turned' (Barad, 2018, p. 86) and reconfigured as an enacted foreshadowing of alternative futures. Similarly, one could consider the intricate object that the *lukasa* mnemonic board represents in its offering of a cartography of the world that does not build upon Euclidian representations of time and space but upon other qualia and layers of more affective and subjective experience through which plans are converted into journeys.[4] One might also take in the mathematics and algorithmics of Chokwe *sona* sand drawings that, like the *khata* knots in divinatory baskets (De Boeck, 2015), suggest alternative ways to think space, mobility, flux and direction, away from linear models (see also Gerdes, 2007). And moving beyond language and writing forms, one could consider many other rhythms that are embedded and embodied in music and dance. Resonating with Yala Kisukidi's proposition, cited in chapter 1, that the flesh can repossess itself as a materialization of spirit, it once again points to the necessity to foreground the body itself as a central unit to understand and conceptualize urban reality and imagine its possible futures. As Mudimbe himself stated:

> Language is the basic expression of a culture and culture can be compared to a body. No, it *is* a body. So in this capacity I make a progression of metaphors, from one to another, 'from language as metaphor' to 'body as metaphor'. From there you can see that an 'I' is established in a particular culture and language and that all this is inhabited and enabled by and *in* a body. If you accept this position, you can understand that we are connected to the

> world, other people and the concrete problems of life. The body must remain vital and healthy and this is possible if culture is passed on.[5]

What do all these intricate discursive and embodied forms of knowing, feeling, breathing and understanding the world tell us about these Central African urban worlds on edge, and how may their inclusion in the Library open up, refigure and expand the archive itself? How can we redirect these 'gatherings' of knowledge away from the amassing of history as linear progress towards something more indeterminate perhaps, but more multidirectional, inclusive, visceral, fertile and co-designed? Where and how to look for these different 'arcs of interference' (Biehl and Adams, 2023) that point to other forms of connectedness and towards an alternative and more inclusive ethics and praxis of care that may be posited against the predatory reality of the urban and the violence embedded in the official visions for its future?

Polyphonic Assemblages and the Notion of '*Reprendre*'

Once again, let me turn to Mudimbe, still one of the most forceful intellectual voices that Congo has ever produced. I realize that Mudimbe's reflections are perhaps a strange place to start from in order to rethink the realities of Central African urbanity. Apart from a brief passage in his autobiographical *Le Corps glorieux des mots et des êtres* (1994) about Likasi, the mining town in the Congolese part of the Copperbelt where he was born and raised as a child, he never mentions the extractivist and segregationist nature of Belgian colonial urban planning, perhaps because it was so much a taken-for-granted part of his own life and of urban life in Congo more generally that it did not deserve a mention and could go without saying. But in between the lines of his own writings, he does have something meaningful to say about alternative modes of connectedness and in-commoning, thereby offering us glimpses of possible novel ways to conceive of this.

To start with, he himself pleaded for abolishing disciplinary boundaries. In 'What is a line?' (2008) he refers to the processes of demarcation which he believes lie at the heart of the crisis now facing the social sciences. 'We are living in the shadow of the nineteenth century', he argues. 'The processes of ordering and classifying which the social sciences adopted as their primary method in the Enlightenment and which in turn created the boundaries between its constitutive disciplines should be thrown into question and dismantled' in order, also, to get rid of the compartmentalized understanding of the world that colonialism called into existence. One model for such a more de-sectionalized and anti-teleological vision comes from Mudimbe's own musical preferences and listening practice. True to his Benedictine formation, Mudimbe has always been a great lover and connoisseur of Gregorian chants, and those who met him know that he loved to engage in long conversations about the history of polyphonic music.

As Anna Tsing has argued, one can consider Gregorian chants as the most perfected form of what she has called a 'polyphonic assemblage', i.e. a particular way in which, in her terms, 'gatherings' become 'happenings' that are greater than the sum of their parts. Polyphony, writes Tsing, is music in which autonomous melodies intertwine:

> In Western music, the madrigal and the fugue are examples of polyphony, as is the Gregorian chant. These forms seem archaic and strange to many modern listeners because they were superseded by music in which a uniform rhythm and melody holds the composition together. In the classical music that displaced baroque (the music of the Enlightenment) unity was the goal; this was 'progress' in just the meaning that I was discussing . . . [namely] a unified coordination of time. In twentieth-century rock-and-roll, this unity takes the form of a strong beat, suggestive of the listener's heart; we are used to hearing music with a single perspective. When I first learned polyphony, it was a revelation in listening; I was forced to pick out separate, simultaneous melodies *and* to listen for the moments of

> harmony and dissonance they created together. This kind of noticing is just what is needed to appreciate the multiple temporal rhythms and trajectories of the assemblage. (Tsing, 2013, p. 23)

What Mudimbe and Tsing thus invite us to do is to rethink and to reinvent along different lines not only the Colonial Library itself, but also the damaged world and the ruins of the extractive landscapes created by capitalism and colonialism (and Congo-Kinshasa is one of the quintessential historical heartlands of this colonialist extractivism) in the form of such a polyphonic assemblage.

Mudimbe also provides us with clues how to proceed with such reconceptualizations, through the notion of *reprendre*, which he offered in an article on the nature of contemporary African art (Mudimbe, 1991). *Reprendre*, for Mudimbe, is grounded in a fundamental attitude. According to him, *reprendre* signifies three things for the contemporary African artist: first, it means taking up an interrupted tradition, not out of a desire for purity, which would testify only to the imaginations of dead ancestors, but in a way that reflects the conditions of today. Secondly, *reprendre* suggests a methodological assessment, through which the artist evaluates their tools, means and projects of art within a social context transformed by colonialism and, later, by other global influences. Finally, *reprendre* implies a meditation on the meaning of the two preceding exercises.

Mutations: Capturing Enactments of Fragmented Pasts to Reassemble the Present and Configure What is Ahead of Us

To a large extent, Mudimbe's thought continues to be inspired by, and remains deeply indebted to, Foucault. For someone like Povinelli, on the other hand, in *Geontologies* (2016), her requiem to late liberalism, the era of Foucauldian biopolitics and its specific regimes of necropolitical power has come to pass in the new Anthropocenic times that we have entered. For her, the main figures of such biopolitical interpretations of power and governance as well as the disciplines they gave rise to (the hysterical woman [psychology], the masturbating child [pedagogy, sexuology], the perverse adult [psychiatry] and the Malthusian couple [demography]) are now being replaced by a new set of characters: the Desert, the Virus (and here she explicitly mentions the Zombie as one of its figurations) and the Animist (in essence the one that I have called the Diviner or the Hunter earlier on).

What unites these three figures is their strong mutational capacity. The Desert is the space *par excellence* that exemplifies how life may mutate into non-life and back again. Similarly, mutations are what most defines the Virus, while the Animist ontology is defined by the fact that it does not discriminate between living and non-living matter, between subject and object, or between spiritual and material realms: everything has a capacity to mutate into, and become and communicate with, all else, in ever-changing in-commoning constellations.

If, as Povinelli argues through her introduction of this contemporary trio of mutant heroes, the capacity to mutate is at the heart of our relationship with this new Anthropocenic world, then what is most needed here is a deep understanding of the specific forms that current cultural mutations and urban transformations take on in this context. As Michel Serres teaches us, the unwanted guest that the Parasite is (and essentially the Virus is a type of Parasite because it must invade a host in order to multiply) generates noise and interference, makes social flows static, takes without giving and weakens without killing. But as such, it is not only the atom of a relation but also the producer of a change in this relation (Serres, 1982).

What is needed here, then, is an ethnographically grounded reflection on the toxic nature of contemporary urban worlds in the Central African context (the city as virus, as poison, pirate, parasite), and the ways in which the Animist (the city resident as diviner of the urban predicament) embodies the possibility for producing a change in the relation with the city. As Danny Hoffman

(2017) states in relation to Monrovia: 'To inhabit a toxic landscape, one must become mutant, learn to grow new and impossible organs' in order to survive. And that is precisely what city dwellers have been doing: transforming themselves through mutational shifts that open up the prospect of imagining and generating alternative orders to be placed against all the urban ruptures, paradoxes, divisions and disasters that cause the city's 'uncommon rhythms' (Wilhelm-Solomon, 2024), i.e. its rhythms of un-commoning.

One possible ethnographic starting point is located in the ritual knowledge that informs healing and initiation rituals that continue to be performed, for example, in Kinshasa's rural hinterlands such as the adjacent province of Kwango, home to an ethnic patchwork that is dominated by the Yaka ethnic group. Because of their vicinity to the capital, the baYaka also constitute a substantial part of Kinshasa's demographics and a large portion of the capital's most pauperized population, most notably in slums such as Camp Luka, or in the vast and overpopulated municipalities of the Tshangu district, nicknamed *Chine Populaire*, that forms the city's south-eastern border with the province of Kwango. Often looked down on by other city dwellers for being *ya mbala* and *ya ngwe*, peasants and village people ill adapted to the city, the inhabitants of Tshangu have indeed often retained strong links with their rural origins, and as such they have also preserved a reservoir of deeply rooted autochthonous knowledge, of ritual and technological know-how that originated outside the city but continues to inform life in the city itself. Think of the divinatory practices mentioned above, for example, but also of Yaka cults of affliction and healing such as *mbwoolu*, described in detail by René Devisch (1990). The *mbwoolu* healing cult treats conditions that show 'lack of form', such as physical disabilities, apathy, paralysis, stiffening, humoral disorders and loss of lust or erection. Nightmares concerning drowning in the river are also a *mbwoolu* symptom, as are certain disorders of a manic-depressive nature. The *mbwoolu* cult enacts a cosmogony which associates some species of catfish with the patient's evolution from formlessness back to form. In the *mbwoolu* treatment, in which river water and the clay of the riverbed play an important role, the patient literally learns how to morph and mutate into a catfish, how 'to grow new organs' indeed, in order to regain health and strength.

As Devisch notes, cults of affliction such as *mbwoolu* 'appear as an unauthored extrahuman management of retaliation and redress that reverses evil – basically ensorcellment – into a process of healing. . . . Ensorcellment feeds greedily on vital forces in people, whereas a cult reverses the evil – both the agent and the misfortune – against itself self-destructively so as to restore the larger weave of forces' (Devisch, 1993, p. 149). This is indeed a very common principle in many of Central Africa's therapeutic traditions, in which the harm or evil that a witch inflicts upon their victim is captured and sent back to its source by the healer. I have often observed how fragments and figments of the bodies of ritual knowledge and expertise that exist within therapeutic contexts such as *mbwoolu*, and which are deeply rooted in the eco-politics and -poetics of an autochthonous pre-colonial cosmogony, still readily find their way into the urban landscape, and into the urban residents' very bodies, thus continuing to inform urban modes of action that one could consider as acts of a spontaneous *reprendre*. If, for many, the urban present is a toxic presence, then rituals such as *mbwoolu* also teach them that this poison might be used to set in motion processes of metamorphosis, and to inform acts of healing along the lines of the therapeutic logic of homeopathic medicine that is applied in local cults of affliction that use the very substance that causes a disease to fight it.

It is clear that none of these traditions resurfaces in the urban context in its original form. Earlier 'autonomous melodies' and sedimentations within the constellation of local polyphonic assemblages never re-emerge as complete and uninterrupted wholes. They do not form full and undisturbed palimpsestic layers covered over by time and by the city and waiting to be excavated again in their totality. As part of more complex layerings of beginnings and becomings, they are, rather, like Freud's breccia in which hard fragments of volcanic rock are caught within solidified lava flows. At moments, this lava brings back up to the surface elements from the deepest sediments: materializations, through different forms, of what Castoriadis has called a magma (Castoriadis, 1997, p. 187): a web of plural meanings, of social imaginary significations through which society (re)creates, institutionalizes and anamnestically recollects itself.

Reprendre also takes place on more mundane levels, involving technical skills and ambient technologies that allow one to shape and scape urban environments anew. The unpredictable pluvial and alluvial cycles that have become more and more common in the Congo River basin as a whole not only cause an aquatic makeover of the city of Kinshasa,[6] but also reintroduce into the city the deeper eco-time of a river world that many of Kinshasa's inhabitants are still very familiar with (as the boundaries between river and city, or 'rural' and 'urban', were never clear-cut for many who inhabit the city, such as the *bana mayi*, the 'water children' who have always lived on and along the river, who arrived in the city by way of the river from more upstream locations, and who have continued to live and shape their home and livelihood in close proximity with the Malebo Pool's water world ever since).

In various ways, ecological disaster pushes Kinshasa's inhabitants to reconnect with environmentally more embedded forms of living that also allow for the reintroduction of action schemes and modes of individual and collective realization that are practically and metaphorically constructed around practices of *capture*, embedded in detailed knowledge of hunting, fishing, trapping, ensnaring, containing techniques. . . I have often witnessed how such technical skills are transferred from rural contexts straight into more urban settings. For years, for example, I followed young Congolese *garimpeiros* who would cross the border into Angola to dig and dive for diamonds in the Kwango River, a transboundary river between Angola and DRC, where it becomes the largest left bank tributary of the Kasai River, itself the chief southern tributary of the Congo River. To get access to the rich alluvial diamond deposits of the Kwango River, these artisanal diamond 'hunters' not only engage in diving, but also in constructing complex and intricate damming systems to redirect the river flow in order to be able to mine directly from pits in the riverbed itself. Fascinating recent research by Simon Marijsse on artisanal gold divers in Eastern Congo shows how, over time, this technological know-how has travelled from one artisanal mining site to another across the whole of Central Africa (Marijsse, 2023). And once these artisanal miners return to their respective towns and cities, they apply the very same damming and impoldering technologies to fight urban erosion sites that are continuously threatening to disrupt the urban tissue. Similar technical spillovers from more rural water worlds into the urban context of Kinshasa and other Congolese cities have also been observed by anthropologist Peter Lambertz, in his ongoing research on histories of river transport, navigation and fishing techniques on the Congo River in which he looks at technologies and 'underwater architectures' of scoop fishing, and how these skills and crafts re-emerge in the urban context to fight floods and erosions (see Lambertz, 2024).

All these autochthonous notions of capture still resonate deeply with and reverberate in urban modes of survival, (gendered) self-making and self-realization, and the possibility for making – and belonging to – a collectivity. The temporalities in which these forms of capturing, scooping and trapping unfold are radically different from the toxic temporalities of plunder and extractive erasure that have characterized the Central African urban landscape.[7] In contrast with the exhaustive nature of the latter, capture necessitates attention, care, patience, reflection, ruse, wisdom and intelligence (*mayele*) and this also shows itself in a knowledge of, an entanglement with, and an attunement to the 'surrounds', to the more-than-human, and to the impromptu and syncopated rhythms of one's social and natural environment. As such, they also engender a new politics of inhabitation that, rather than being inscribed in the linear temporality of modernist progress, is attuned to more organic cycles of rise and fall, waxing and waning, accumulation and dispersal, growth and decay, flow and blockage, effervescence and stillness, renewal and loss. . . that have always been at the heart of Central African urban life as well, even though such rhythmicalities have never been recognized by, and even less incorporated into, the discourse of officialdom.

What is needed here is a sustained research into various practices and notions of urban hunting, capturing and trapping as very specific, culturally constructed, and organically decolonial, forms of care that enable individual but also more collective accumulations and (re)distributions beyond (conspicuous) consumption in the peripheral (and peri-feral)[8] spaces of the city that are its most central ones at the same time: its gaps, voids, folds and recesses, its rifts and hidden holes, its undergrounds, wastelands and swamps. It is in all those Anthropocenic patches and ecological corridors that relations, mobilities and temporalities are designed that suggest the possibility of an emergence of incipient alternative urban orderings and the appearance of spaces of retreat and escape, of reflection and resourcing that hold promise for renewed mutations and transformations of the conditions of urban living.

3
Hope without Future? Eko Atlantic, Climate Urbanism and the Self-Devouring Growth of Lagos*

In July 2023, I toured the private enclave of Eko Atlantic City with Nneka, a sharply dressed environmental marketer whose polished British accent seemed engineered to persuade. Here, 'all na packaging', as Lagosians say. From our coastal shuttle, the emerging city's desolate and almost ghostly landscaping stretched before us. We paused briefly at the so-called 'Great Wall of Lagos', then pressed on along Eko Boulevard, an eight-lane avenue billed as 'Lagos's grandest in the making' – a future rival to Paris's Champs-Élysées or New York's Fifth Avenue, though its towers remain skeletal and its sidewalks eerily silent. Nneka boasted – again and again – that every 'who's who' in Nigeria, even the US Consulate, has snapped up plots here. Yet as we glided past empty facades, Eko Atlantic unravelled into something less visionary than a shimmering architectural mirage: dazzling at a distance, hollow at its core.

By the tour's end, Nneka's enthusiasm wilted when she learned I was an academic, not a buyer. This disappointment spoke volumes. Eko Atlantic is a citadel of coastal exclusivity, conceived for some 250,000 affluent residents – most outsiders – seduced by its tree-lined boulevards, waterways, manicured gardens, elegant

* Drafted by Daniel E. Agbiboa.

plazas, three marinas and pristine oceanfront promenade. In one twenty-four-storey tower, two- and three-bedroom apartments command $700,000 to $3 million USD, staggering sums in a country where a middle-class family of four earns, on average, between $14,600 and $29,000 per year (Renaissance Capital, 2011).

These exorbitant prices consign the vast majority of the Lagos population ('Lagosians'), especially those inhabiting waterfront settlements, to the status of 'recognized strangers': ever-present yet marked as outsiders (Ahmed, 2000, p. 21). Their exclusion from this so-called 'Dubai of Africa' exposes Eko Atlantic's true nature as a 'witch', as we argued in chapter 1: a 'harbinger of good things to come' even as it unravels lives in the present.

Lagos's reputation as a 'city of the future' has long captivated architects, urban theorists and colonial planners. In 2001, Dutch architect Rem Koolhaas hailed the city not as backwardness but as 'an announcement of the future', a tribute to the improvisational ingenuity of ordinary Lagosians (Packer, 2006). Yet that celebratory gaze has since been appropriated by developers, who deploy it to justify a glossy, utopian blueprint that severs bold visions from everyday realities. Beneath this gleaming edifice lies a harsh calculus: aesthetics mask mass expulsion, ecological risk is privatized, and elite dreams erase social memory.

In this chapter, I represent Eko Atlantic as a paradigmatic case of exclusionary climate urbanism – one that transforms Lagos's shoreline into a monastic enclave for the heinously wealthy, while displacing and endangering its most vulnerable residents, the so-called *ara Eko* (body of Lagos). By centring the 'surrounds', those waterside communities pushed to the margins, I show how the project legitimizes itself through the obliteration of memory, the privatization of coastal protection, and the deepening of social and ecological precarity. Rather than equitably mitigating sea-level threats, Eko Atlantic constructs a barrier of climate privilege, where safety becomes a luxury commodity and exposure is outsourced to those unable to pay.

Dreamscapes of Displacement

Across Africa, high-profile 'smart city' and 'green growth' initiatives often serve elites at the expense of the urban majority. Under the guise of progress, they inflict a triple loss – of property, personhood and memory (Roy, 2022) – while eroding the everyday networks of care that sustain life in the present, in what António Tomás (2022) calls 'the skin of the city'.

For investors and politicians, these megaprojects promise to cure 'urbanization without development' (Nugent and Locatelli, 2009, p. 2) and transform African cities into global showcases. Yet for waterfront residents, renewal translates into expulsion. Their neighbourhoods – once vital arenas of socio-economic life – are cordoned off to make way for a high-modernist fantasy still in the making. In this urban dialectic, hope and despair intertwine: modernity's power to expand possibilities simultaneously deflates the expectations of those it excludes.

Home to more than 20 million mostly self-styled hustlers, Lagos is poised to rank among the world's three most populous cities by 2050. More than half its land is wetlands – a nod to the lagoon island that early Portuguese maps labelled 'Lago'. Yet those sixteenth-century voyagers made no note of its small fishing villages, suggesting the settlements then seemed inconsequential. In fact, an 1883 map of Lagos Island left interior areas blank, only for those 'empty' spaces to appear as bustling settlements by 1885 (Hopkins, 2024).

Today, writer Chimamanda Adichie reminds us that nothing in Lagos was crafted for tourists; its allure is raw, uncurated (Adichie, 2019). Eko Atlantic, by contrast, is nothing if not curated. Rising along the sandy stretch known as Bar Beach in Victoria Island, Eko Atlantic reclaims some 6.5 million square metres 'seemingly out of thin air'. Shielded by an 8.5-kilometre coastal revetment – dubbed the 'Great Wall of Lagos' – and backed by South Energyx Nigeria Ltd (a Chagoury Group subsidiary), it boasts a 'full and comprehensive' Environmental Impact Assessment (EIA). Promoted as 'Africa's future Hong

Kong', its footprint rivals Manhattan's skyscraper district and echoes the renderings of Hudson Yards, New York, positioning itself as Africa's next financial capital.

But Eko Atlantic is also emblematic of a broader surge in fantasy urbanism: pre-packaged enclaves – from Nairobi's Tatu City to Abu Dhabi's Masdar – that arrive as self-evident solutions yet disregard local lifeworlds (Guma et al., 2023; Watson, 2013). This phenomenon reflects the 'worlding' of African cities, a privileging of Euro-American master plans and citation practices that sidelines scholarship and experience from the Global South (Roy and Ong, 2011).

Paradoxically, many Lagosians both critique Eko Atlantic's exclusivity and yearn for its symbols of modernity. Displaced waterfront communities aspire to the very skyline that erases them. 'When I went there last week,' said a former Bar Beach vendor displaced by Eko Atlantic, 'I saw it. It's very fantastic. I dream about that place. It's fine' (as cited in Emezi, 2018). The tension between critique and longing expressed by many displaced residents resonates with what Achille Mbembe calls 'mutual utopias': shared 'hallucinations' that entangle elite visions of the future with the aspirations of those displaced in their realization (2002, p. 263).

These mutual utopias do not dissolve inequality; they intensify its contradictions. Rather than dismissing master-planned futures outright, we must attend to these entangled surrounds – zones of rupture and endurance at the margins of tomorrow's city. Only by sustaining productive friction among the displaced, the ruined and the 'more-than-human' can an urban future emerge that does not depend on their erasure.

City Doubles

Beneath Eko Atlantic's glossy promise of protection and 'happiness' lie the precarious shoreside settlements grappling with the fallout of dredging, land reclamation and nonstop construction. These shadowlands – neither fully inside nor outside the city's formal grasp – are 'sacrifice zones' where the city's strugglers disproportionately shoulder the ecological and social costs of elite-driven fantasies. Here, people are expelled from longtime homes, erased from official plans, and cast as 'proof' of progress, forced into a constant state of uncertainty and readiness. In these surrounds, survival remains precarious and mobility bends sideways or slips downward.

These margins also underpin Eko Atlantic's own identity as a 'city double' – an ordered city built from scratch to contrast with the chaotic unravelling of informal settlements (Murray, 2015). Unregulated traffic gives way to manicured boulevards; open-air markets to 24-hour security; history-rich neighbourhoods to blank-slate luxury. This intimate proximity of order and disorder underscores the master plan's high-modernist logic: one cannot exist without the other. The uninhabitable becomes the very grounds of the habitable. In other words, as noted in chapter 1, 'the ultimate location is an effacement of location'.

And yet, as nearly two-thirds of Lagos's residents continue to live in precarious, underserved communities, a different question emerges: Whose future is being built, and at whose expense? The official language of *Itesiwaju* ('march into the future') rings unevenly across the city. As William Gibson observed, 'the future is already here – it's just not very evenly distributed' (as cited in Spurling and Kuijer, 2016).

Self-Devouring Growth

Eko Atlantic's gleaming promise of coastal protection belies a harsher reality: in reclaiming land for luxury living, the project is literally driving neighbouring shoreline communities into the sea. Its 'barricade of adaptation' masks zones of hyper-extraction – dredgers and incessant landfilling swallow homes, erode cemeteries and devastate informal economies – while the Great Wall of Lagos deflects storm surges only to amplify erosion elsewhere. Unregulated night-time dredging deepens the seabed, drawing tides ever closer to makeshift dwellings. 'The sea is more angry now', an elder warned, pointing towards a family cemetery that had slumped into the surf, its dead mourned twice – once at death, again at displacement.

Once-vibrant fishing villages on Lagos Island now watch as their streets – and even their graveyards – slip beneath the waves; yet these precarious settlements scarcely register in any official plan. Caught between blueprint utopias and the ocean's advance, these communities inhabit a relentless cycle of crisis, adaptation and uncertainty. Their struggle lays bare the cruel irony of climate urbanism: the very measures meant to safeguard Lagos's future depend on uprooting those who form its body – a process Julie Livingston (2019) aptly calls 'self-devouring growth'.

To see how this pattern began, we need only look at Bar Beach. Once the bustling public realm of Lagos, Bar Beach provides the earliest and most poignant example of climate urbanism as violence. Cast as an ecological emergency site to arrest coastal erosion, the state recast the sandy stretch into a stage for high-modernist spectacle. In its heyday, Bar Beach was the setting for birthday picnics, lunch-hour strolls, first dates over ice-cream cones, and the sunset prayers of Aladura 'White Garment' churches dancing in the surf. It was where children mounted their first horses and entire families forged collective memories. 'Bar Beach means a lot to people in their mid-thirties and above', recalls one resident in her mid-fifties. 'It helped me relax, it was a period I cherished. They could have built Eko Atlantic without taking that huge chunk of beach.'

Instead, the shoreline was excavated, reclaimed, and locked away behind luxury towers, an erasure of both ordinary pleasures and the darker echoes of its past: the 1971 military executions that once turned the sands into a firing-squad amphitheatre. As Wole Soyinka later reflected, 'I knew of no other place where humanity interwove with water in such an organic, understated flow' (Soyinka, 2020). Today, that layered history lies buried under concrete and glass.

Bar Beach is not an isolated incident but part of a broader pattern. In 2016 and 2017, over 30,000 residents

Figure 3.1 Okun Alfa community
(Photo: Adolphus Okpara 2023).

of Otodo-Gbame and Ilubirin watched bulldozers reduce their homes to rubble. Some drowned while fleeing tear gas and gunfire; others drifted on fragile boats – homeless, traumatized, abandoned by the very legal system meant to protect them. A Lagos High Court later declared the evictions unconstitutional, but the ruling proved hollow, as they so often do in Lagos, nay Nigeria. Today, Imperial International Business City and Periwinkle Residences rise where fishing nets once dried in the sun. Taibat Lawanson calls this a 'political act of classification': the bureaucratic rendering of informal citizens as non-persons, clearing the way for luxury capital (cited in *The Guardian*, 2022). As one survivor put it simply, 'Our only crime is that we are poor.'

On Alpha Beach, villagers watch as dredgers steam in to harvest sand for Eko Atlantic's foundations: 'Our fathers' land – gone', one lamented. Over ten years, Okun Alfa has been halved; what was once safe ground now lies perilously close to the surf (figure 3.1). In Okun Alfa, residents live in constant fear, unsure when bulldozers will raze their homes or dredgers will 'swipe' their lives. Fishermen describe empty nets and poisoned lagoons, forced into subsistence fishing as commercial livelihoods collapse. In 2025, at dawn, bulldozers razed the waterside community of Ilaje-Otumara – whose very name, *Otu-milara*, means 'a place of comfort and peace' – evicting more than 9,000 people with no warning (Akinwotu and Bright, 2025). The irony is stark: the community built for solace was destroyed in the name of securing luxury.

These local tragedies reflect a global pattern: gated 'world-class' enclaves rely on the dispossession of the poor. Foreign investors and visiting Global North scholars slip through secured perimeters in Ikoyi and Victoria Island, insulated in luxury hotels while outsourcing the 'messy' work of field research to local academics. In this sanitized circuit, climate adaptation transmogrifies into climate violence: elite protection built on the devastation of those least able to resist. The stark conclusion is unavoidable: Eko Atlantic and its peers do not plan for the poor – they plan them out. At best, they relocate poverty; at worst, they convert ecological crisis into what Julie Livingston (2019) calls 'self-devouring growth'.

Between World Class and Working Class

Eko Atlantic epitomizes Lagos's post-1999 drive to recast itself as a 'world-class' megacity. Following decades of military neglect, Governors Bola Ahmed Tinubu (1999–2007) and Babatunde Raji Fashola (2007–15) unleashed sweeping reforms to secure fiscal autonomy, attract foreign capital and modernize infrastructure (Agbiboa, 2018, 2022). Tinubu overhauled taxation and forged public–private partnerships that rejuvenated Lagos Island; Fashola, styling the city as 'Africa's Big Apple', doubled down with glossy marketing campaigns promising 'untold opportunities'.

Guided by what chapter 4 calls 'ambivalent illegality', laws switched on or off to suit elite designs, Lagos State authorities razed informal settlements without resettlement plans, expelled vendors, banned informal transport workers, and bulldozed working-class neighbourhoods in the name of *Itesiwaju Ìlú Ẹ̀kó* ('Lagos's march into the future'). These moves were generally applauded by the global press. Seth Kaplan (2014) hailed Lagos as a 'model city' in *The New York Times*; *The Economist* (2015) praised its capacity to 'kick-start wider change'; John Campbell (2012) called it 'a success story' for the Council on Foreign Relations; and Alex Perry (2011), writing in *TIME*, gushed that the city was 'emerging from its Dickensian squalor and rediscovering its soul' (Perry, 2011). Yet the soul they celebrated excluded the urban majority, recast by the state as a pathology to be eliminated or 'ensconced in places not of their own choosing' (chapter 1).

In subtracting people from the present, the blueprint utopia dubbed Eko Atlantic invariably strips away the capacity to imagine a plural future. Eko Atlantic does more than redraw shorelines: it purges the city's capacity for alternative worlds. Here the question is, futures for whom? Who will be left to entertain a future, when certain inhabitants across the world are being 'absented' from the process of future-making altogether? As we showed in chapter 1, these absented lives are precisely the ones that urban master plans write out of existence.

At the urging of theorists such as Hernando de Soto, Lagos officials promised to 'formalize' the informal, a euphemism that often meant disciplined eviction. As bell hooks reminds us in *Where We Stand*, the poor constitute 'a predatory class to be both despised and feared' (hooks, 2000, p. 48). Lagosians, however, heard the subtext. 'Making a megacity doesn't mean banishing the poor', one resident snapped. Another mocked the governor's boast of planting 4 million trees: 'Na flower I go chop?' (meaning 'Will I eat flowers?'). A third put it bluntly: 'They want a Lagos that glitters, but Lagos is Lagos because of its people.'

These outcries from the surrounds cut through the spectacle, revealing the lie of a neoliberal order that claims inclusion even as it banishes its most vulnerable; or, as Stefano Harney and Fred Moten put it, a project that 'soldiers on, claiming to defend what it has not enclosed, enclosing what it cannot defend but only endanger' (Harney and Moten, 2013, p. 8). They remind us that true city building begins not with blueprints, but with those who dwell, labour and dream within its ever-contested borders.

Makoko: Against the Current

Makoko – a century-old stilt settlement of nearly 100,000 residents – is now ground zero in this intensifying war for waterfront land. With property values soaring, Makoko's future hangs in the balance. In early 2025, fears became fact: the Lagos State Government, in partnership with private investors, launched FBT Coral Estate, a 55-hectare luxury development on Makoko's fragile shoreline. Touted as 'the new face of Lagos smart city', the project was greenlit via a 75–25 state–private agreement, with little warning, no community consultation, and no publicly disclosed social impact assessment.

'They gave us two or three days' notice, told us to go back to where we came from. But we were born here', said one community elder. Even those brandishing court injunctions could only watch as concrete crept across their homes. Drying racks for fishing nets have been reimagined in blueprints as malls, hotels and yacht clubs. Makoko's 2012 eviction – when then-Governor Fashola gave residents just 72 hours to vacate – still haunts the community. That lightning-fast demolition underscores our claim in chapter 1 that 'the speeds at which things are undone come to exceed those that would contribute something perhaps truly reparative'.

'Makoko was called an eyesore', said Taiwo, son of the community chief. 'Because visitors crossing the Third Mainland Bridge could see us.' He added, his voice sharp with the memory: 'That year, there was a massive shooting. We lost some of our men.' Taiwo and I moved through the floating infrastructure of everyday survival: canoes ferrying schoolchildren, sachet water, mosquito repellent, condoms (figure 3.2). 'If they sandfill Makoko, we lose everything', he said. 'No fishing, no home, no life.' 'The government does nothing for us', Taiwo added. 'The only time we see them is during elections.'

Figure 3.2 A makeshift bridge in Makoko (Photo: Adolphus Okpara).

The community responded with protest marches to the Lagos State Secretariat in Alausa, submitted regeneration plans when asked, even met with state lawyers. 'We followed their procedures', Taiwo tells me. 'But we never heard back. Instead, we heard rumours – then announcements – of new developers.' The message was clear: no matter how you comply, the bulldozers come anyway. One lay preacher in Makoko summarized the stakes, telling interviewers: 'We are not farmers, fishing is our own farming. If they sandfill this place, our occupation is destroyed. We are fishermen. We must live near the water. We, the community, say no to forced eviction. You cannot take our community. Where should we go if you take it from us? If you are to kill us on it, then we would still live here' (as cited in Olaoluwa, 2022).

This is not just a material struggle. It is symbolic, spiritual even. At the entrance to Apollo, one of Makoko's six constituent communities, the phrase 'Sea Never Dry' is painted three times on the back of a minibus taxi (*danfo*) – a vernacular theology, a plea and prophecy at once. But the sea does change. Dredging and sand-filling alter its rhythm. And the state's vision of a Lagos that 'looks like London' threatens to erase not just livelihoods, but histories and cosmologies.

Human rights advocate Nnimmo Bassey, director of the Health of Mother Earth Foundation, denounces the Coral Estate megaproject as textbook 'accumulation by dispossession'. He urges Lagos to stop weaponizing 'development' against its own people: 'These are communities whose ecological knowledge and labor have long sustained Lagos. Displacing them for profit is violence – not progress' (Ganic, 2023).

Jacques Rancière's notion of the 'partition of the sensible' helps us see how the excluded, those with 'no part', can nonetheless become agents of political rupture (Rancière, 1999, p. 11). Echoing the 'popular planners' of the 1950s (Somotan, 2025), today's residents – fisherfolk, traders and community elders – leverage every legal tool at their disposal. In 2016, the Legal Defence and Assistance Project (LEDAP) sued to halt Eko Atlantic's destructive encroachment, arguing that the project violated both marine ecosystems and the livelihoods of thousands. Under the umbrella of the Nigeria Slum and Informal Settlements Federation, waterfront communities issued a collective declaration: they belong to this city, they have rights to shelter and livelihood, and forced eviction is neither lawful nor effective (ICIR, 2015). Still, bureaucratic inertia and endemic corruption have stalled redress.

Hope without Future?

The coastal community's resistance, their refusal to be rendered refuse, is not a plea for progress but, as AbdouMaliq Simone describes, a 'sense of maybe – maybe I make it or maybe I don't'. This maybe is not mere uncertainty but a temporality of improvisation – a life lived *pro tempore*, without guarantees: 'rebellion without redemption' (Simone, 2022, p. 103).

Yet in the face of Lagos's suspended futures, not all responses take the form of refusal. Some, particularly among the religious middle class, attempt to construct parallel orders entirely. One such example is Redemption

City, a Pentecostal settlement developed by the Redeemed Christian Church of God. Established in 1983 as a prayer camp, it has since grown into a functioning city of at least 12,000 residents. In contrast to the chaos of Lagos, Redemption City offers gridded streets, reliable electricity and uniform housing – each complete with a 'mission room' for church work. Rules are clear: no hawking, no loitering, no irregularity. In this camp of salvation, hope is not deferred but designed. 'We make life easy', one pastor explains.

Redemption here is spatialized – orderly, infrastructural and moral. And yet, even this sanctified space cannot escape commodification: though homes are intended for the faithful, they increasingly appear on commercial real estate platforms (*The Economist*, 2018). Redemption City thus mirrors Eko Atlantic in curious ways. Both are gated utopias, both curate order through exclusion, and both offer redemption, albeit through different registers: one through capital, the other through Christ.

Whether through refusal or reinvention, these urban experiments converge on a fundamental question of personhood: who counts as human – who is seen, protected, mourned? And who is a 'mere dangler', suspended beyond the bounds of recognition? As Simone (2022, p. 103) asks, 'How has the "human" been used to reduce large swathes of human life to the status of the inhuman?'

Drifting in the Abyss of Expulsion

From the margins, Eko Atlantic's promise of protection and happiness dissolves into a nightmare of abjection. No blueprint – however total – can erase those it casts aside. Even as Eko Atlantic's seawall rises, the dead, the displaced and the feelings they leave behind persist: washed-over burial grounds, whispered stories, unatoned wrongs, mothers' naked grief, elders' curses. These spectral traces summon new ethical and political horizons, proving that every utopian plan drags its own ghosts. Chapter 5 reminds us that 'the present actuates beyond what is to be seen or cognitively understood';

it is precisely this surplus – lingering affects and restless spirits – that punctures the master plan's claim to finality.

The ghosts do more than haunt; they rouse the living. Eviction is rarely disappearance. Communities are never truly 'gone', certainly not in the blunt terms of the NPR headline, 'A Lagos community, destroyed in one day' (Akinwotu and Bright, 2025). Residents wait, return, rebuild – and rise again, like boxers steadying for the next blow. What looks like aftermath is, in fact, an 'untimely contemporary' (chapter 6), where eviction pens an ending that waterside residents immediately rewrite as prologue – 'endings that are not over', in Avery Gordon's (2008) sense. The stubborn resolve of the surrounds is distilled in the refrain *Eko ò ní bàjẹ́* – 'Lagos will not spoil'. Displaced residents play the long game, insisting 'in the *meanwhile*, we are here' (chapter 1). We refuse to become the conspicuous void on which your blueprint utopia depends. Families point to the cracked foundation slabs that remain – relics of their homes – crying, 'This was someone's property – stop the dredging ship!' even as bulldozers growl at dawn, unleashing shuddering sonic violence.

Denied both present safety and belonging in the future tense, surrounding residents drift unmoored from Lagos's sanctioned modernity. Édouard Glissant's question echoes: 'The banks of the river have vanished on both sides of the boat. . . . What kind of river, then, has no middle?' (1997, p. 7). Yet even here, in this suspended state (chapter 4), voices endure – not as plaintive laments but as defiant claims to memory and place. Their appeals lay bare a simple truth: the right to be seen, to remember, to belong – these are inseparable from the *right to the city* itself.

4
To be Suspended: The 'Black Heart' of Naples*

Introduction

In the final pages of Italo Calvino's book *Invisible Cities*, Marco Polo allays Kublai Khan's fears for the future by revisiting the present. He tells him the 'inferno of the living is not something that will be; if there is one, it is what is already here, the inferno where we live every day, that we form by being together. There are two ways to escape suffering it. The first is easy for many: accept the inferno and become such a part of it that you can no longer see it. The second is risky and demands constant vigilance and apprehension: seek and learn to recognize who and what, in the mist of the inferno, are not inferno, then make them endure, give them space' (1977, p. 148). Through Marco Polo, Calvino is telling us that any dismal urban present has the dual character of inertia towards the infernal and signs in ongoing relations of a different future that must be grasped.

This is the tension explored in this chapter on Castel Volturno, a littoral settlement north of Naples that onlookers describe as infernal for its many perceived failures and degenerations. Here is a place of dumped waste, agricultural exploitation, dilapidated buildings, half-built infrastructures, racial tensions, migrant poverty,

* Drafted by Ash Amin and Enrica Morlicchio.

corrupt governance, drug and sexual trafficking. Stock phrases that circulate are that over the last forty years, Castel Volturno has become an 'inferno without hope', a 'powder keg waiting to explode', a 'theatre of war',[1] a ruined holiday destination. Yet these are phrases without history, negligent of the social efforts to make infernal life endurable through the care of religious and civic associations, informal arrangements and solidarities among the marginalized, the spaces of shared habitation, and the sheer will among migrants to believe in the possible. In the ruins have emerged practices of affiliation in the shadows tempering time's recursions of the infernal.

These practices are forever sabotaged, leaving Castel Volturno's troubled residents in a constant state of suspension. In a literal sense, they are cast out in so many different ways, including evictions and house arrest for minor crimes, stigmatization and violence, invisibility due to the absence of legal documents. But in penury, they are also stuck in a long middle time between damnation and salvation in which an ecology of survival forms. It is an ecology of minor adjustments to condemnation in the repeatedly conjunctural that settle into a life form in its own right of opportunities, gains, disappointments and movement. The state of suspension has its own ontology of habitation, connection and provision tilting the balance of gain and loss, alienation and sociability, disappointment and hope. Its texture is consequential, less in the sense of a deferral of expectations by African migrants and displaced Neapolitans (in the way Xiang [2021] explains rural migrants in China working all hours in cities to earn the means to return to a 'normal' life), than as a condition of inhabiting marginality with its own call and response. As AbdouMaliq Simone puts it, 'Castel Volturno not so much avoids detection but obscures all sense of proportion. For, what if it was unclear the extent to which existent realities on the ground were at one and the same time self-destructive, virtuous, frivolous, necessary, generous, and manipulative? What if it were impossible to tell exactly what is virtuous or debilitating?' (2020, p. 3). Suspension works in much the same way as an interstitial condition of denial and affordance, as do the motifs of *reprendre* in Kinshasa and extensibility in Mexico City.

After forty years of migration, Europe's allegedly densest concentration of Nigerians and Ghanaians lives in the ruins of urban speculation in Castel Volturno, negotiating racial hostility, legal unrecognition, municipal indifference and organized crime to beat the streets, fields and roads to Naples for meagre returns. Yet over time, the rawness of early racial violence has receded because of some accommodations of difference, the campaigns of religious, anti-racist and civic bodies, and of Africans coming together in protest, faith and community. These openings have created fragile possibilities in the permanence of racism, deprivation and illegality. In a similar state of suspension is another set of migrants to Castel Volturno, who have inhabited stasis differently as bearers of citizenship rights. These are impoverished Neapolitans who have ended up in Castel Volturno to escape higher costs of living and earthquake tremors, squatting in abandoned houses, pirating electricity and water utilities, eking out a meagre existence without work, opportunity or hope. Trapped by poverty, illness, house arrest or social neglect, they have made home and hearth through their courage to squat, pirate services, and dream of a nostalgic past. They have made claims in ways that the Africans, denied Italian residency and cultural legitimacy, could not dare. Living in different parts of Castel Volturno, the black and white migrants bear the endless present of denial differently, the latter looking back in defiant entitlement, and the former looking forward in expectant hope.

This chapter explores the dynamics of black and white suspension, examining how time and place, law and association, and personal biography mediate the balance between surrender and hope. It opens with a summary of the subtractions of place that have both constrained and enabled life in abandonment. It then considers the ambiguities of suspended law – the denial of citizenship, the illegalities of work, the push towards the irregular. After turning to the ghosting of black migrants and the phantom existence of displaced Neapolitans (drawing on field research,[2] published ethnographies and films and documentaries), the chapter looks at how, amid denial, an ecology of self-organization and solidarity has grown over the years to make African lives that much more bearable.

A Fractured Place

A portrait of Castel Volturno based in its natural surroundings would paint an exotic picture of the shores of the Mediterranean Sea and the Volturno River, Emperor Domitiano's castle built in AD 95, a countryside of buffalo, rare ibis and plover, nesting turtles, exotic palms and tomato fields, and pine groves that extend for kilometres. Yet Castel Volturno is a place of ruination and decline. It has suffered a continuous, often irreversible replacement of the original settlement through construction sites, most often due to illegal speculation, best symbolized by the eight towers that rear up on maritime state property and the houses built at the head of the Volturno River. Houses which have seemingly sprung up from the sand. The devastation has been made worse by the extensive pollution of irrigation channels and the river by illegal discharge from the Regi Lagni pipelines[3] and from landfill sites controlled by Camorra clans and notorious for the high incidence of cancer deaths, but turning 'trash to gold' for the beneficiaries of dumping.

In this altered landscape, social fractures have deepened, with old residents separated from their original social and territorial moorings, and then later from migrants arriving from the Maghreb at the end of the 1980s for summer work, and in the following years, larger waves of sub-Saharan and East European migrants. The migrant traces, no longer only seasonal due to year-round demand in agriculture and in construction, have been ghostly, not only because of spatial segregation from white areas, but also because of the laxity of official statistics. Municipal representatives or the *carabinieri* (the national police force), when asked how many illegal migrants there are in Castel Volturno, always give the same answer: there are no numbers, there are no reliable data. So, random numbers pass from mouth to mouth, becoming fact, estimating migrants not legally registered in Castel Volturno to be between 15,000 and 25,000, more than half of the resident population.[4] In contrast, research-based enquiries (e.g. De Filippo and Strozza, 2012; Petrarca, 2016) put this number at no more than 20 per cent of the population.

Today, Nigerians (60 per cent female) and Ghanaians (80 per cent male) together make up more than half of the legally resident foreign population, followed at a distance by Ukrainians, Poles, Romanians, Gambians and Togolese. Among this largest group, there are those who arrived over thirty years ago and have spent most of their lives in Castel Volturno, those who were born there, and those who arrived a few months ago. There are those who would like to settle down, those who have left to return one day, those who consider themselves just passing through, and second-generation African Italians who, as one informant puts it, 'call themselves brown, while they call other Africans black, but at the same time, they don't call themselves Italians'. The Castellani have made claim to the historic centre close to the river, separated from the Africans, but also from the Neapolitans who relocated for a life by the sea during the 1970s or to escape seismic instability a decade later (see figure 4.1). Parco Saraceno, a new residential complex built in Pinetamare, also known as Villaggio Coppola after the realtor's name, was intended to be the flagship to entice the middle classes wanting to escape the smog, traffic and crime of Naples. Twelve thousand apartments were planned, together with health centres, schools, a cinema, a police station, restaurants and a large luxury tourist port. The Neapolitans would cohabit with the American soldiers stationed at the NATO complex in this Italian 'Miami'. The dream evaporated, with the plans only half realized, their legality contested by the authorities, resulting in even basic services never being put into place, buildings soon falling into disrepair, and apartments illegally rented out, as Salvatore Porcaro (2019, 2021) shows in his detailed history of the development.[5] Here and elsewhere, an informal system

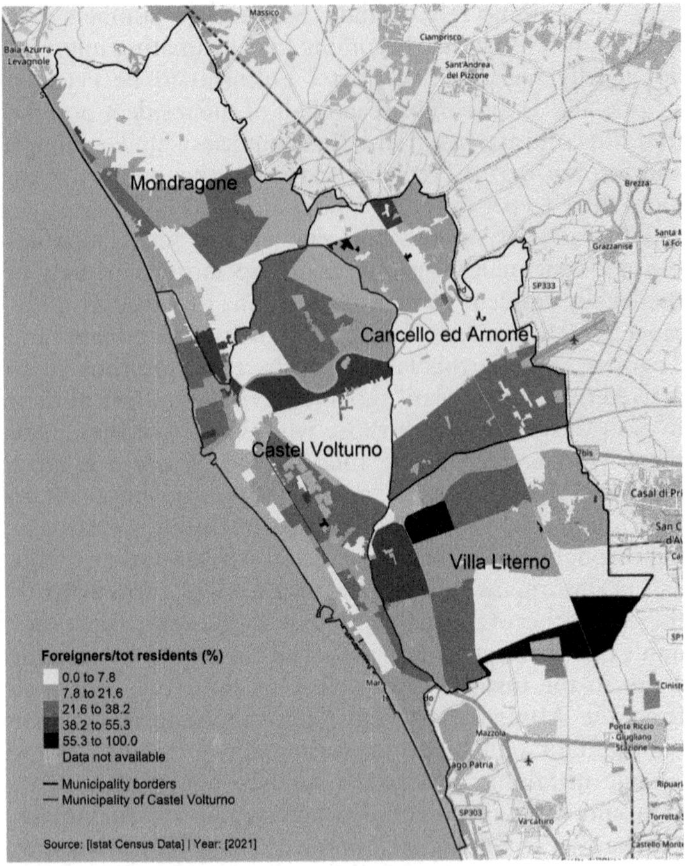

Figure 4.1 Distribution of foreign residents in Castel Volturno and nearby municipalities

of filling empty houses under the control of local bosses and disreputable intermediaries has grown, regulating migrant and non-migrant access to housing. There are no rental contracts, and every transaction takes place within a moral economy of corruption, often resulting in people being arbitrarily moved out.

In this coded landscape, a history of racialized blame has grown, often accusing African migrants and even displaced Neapolitans of running down the built environment, when in reality, without their rents, there would be no housing economy, nor the corrupt allocation system in place. Amid the dilapidation, migrants have kept things going, despite local authority disengagement, the absence of public transportation and lack of maintenance of the housing stock by sometimes untraceable Italian second-home owners. It is the owners, one Tunisian bricklayer tells us, who fail to maintain their mouldy and crumbling houses, while migrants take care to paint them in bright colours, make vegetable gardens and undertake small repairs, even without having any stake in the housing. Yet, as clandestine migrants without papers, they remain under the radar, in a 'darkness in which you can hide your tears', according to one young Nigerian, contributing but without much hope of obtaining rights. The invisibility is also spatial, with African communities concentrated in the neighbourhoods of Destra Volturno, Bagnara and Pescopagano (figure 4.1). The history of violence against Africans has played its part in ensuring their concealment in Castel Volturno's less visible places, where it is easier to hide from criminal actors and the police.

Rogue urbanism has left Castel Volturno without the tissue to bind it together. There are no buses, road names do not exist, public infrastructures are incomplete, and the only cinema has been closed for a few years. It comes as no surprise to hear from one resident that 'after 7.00 pm there is no one to be seen out and about, Castel Volturno becomes a ghost town; or that in winter you can't even go out: at five o'clock it's all dark, it's scary to go out, because in the streets there is no public lighting, and you don't know who you might encounter. If there is daylight, you can go out, but when it's dark we lock ourselves inside.' On the main desolate roads (figure 4.2), there are a few bars, shops and hotels, but they are racially coded, avoided by Africans, who gather in churches and mosques and their own meeting places and shops, or simply minimize stepping out at all, especially single women. With its arrivals from all around the world and from Naples, its NATO and vacationing history, and its legacy of seafaring, agriculture and villas from different epochs, there is something ghostly

Figure 4.2 Main road in Castel Volturno (Photo: Enrica Morlicchio).

about Castel Volturno in its ruination and segregation – a ghostliness that simultaneously curtails and enables.

The Suspension of Law

This duality is evident in the workings of illegality, which both sustains racial violence and dispossession, and provides migrants with opportunity. Filmmakers, writers and journalists, drawn by stories of organized crime, prostitution and drugs, have played their part in labelling Castel Volturno as lawless.[6] But in this suspension, strategies of survival, resistance and escape have been forged, as have skills and resources to meet the opportunities that present to settlers and migrants alike. Illegality operates as a kind of vice that nobody ever manages to rid themselves of completely, according to a brothel 'Madam' in the film *Il Vizio della Speranza* ('The Vice of Hope') by Maurizio de Angelis.[7] In the normalization of illegal work and housing, migrants find an 'existential reciprocity' (Lucht, 2012) of exchange, defiance and solidarity (elaborated below) that helps them negotiate difficult and often violent times.

These reciprocities build on a history of refusal of the terms of organized crime. One example is from 2008 when Daniele Manzo, owner of the Crazy Horse bar, refused to sell a specific brand of coffee. The Camorra machine gunned the bar's shutters, yet Manzo went on to establish an anti-racket association named after Domenico Noviello, the owner of a driving school who had been killed after refusing to pay protection money (*il 'pizzo'*). Manzo maintains that 'thanks to the fluidity of this place we have developed antibodies'. But in the process, a high price has been paid by Africans: for example, the burning down on 17 September 1994 of a reception camp in Villa Literno, a nearby town, opened by Caritas to house a thousand African workers, in which twenty-one caravans and twenty-one newly installed containers were destroyed. Five years earlier, on the night of 2 August 1989, a group of migrants had been sleeping in an abandoned farmhouse in Villa Literno, after picking tomatoes from early morning to sunset. At dawn, when the day labourers were still groggy, four members of the Casalesi Camorra clan burst into the building demanding money, attacking a Sudanese worker who tried to sound the alarm, and killing Jerry Masslo, an anti-apartheid activist, by shooting him in the abdomen. In his dying words Masslo was heard to ask 'why', chillingly prophesized by his comment in a TV interview a few days before:

> Having black skin in this country is a limit to civil coexistence. Racism is also present here: it is made up of bullying, abuse, daily violence with those who ask for nothing but solidarity and respect. We are contributing to the development of your country, but it seems that this has no importance at all. Sooner or later some of us will be killed and then you will realize that we exist.

Masslo's death was a turning point. The left-leaning union CGIL demanded, and obtained, a state funeral. On 7 October 1989, the first national demonstration against racism and illegal hiring (*caporalato*) took place in Rome, and in 1990 the first positive regulatory intervention in Italy on migration was introduced, the Martelli Law (named after its proposer). One year later, in Pescopagano, a settlement bordering Castel Volturno, a Camorra commando fired into a bar, killing two people and injuring six other locals and migrants. Immediately afterwards, the killers mowed down three other migrants in a car near the bar. There was an explosion of migrant outrage on the streets, a warning that their illegality was not going to stop them from demanding justice. In 2008, six young Africans were murdered at a tailor's shop in Lago Patria, a suburb of Castel Volturno, in a revenge Camorra act; though it later emerged that none of the victims was involved in criminal activities or was a member of any criminal organization (including the 'Nigerian mafia'[8]). Similar protests followed, and slowly the killings have stopped, not because of political opposition (which in fact diminished after the 1990s), but because of Africans demanding justice as well as forming solidarities that did not stop racism and maltreatment but have checked the brazen violence that typified the early years of African arrival.

There is another important dimension of ambivalent illegality. In the 1980s and 1990s, young Nigerian and Ghanaian women in their thousands ended up in Castel Volturno as the trafficked women of drug and prostitution rings, working the streets and brothels known as connection houses. They were sexual slaves, owned by 'Madams' who paid for their journey to Italy, unable to flee without money or official papers, terrorized by threats of reprisal and curses of black magic, and reliant on other working girls, clandestine friendships and church organizations to find some breathing space in such dire circumstances. After years of campaigning and support from especially the Comboni orders, the sex trade has declined, and some women have managed to pay off their debt or escape. Today's connection houses don't pour young girls onto the street but mix indoor prostitution with entertainment. They have become spaces where tired labourers gather to drink, eat, remember 'home' through regional music, film and television. Mostly for men, but also for a minority of women, these connection houses – with their continuing illegalities of black market goods and clandestine trade – have become important centres of black socialization.

Emancipated from criminal circuits, the Madams remain formidable figures as businesswomen and protectors of their charges. They set the law in their own world. In the past, they had the power to beat their girls, force them to work even when ill or pregnant, and threaten families in Africa if debts were not paid. But they were a cog in a bigger chain of vice. In 2018, when the Oba king in Nigeria passed an edict invoking voodoo rituals to break the Madams' hold over trafficked women and their families, the traffickers simply shifted recruitment to new Nigerian regions, ignored the edict, and recaptured freed girls with even more violence, knowing that there would be no reprisals. Sometimes girls who pay off their debt become Madams themselves, or struggle to find work as carers, cleaners or bar workers because of their poor Italian, lack of money to travel to work, legal invisibility and stigmatized reputation as Nigerian women. Other sex workers have managed to find a life outside prostitution by running away to Northern Italy or elsewhere in Europe, facing huge risk of capture, despite the protection of religious missions, social workers, or even clients. And ironically, women who pay off their debts often retain links with the Madams who shaped their lives from a young age, massaging exploitation as care.

Black Ghosts

This suspension of the law, including in the area of work and residential rights, as discussed below, has kept black Castel Volturno in the shadows. The many Africans working the fields and construction sites, filling the buses to Naples, walking the highways before dawn and after sunset, crowding certain neighbourhoods, attending connection houses, churches and mosques – in short making up so much of the daily life of the settlement – remain ghosts. They are made invisible by their diurnal timings, segregated living and absence from public space. They are considered to have no claim because of their continual arrival and departure and lack of official papers, to not belong because of their race and ethnicity, to be contaminants because of their involvement in crime, drugs, prostitution and dirty work. Even when possessing citizenship and work rights, white Castel Volturno considers them as anomalies in its history of rich agriculture, coastal scenery, Roman villas, holiday homes and NATO investment, conveniently forgetting the role of organized crime, corrupt government, building speculation and economic illegality in bringing the Africans to Castel Volturno. It is in this history that the Africans have endeavoured to find possibility, amid all its miserable precarity, as dispensable surplus sustaining illicit profits, and shouldering the blame for the corrosion of illegality (Baldascino and Casale, 2005; Lucht, 2012; Porcaro, 2021; Simone, 2020).

African migrants have learnt to inhabit this state of suspension between recognition and rejection. Second-generation Italian Africans possessing citizenship or residential rights, older migrants who have been in Italy since the 1990s, and recent arrivals without permits doing the beat for the most meagre returns, share this constancy of being remaindered, enduring unbelonging. As Hans Lucht (2024, p. 1) observes after more than a decade of research in Castel Volturno: 'these migrants are shackled by an excess of relentless reality. Consumed by the demands of this moment and the next, migrants increasingly inhabit hyporeal worlds where distances grow, obstacles become insurmountable, and the waiting becomes endless. . . . Living and working in hyporeality, a widespread and mundane experience, . . . has certain implications for migrants' sense of time, space, and agency.' There is a shared perception that while a closed horizon promises only a repetition of disappointment, living the arduous present creates new openings, requires skills that might lead to another outcome.

This is especially so for second-generation migrants. Sabrina is the daughter of a trafficked Nigerian sex worker forced by her Madam to give her away shortly after giving birth, to supplement the brothel's earnings. A Neapolitan friend living opposite the connection house took the baby and brought Sabrina up as her own.[9] Benefiting from a secure upbringing, eventual citizenship and excellent educational qualifications, Sabrina is the author of five novels and is completing a degree at Naples University. She is only in her mid-twenties, already a minor celebrity speaking out for a new generation, forging a future for herself, and playing her part in making Castel Volturno a better place for migrants. Yet Sabrina sees her future to lie elsewhere in Europe, away from Italy's suffocating racist stereotypes and limited opportunities for black writers. She craves a time and place where she can be 'Sabrina', not the black migrant or the object of the *occhio bianco*, the denuding white gaze;[10] yet she is saddened by the thought of leaving the people and place she loves as an African Italian (Efionayi, 2022). Sabrina possesses that rarity for African migrants: Italian citizenship, which allows her to travel in Europe, looking into a mirror that both affirms and denies her identity.

Matar, another key interlocutor in our research, does not have Italian citizenship but only temporary residency with all its restricted entitlements and continual burdens of proof for renewal. He is in Italy because of his fascination growing up in Senegal for the novels of Giovanni Verga and Giuseppe Tomasi di Lampedusa, which after many attempts secured him a visa to read Italian Studies at the Oriental University in Naples. A decade on, Matar also seems to be on his way with a degree under his belt, shared housing in Castel Volturno, intermittent work as a writer, researcher and tutor at Black and White (a language and after-school centre for migrants in Castel Volturno), roots in the local black community and religious networks, and an insatiable optimism. Matar refuses to accept the limits set and seeks recognition for what he can contribute, and not as the black migrant. But this is what he remains, chasing permanent residency on which so much depends, keeping afloat his large family in Senegal, tirelessly staying one step ahead to meet opportunity. So many cigarettes smoked, and so little in Matar of his Imam's tranquillity gained from prayer and shepherding his congregation, and who explains away his arduous journey from Ghana as a call of destiny.

The Imam is one of a small generation of African migrants who have survived the odds to make Castel Volturno their home. It is cohabitation that has made the difference: the barbs of racism have not abated, only the hurt caused by them; the horizon has not opened, only the ability to occupy the void between Africa and recognition, between invisibility and personhood. For this older generation, at critical moments, the mobilizations of anti-racist organizations and the help of religious bodies such as the Centro Fernandes with food, shelter and permits have played their part, as have serendipities yielding residential rights; but it is in blackness that any sense of belonging has grown. A right of place has come from the expansion of the African community, the solidarities and friendships built, the connections and protests made together, the sanctuaries of shadow existence with others in the illegal economy, the singing and reminiscing done together in exclusion. This right has been tested constantly by adverse circumstances, white exploitation and hostility, and maltreatment within the black economy by housing, drug and prostitution overlords, but in the biding of time has grown a strength of experience (rather like the habits of resumption described in the chapter on Kinshasa) that finds no place in public discourse on migration and asylum.

Yet it should, because the testimony is powerful and instructive. Kojo (pseudonym) is a Ghanaian in his mid-forties who has lived in Castel Volturno since 2008, having only recently obtained an official work contract that might convert his temporary residential permit into something more permanent. For him, it has been nearly two decades of irregular and underpaid illegal work in the fields and living in squalid accommodation without services and utilities to maintain a wife and daughter in Ghana. Slowly, better work and housing have come his way, and the memory of the dangerous crossing across Africa and the Mediterranean has receded, but not the pain of separation from his family, of living alone, of chasing the permits to get official work, to remain in Italy. Yet he has refused to be cowed, coming out to protest against the murder of six Ghanaians in 1998, helping to establish Black and White, becoming a mediator in race conflicts through the Comboni and Caritas missions. He is known for helping Africans in need, contributes to church activity, and has put down roots, yet he is ready to leave for better work in the North if he can obtain permanent residency; willing to trade in the congeniality in black Castel Volturno for escape from the exploitations sustained by illegality.

Akin's (pseudonym) biography is similar. A Nigerian in his late fifties, he has spent thirty-five years in Castel Volturno, recently joined by his wife and daughter after a long struggle to obtain the right to work and live in Italy. Akin arrived in Rome in 1986 with a student visa to study for a master's degree in political science, which he had to abandon when the Nigerian government unexpectedly withdrew funding for its overseas students. Facing destitution, and without a visa, he arrived in Naples in 1988. Finding it impossible to get work as a black man, he eventually worked his way through the agricultural fields of Campania to end up in Castel Volturno as a procurer of drugs and sex workers for soldiers at the NATO site. Arrested in 1993, and imprisoned for sixteen months, Akin slowly built a life beyond criminality, finding different types of work, social connections and community roles to improve his chances of obtaining the right to remain. Today Akin has what he needs in Castel Volturno, yet he dreams of returning to Nigeria, dismayed by the decline in

Italy of a collective politics that once brought out unions, churches and social movements to campaign for migrants. He laments the loss since the 1990s of a pan-African solidarity, when 'an African was an African, there was no Nigerian. As soon as an African saw another black African, he asked how are you brother, how long have you been here, where have you been sleeping, what do you need, water and food, do you know where to find them? Come on, I'll help you.' For Akin this was a time when Africans – browbeaten, ghosted, exploited, vilified – knew of the 'importance of telling our story as migrants. With Mary Osey[11] we said let's not let them invite us to speak, let us invite them, let us speak the voice given to us.'

As political collectivism declined, the role of self-care and religious or civic intermediation became more important, again with frayed protective boundaries. Eniola (pseudonym), who came from Nigeria twenty-five years ago and now lives in Naples with her Italian partner, has spent the last ten years working as a translator at Emergency, an advice and treatment clinic for migrants in Castel Volturno. Emergency has become a place that migrants lacking papers, confidence and proficiency in Italian have come to trust. The clinic offers basic nursing, health guidance and home support to patients and carers referred to it by family doctors and the social services. Eniola is respected by patients and in the health sector, yet outside the workplace she remains the black face, looked at disparagingly in the street, addressed as 'tu' in public spaces instead of the polite 'lei' or 'voi' form used in discourse among strangers. Her memory of having insults hurled at her or being spat at while waiting at the bus stop lingers: her earlier rage is replaced by detached self-preservation. But she knows that holding off has come at a price; that not being known for what she does hurts; that things must turn out differently for the next generation of African Italians with citizenship, who will be educated, fluent in Italian and more savvy than her. These are things Eniola wants us to know.

If these individuals have managed to find some equilibrium, most African migrants remain on the edge of desperation, despite their years of graft. Amma (pseudonym), a Ghanaian woman in her late fifties, is a typical example. She would give up on life were it not for her son. She is exhausted by thirty years of chasing jobs in Italy, running away from groping men and easy solutions in the sex trade, doing time for being caught with a false passport, enduring the barbs of her father back in Ghana. Her record is one of achievement, not shame, just like that of the vast majority of African migrants remaindered in the shadows of legal unrecognition. After a gruelling crossing across Africa, after failed attempts to claim asylum at detention centres, after struggling to find work in regions demanding papers, the Africans arrive in Castel Volturno with the expectation of finding clandestine work, low-cost shared housing, other Africans to live with, help from organizations such as Caritas or the Centro Fernandes. Their illegality shapes everything. There may be work in the fields, but it is backbreaking, sporadic and underpaid, controlled by gangs, and involves hours of walking to get to pickup points of hit-and-miss day labour. Without a written contract, the work counts for nothing in building the case for residency or access to welfare and other services. Others, again in large numbers, end up in the drug economy often as user-runners for the lack of other income opportunities; and any easy money is marked by the violence of rivals and bosses, the debilitations of addiction, the degradations of living rough in desolate spaces, and the consequences of getting caught and left with a criminal record.

In turn, as already mentioned, swathes of young women have been trapped in sexual slavery without much prospect of escape for fear of retribution, or failing to find the 'giant in themselves' (Doe, 2023), willing collaborators or protective missions to escape to other regions (with their own burdens of illegality, racism and informants). Now there are young women like Abina and Mary (pseudonyms), arriving in Castel Volturno respectively from Nigeria and Ghana to join partners or parents, who do not want a life in drugs, prostitution or agriculture. Yet their desire for service work, education or a small business is stymied by poverty and isolation, their lack of social contacts, official papers, Italian proficiency and appropriate experience. For them, the comfort of weekly calls to family in Africa and prayers in church or mosques, the rewards of the occasional walk to African shops or the class in Italian, the support of intimate others close by or far, or the daring to dream another future, don't quite stack up against that urgency to earn money that leads to degrading clandestine work. As a woman trapped in casual work in the fields says, for African women 'it is more difficult to find work . . . you have to mix with illegal or horrible things to get anywhere'.

The right to stay in Italy affects every move and every possibility. It frames the horizon and it overshadows the present, as illustrated by Eniola's comment that in her years working at Emergency, patients only talk about how to get their papers and not their health. Kojo tells us he has seen people going mad without documents, stuck in a place with nowhere to meet, eating and drinking alone, living in abandoned houses without electricity, without money. Adelola (pseudonym), a Ghanaian woman in her forties, who has worked the fields for many years, calls it a 'life worse than in Africa', where the right to belong is not in question, and daily poverty comes at least with the compensation of community. In prolonged legal suspension, prospects for African migrants have become accidental, tied to the brutalities of the clandestine economy from which there is no escape unless residency or a work contract can be secured. The ironies are glaring: migrants arrive in Castel Volturno because without papers they can find work, however bad, and the informalities of black cohabitation provide some alleviation; while there, all they seek is official papers in order to find better work in the North or elsewhere in Europe, while losing the comfort of black ties and religious or civic support that have grown during the forty years of concentrated migration from West Africa.

In the ethnographies of Castel Volturno by Salvatore Porcaro (2021) and Hans Lucht (2012), and in the memoirs of the victims of sexual slavery (Baldascino and Casale, 2005; Doe, 2023; Efionayi, 2022), there are countless testimonies of the horror of dangerous migration journeys and continuing brutalities of different kinds of dispossession. They are testimonies of dehumanization, even at daybreak at pickup points on the highway and on buses, where there are fights between Africans, dangerous offers, racist bus drivers who don't stop, deliberate accidents involving blacks: brutalities repeated during the horrors of the illegal day job. The temporality is one of always waiting, killing time, trying, but with not much changing. But our study has also found testimonies of hope and determination, commitment and generosity, revealed in the labour to find ways out of toxic work and entrapment, in the reciprocities of faith, friendship and commensality, in the obligations towards distant family through remittances and phone calls, in the will to change things for the better. They signal a refusal to be dehumanized, a will to rebut the suspended sentence learnt in inhabiting the shadows, to forego and foreshadow in order to refute a future of foreclosure.

Phantom Whites

The living conditions of the poor and displaced Neapolitans in the abandoned buildings of Parco Saraceno (figure 4.3) aren't any better than those of African migrants, and their conditions of 'non-existence' at an institutional level are the same. However, their state of suspension is different, in that in abandonment they feel angry and let down as citizens, while the Africans, with little chance of obtaining residency or citizenship rights, have few illusions. Black suspension is a continuous aspiration without delusion, and white suspension is a persistent nostalgia preventing recuperation. In the squatted houses, the displaced Neapolitans have built a home in the most precarious circumstances, as one woman from Scampia in Naples reflects, 'obviously I knew it was illegal, but . . . little by little you still get attached; when they bricked up my house in Scampia I didn't want to be here. I felt bad. . . . there is a piece of my life there. We made everything, the

Figure 4.3 Parco Saraceno in Castel Volturno (Photo: Erica Ciccarelli).

windows, the toilets, everything. My husband and father did the work. It was as if you had to build your own house.' Forced to move to Castel Volturno, they made a community, as she explains: 'At first I didn't want to be here because I was afraid, but once you are inside you begin to understand, because there are really deprived people, who don't know where to go . . . people who washed stairways for 10 euros a month to put food on the table [but] it is like family. Even if they don't belong to you, it is like a family.'

The same feeling of attachment can be found among people who just before Christmas 2024 were evicted from Parco Saraceno. The complex was built in the late 1970s by the influential Coppola family, opposite the Saint Bartolomeo dock. For about fifteen years, its thirty three-storey buildings housed the families of American soldiers working at the nearby NATO base. When the base closed, Neapolitan families, to escape the danger of frequent earthquake tremors, moved in, along with people under house arrest electing to move to a place by the sea (living off petty crime or Camorra employment in drugs or extortion) rather than in a dingy alley or an impoverished periphery of Naples.

In these early years, the dare to squat paid off. The buildings were in good condition: the apartments were furnished with marble or parquet flooring, large well-equipped kitchens, and terraces overlooking the sea. They were illegally occupied, but with not much threat from the authorities or owners, and rents either avoided or set low by Camorra gatekeepers or remote owners nervous about leaving the properties empty. The occupants paid no bills, relying on pirated water and electricity, finding ingenious tricks to reconnect when cut off by the utility companies or police. Moving to Parco Saraceno was a good solution, financially and otherwise, for working- and lower middle-class Neapolitans threatened by extreme precarity. One resident, whose prospects had declined from stable white-collar work to low-wage manual work, reflects that although he went from the desk to the broom, as he put it, he could still make ends meet because of the negligible housing costs, while hoping for better prospects when the new tourist harbour promised by the political authorities opened. There grew a strong sense of place among the displaced Neapolitans, marked by trust and sociability between the squatters, and an attachment to the neighbourhood, touchingly captured in *Ritratti Abusivi*, a docufilm by Romano Montesarchio (2013).[12] In one scene, an early resident remembers: 'all doors were open, and you barely knew who were the parents of the children scattered everywhere'.

The overlap between place nostalgia and personal hardship is illustrated in Francesca Leonardi's podcast *Il mio posto. Un incontro a Parco Saraceno.*[13] Its protagonist, Claudia, has experienced tragedy after tragedy: sold by her mother to a family in Modena when she was sixteen months old, reunited with her alcoholic grandmother after moving through various forms of care, running away at fourteen, and four years later meeting the father of her two daughters, a pizza chef and handyman for the Camorra who ended up in prison, and later pairing with another man with whom she endured an exhausting legal war over the custody of their child. Claudia had to leave Parco Saraceno, her home for twenty years, which she remembers with affection in the podcast as a kind of sanctuary:

> I had to face my husband's imprisonment, occupational precariousness, and they [neighbours] always helped me. Sometimes if we heard someone arguing we went to see what was happening even in our pyjamas, to make peace; if an ambulance passed by on the street, we ran to see who had felt ill or got injured; if a person didn't have money for groceries, to avoid offending them we went to their home and said, 'look I made meatballs, there were some left', but we had made more on purpose. I was twenty-one when I came here. That is my place. (our translation)

Today, after a series of evictions and desperate departures, Parco Saraceno has become a ghostly place of furtive occupancy only by the few. We struggled to find people to talk to, but when we did, their narrative was similar to Claudia's. Jerzy (pseudonym) is Polish, addicted to crack and alcohol, with a past of family abandonment and juvenile prison. His life has been difficult, but he too remembers Parco Saraceno's early years with fondness:

> We all were like a family: Poles, Neapolitans, and even a few Africans. We ate and got drunk together. We were only people trying to survive, not the criminals they showed on TV. They accuse us of not paying the bills, but no one says that the Coppola brothers built all this without permits. They are the real squatters, but they can break the law since they have a lot of money.

Drugs and alcohol anaesthetize his unbearable present and prefigure his future, but he also draws on the memory of how this abandoned locale was home in more senses than one. More fortunate is Marco (pseudonym), a skipper who landed in Parco Saraceno after losing his job and facing huge debts. Today he works as a mechanic in a nautical workshop elsewhere, but from time to time he returns to Parco Saraceno, drawn by the memories of neighbourliness, telling us that: 'when all my "friends" no longer answered my phone, they [neighbours] were the ones here who gave me a hand'.

Today the fabric of neighbourliness has crumbled due to decline and abandonment, leaving those who remain with no hope or solidarity, no prospect other than a fond memory that can't deliver. Over time the houses have suffered from a lack of maintenance, rising damp, crumbling walls, floors and balconies, while the sense of community has eroded due to the departure of neighbours and the arrival of hyper-marginals (e.g. Roma families, young addicts and micro-criminals), who are different from the first families of 'survival' squatters. Parco Saraceno was turning into Beirut, according to Claudia, suffering rounds of eviction helped along by builders paying families money to move out. A few days after the last eviction two weeks before Christmas 2024, only empty homes, abandoned toys and furniture, strewn Christmas trees and wrapping remained. A few months later, a few residents have returned, the only signs of them in the empty homes a bottle for crack consumption, a jacket hanging out to dry, a broom and a dustpan in a corner. They are the new phantoms, no longer the outlaws of old who defied the law by daring to squat and live a better life, but shadow figures who materialize in the night when they return with leftovers and unsold bread put out by restaurants and bakeries, a tetrapack of bad wine, a sachet of drugs.

The combination of changes in social composition, physical abandonment and community collapse has left white suspension without agency. The cruellest irony is that the evicted squatters, hopeful of the fruits of a port redevelopment that never came, have seen all their investment, security and sense of place destroyed at a stroke. They have been dispersed to nowhere, isolated in ways that we could not say of the African communities. Those who remain and the new arrivals are left to their own devices, without horizontal associations and collaborations, ill-served by nostalgia and the illusions of citizenship.

Conclusion: Shadow Infrastructures

It's in Castel Volturno's character as shadowland that migrant lives have unfolded, its shapeshifts leaning in as both subtractions and additions. In the suspensions of law have arisen work and housing opportunities, while prolonging precarity, exploitation and lack of recognition. From the hidden hands of the Camorra and trafficking networks, and the silent collusion of the authorities, have come bodily violations, deprivation and neglect, but met also with resistance through flight, kinship and response from religious and civic organizations. The lines of spatial segregation and degradation have severed the territory and society, keeping town centres, peripheries and neighbourhoods apart despite their working connections. They have reinforced an apartheid with no care for the common, but have also allowed separated communities – old settlers, African migrants, displaced Neapolitans – to make their own habitats and ways of life. In fractured Castel Volturno there is no shared sense of place, no coming together in public space, no common provision of services and public goods, no overlap in the housing, labour and retail markets, no municipal governance in the general interest. These absences sustain sharp class and racial differentials in wellbeing, but also their own countercurrents.

If the countercurrents in places such as Parco Saraceno started out with more solidity than those working for African migrants, the tables have turned in the course of time. The outcast solidarities among the displaced Neapolitans have been put to the test by the closure of the NATO base, the mounting desolation of addiction, detention and unemployment, and the departure of people. The countercurrent of defiant citizenship could not endure once the housing stock and its surrounds started to deteriorate, once the threat of crime and violence forced people to leave or lock themselves indoors, and once the authorities finally decided to tear Parco Saraceno down. All that remained was wistfulness, crushed by signs in the rubble of how fragile the citizenship claims of marginal subjects can be. But the Africans have never had this right. They have no access to social and welfare benefits; they cannot march into unoccupied buildings and pirate utilities, for fear of imprisonment and expulsion; and, except in rare moments of collective outrage at wanton killings, they cannot make public demands as the unentitled. Crowded into rooms accommodating sometimes ten people, within high-rise blocks or villas far from the highways to access work, they have had to pay for everything, dare nothing, and risk the consequences of injury, illness and destitution because they aren't covered by welfare protections.

In this condition of overwhelming lack, and with their numbers rising, different outcast solidarities have emerged, breathing care into an otherwise suffocating atmosphere of place. In churches and mosques, shared houses and meeting places, ethnic shops and salons, crowded buses and jalopies, drinking dens and illicit spaces, outdoor Sunday gatherings and congregational celebrations, migrants from Nigeria, Ghana and Senegal have given each other help and hope, and affirmed their cultural legitimacy in a hostile environment. The solidarities are fragile, constantly tested by the scramble for jobs or seats on packed buses, the stresses of entrapment, the violence of racism and the dejection of forever waiting for fortunes to turn. Yet they have made the burden of precarity that much more bearable, the hope to dream that much more possible. In entrapment and destitution something lingers from the notes of friendship in a shop, church or mosque, or a drinking hole. Something remains of the joy of watching Nigerian soaps and listening to Afrobeats in Mussa's barbershop while being made to look good despite the humiliations outside. It's in the interiors where the black solidarities are rehearsed, not in the public spaces avoided by Africans to not attract attention. As a place of such high African concentration, Castel Volturno's exteriors are eerily white, without expressions of black culture in the sounds, bodies, goods and rituals that circulate. But the interiors are different, benefiting from spatial segregation and ruination making room for outcast culture in neglected spaces.

A social infrastructure of support for black migrants that displaced Neapolitans do not have has also grown over the years. Mosques and evangelical or Pentecostal churches have sprung up, offering Africans a space to congregate and rejoice. They supplement the pioneering activity of religious orders such as the Combonians and Waldensians, whose organizations have helped women out of sexual slavery, given succour to new arrivals, helped with residency applications, campaigned against injustices towards migrants. These religious orders have challenged public and political perception of Africans as contaminants, showing them to be victims not the perpetrators of degradation in Castel Volturno, and whose faith and endeavours are sources of moral and economic vitality. Alongside the religious networks have emerged civic initiatives offering targeted services. Tam Tam, a tournament-winning basketball initiative created by a retired professional player, has given black youths – often walking miles to get to training on time – the opportunity to keep off the streets and grow in confidence. At Black and White's after-school activities, young teenagers have started to define themselves as different from earlier generations of African arrivals, but also from the locals, who they see as lacking in ambition. The social enterprise Made in Castel Volturno helps Nigerian women to learn sewing skills and to find company, and many now work with professionals to exhibit and sell garments in Naples.[14] There are meeting spaces opened by individual pastors, respected 'old-timers', or women running ex-connection houses providing Africans that small moment of respite. The Miriam Makeba Association continues to be a symbol of black cultural expression, a reminder to young Africans of possibility in the arts, and to older Africans of a time of political song to denounce racial violence. There are clinics such as Emergency offering health and social care to migrants. 'One Euro' minibuses have appeared, their black drivers ferrying children to school or workers to the fields or trunk roads because of the absence of buses.

This black infrastructure, however, lacks institutional solidity, reaching the lucky few and only for a while;

it falls well short of the integrated services required to address the multiple obstacles faced by migrants. The provisions are threadbare and disconnected, unsurprisingly because of the absence of an overarching institutional framework. How much more could be done by a network of centres offering legal support, drug, alcohol and mental health rehabilitation, business outlets and training in skills valued by migrants, facilities for sports and the performing arts, opportunities for social encounter and respite? But the absence is hardly surprising, given the bias of the local administration and Camorra interference, and the perception in a region of white poverty of African migrants as undeserving. Populism, corruption and ineptitude have left Castel Volturno with no political interest in facilitating migrant integration, because keeping them down ensures continued profits in sex, tomatoes, mozzarella and drugs. Pockmarked development and degradation have left Castel Volturno without general services; the physical infrastructures and utilities reach only some people and places; and the theatres, bookshops, cinemas, libraries, retail centres, playing fields and parks are nowhere to be seen. Even a broken bridge on a trunk road causing lengthy detours has taken years to fix, in the knowledge that necessity will find its own solutions. The cost to those most likely to benefit from a functioning commons – migrants, displaced Neapolitans, struggling families, people without private means – is of little interest to a municipal authority aligned with other sectional interests.[15]

In the competition for survival, the black countercurrents have also fragmented. An older commitment to political mobilization has given way to organizing to deliver services. Little remains of the joint action of unions, religious bodies, lawyers, black and white anti-racists, and civic associations to demand rights and justice for migrants – such as the successful campaign by the ex-Canapificio social centre in the early 2000s to process residency applications under a temporary government amnesty. A collective politics of liberation no longer exists, which is much lamented by pan-Africanists such as Akin and Kojo and by activist-intellectuals such as Sabrina and Matar, who see the limitations of service-based organization. Its renewal could work across the urban shadows, breathe air into struggles, bring the subjugated – white and black – into relation. It would expose the connections between the evisceration of Parco Saraceno, the pockmarked divisions of Castel Volturno and the perennial unbelonging of Africans. It might bring the diverse damaged communities together to call time on the interests benefiting from illegality and corruption. It could add traction to new spaces of social congregation such as sports and music ventures, and repair old informal networks of neighbourliness that, as Mercedes González de la Rocha argues, are 'not offered to the poor, but are created by them' (1994, p. 13).

The energies of *reprendre* (chapter 2) are differentiated by the type of suspension endured, but both displaced Neapolitans and West Africans bear time in the gap between foreclosure and possibility, in the constant urgency of day-life. As revealed for Mexico City in the next chapter, a continuous present lacking a horizon of possibility is textured by small passages through this foreboding horizon formed in lives where horizontal relations are needed to deal with discrimination, abandonment, illegality, failed infrastructures and services.

5
Extendable Present: Making the Future through Smart Buildings, Sacred Mushrooms and Ghosts in Mexico City*

Introduction

On a bright day in Mexico City, when we wake up in the morning after a night of rain, when the smog and the fog have not yet reconquered the city, I can see from my window the shape of the Popocatepetl volcano (figure 5.1). When this happens, we are all excited at home because, in this city, we usually live through thick smog, literally and metaphorically. Beyond air pollution, which in itself is not easy to manage on a daily basis, fog could be said to characterize our relationship to the future. Indeed, when the future is foreclosed by the uninhabitability of urban life, people tend to focus on the present. The impossibility to plan, project or prepare for a future that scientists and politicians continue to conceive as the endpoint of a linear process extrapolated for the present, in a city where state capacity and resources just do not allow efficient planning, renders the present much thicker. The impossibility for intervening in the future, or the lack of belief in any promise that we can actually be prepared

* Drafted by Julie-Anne Boudreau.

Figure 5.1 A view of the Popocatepetl volcano (Photo: J.A. Boudreau).

(for the end of water, for the next earthquake, for massive death caused by air contamination, for the devaluation of the peso or uncontrolled inflation), makes the present more significant. It is as if we were stuck in a temporal vortex, an endless present. A thick, foggy and smoggy present would apparently mean stillness and the impossibility for change (for progress, development, utopia).

Yet, Mexico City, long on the brink of catastrophe, is a place where the impossible is constantly reinvented. The city continues to function, contradicting the many scientific forecasts and scenarios. It is under repair every day, in all its interstices. Humanity's urban future, as I have suggested elsewhere, is to emerge from cracks in the sidewalk (Boudreau, forthcoming), because there are always various interstices of future-making in the city, from pollinating gardens to street altars, from political graffiti to homemaking in the thresholds between the house and the street. This is what we have referred to throughout this book as blackness, as residual, incipient and generative life. By moving about the city, defying any form of coherent narrative about their life, people 'forego' the future, as AbdouMaliq Simone suggests. People make the future without projecting it. They attend contingencies, adapt, connect and repair. They do not need to see beyond the smog.

One characteristic of this future-making is that it works at a micro spatial and temporal scale. It appears in small in-between spaces, and these ephemeral appearances can cumulate and reconnect, thus producing duration. Yet, these shadows, these ghostly future-making instances, are difficult to see, even if they are all over, surrounding us. In Mexico City's world of failing infrastructures, expert utopias and revolutionary policies, (dis)ordered streets and densely populated peripheries, there are multiple thresholds that open onto alternative futures. In order to perceive these shadow interstitial future-making gestures, we must pay attention to the unexpected, be disposed to be affected, with all senses alert. We must be attuned, as chapter 6 suggests, to the ethics of surfacing. Only then can we see the future that emerges from the process of urban becoming, from the duration of the present. We make the present inhabitable, and by doing so, we make the future.

Because this endless present is far from simply being a thick fog that makes movement impossible. The present is multidimensional. The present is extendable. It is peopled by ghosts, creatures of all kinds surfacing from the underworld; it is simultaneously lived online and offline.

It appears in stones and walls stuffed by legends, water marks from past floods, or cracks from the last earthquake. The present actuates beyond what is to be seen or cognitively understood. It can contract and extend. This is what I want to describe in this chapter: examples of how people live in an extendable present, how they juxtapose its multiple dimensions, switch between them, make them coexist, extend the visible into the ghostly and the shadows into the light. The argument being that only by understanding this process can we understand that the heaviness and thickness of an apparently still present is in fact pregnant with future-making gestures. It is embedded in a process of becoming.

I will start with three short vignettes, travelling from a smart building for digital nomads, to a conversation with a transpersonal therapist who describes her use of hallucinogenic mushrooms in her practice, to a Day of the Dead altar. Through this voyage, I wish to describe how we, inhabitants of this uninhabitable city, move through the thick fog of the present by *switching, traversing and mattering* its extendable dimensions. Using what I have elsewhere called a street epistemology, these descriptions seek to make visible and bring to the surface the ontological plurality of the present by focusing on how switching, traversing and mattering practices enact different realities and, hence, work to assemble different futures (Harrison, 2016).

Mexico City is a vast, low-rise, extended, dense place, nestled between active volcanoes. From the edge of this densely inhabited landscape to the historic centre, one has to take at least three different modes of public transport, paying each time there is a change from a moto-taxi to a semi-informal microbus to a cable line bus or to the subway, spending up to half a day's salary and a minimum of four hours in the journey back and forth. Mexico City is the epitome of extension. But the extensibility I wish to underscore in this chapter does not refer to Mexico City inhabitants' specific relationship to distance and endurance. In fact, the following three vignettes take place in the centre of the city.

Extendability refers here to a constant movement of stretching and releasing. Simone et al. (2023) speak of 'acts of extension', whereby people stretch the urban so thin it becomes something else. When you stretch something so thin, it produces openings, little holes in the matter. These are extensions and interstices. These little holes are where and when the fog dissipates and people can switch, traverse and matter somewhere, somewhen else. Extending the present means gaining 'increasing manoeuverability through exploring lines of connection among disparate materials and situations' (Simone et al., 2023, p. 6).

In Mexico City, as I will describe in a moment, people always seek a new position from where to orient themselves in the fog. We know from Lynch (1960) that orientation is a collective form of knowledge. How people spatially orient themselves depends on how they learn to read landscapes and visual cues; how they weave paths and read the clouds, the buildings; how they trace imaginary connections that unite points of the landscape and project their way beyond what is visible. Orientation is a way to fix a point and decide where to go next. Through acts of extension, people look for new possibilities of operation across time and space. They invent ways to reorient their actions and movements, to read 'where things are heading, increasingly hedging their bets across multiple locations and affiliations' (Simone et al., 2023, p. 5). They switch between geographies, traverse various versions of themselves, and make the immaterial matter. They extend the present and break its stillness.

A Smart Building for Digital Nomads: Switching Between Material and Digital Dimensions of the Present

La Roma-Condesa has become one of the most cosmopolitan and hipster districts of Mexico City. It figures in most urban influencers' content as the place to be and is where most Airbnb offers are located across the city. At the beginning of the twentieth century, it was urbanized for the middle classes, and by mid-century it had become the place where European bohemians and leftists fleeing fascism would arrive. Cosmopolitan, artistic and bohemian has always been its flair. The Oscar-winning capture of the life of this place in the early 1970s by Alfonso Cuarón (2018) in his beautiful movie *Roma* reveals the intersectional class, ethnic and gender tensions that this implies. And as we close the first quarter of the twenty-first century, this has only expanded and accelerated with its prominent appearance on our mobile screens. The content about Roma-Condesa generated by urban influencers is continuously increasing, and this attracts more and more young creatives to the neighbourhood.[1]

There are approximately 2.5 million Americans living in Mexico, some of them in the retiree communities of Baja California and San Miguel Allende, others in the digital nomad meccas of Tulum (near Cancun) and Roma-Condesa (Mexico City).[2] The duration of their stay will vary from a few months to a permanent installation. We are not talking here of tourists; this is a population that has come to live in the country. Two important events have triggered this influx. First, during the pandemic the Mexico City government struck a deal with Airbnb and UNESCO in order to encourage digital nomadism, which was seen at the time as a good source of income for the pandemic city.[3] Secondly, Trump's election in November 2024 has accelerated the departure of many people from the United States to Mexico, voluntarily or not. The profile of this population is diverse, ranging from young digital nomads working for foreign tech companies and various other types of contracts within the creative economy, to second-generation Mexican Americans who want to 'reconnect' with their roots, to retirees who seek eternal sunshine and cheap care services. These arrivals generate a tight squeeze on the housing market, they change the ambience of certain targeted areas where English becomes the common language, they change the local commercial offer, they generate a digital aesthetics on social media, and they make visible bodies that are differently dressed or tattooed on the streets of the neighbourhood.

More than simply gentrification, these new inhabitants generate an 'arrival infrastructure' (Felder et al., 2020), an infrastructure that is organically emerging, visible for instance in the introduction of English translations for menus in restaurants and the few words that street vendors have learned in that language. This arrival infrastructure can only function by articulating a very specific digital map of influencers, short-term accommodation platforms, real estate and immigration brokers, and mutual help groups for newcomers, with an urban map made of specific locations that are considered 'safe' for them.

At 6.30 am on a Friday morning, we were standing in front of a select cafe where each table has its own electrical outlet for laptops and good Wi-Fi, open for digital nomads who work for companies of the European time zone. There is a small pocket of Zurich and London on the streets of the Condesa, mediated by flat white coffee, fibre optics and computer screens. The staff of these cafes speak English, and the walls are plastered with ads offering Spanish or dance lessons for Americans and Canadians interested in knowing how to move with a Mexican rhythm, although they spend their lives digitally connected with northern political, cultural and economic power centres and have their pockets (or rather their digital credit cards) filled with dollars and euros.

Passing yoga and wellbeing centres where you can get Ayurveda treatments and your chakras realigned, where all information is posted in English, on a beautifully landscaped Condesa street, at about 11.00 am, there is a long line of young, elegant people, some of them with their suitcases on their way to the airport, all of them taking selfies and eating the delicious pastries as they come out. Odette's is a high-end patisserie that attracts hundreds of North Americans who follow that famous chef on Instagram. As we joined the queue in order to understand *why* this gathering of foreigners, I chatted with the woman in front of me, a tech worker from Texas. We bought our outrageously over-priced croissants (but hey, they are meant to be paid for by people who have access to dollars), trying to understand what this supposedly

Figure 5.2 Queue of foreigners to buy quesadillas from a street kiosk in Roma-Condesa featured on Instagram (Photo: J.A. Boudreau).

authentic Condesa experience meant, when none of the Mexicans I know from the neighbourhood had ever heard of this place. There are a number of such spots in the neighbourhood, where you see strange queues of North Americans invading the sidewalk and taking selfies in front of specific shops or street kiosks (figure 5.2).

Allow me to stop for a moment in one of these places. It is a short-term rental building recently renovated after the damage caused by the 2017 earthquake. Built in a stunningly beautiful brutalist architecture, it is located in front of Parque México, in the heart of the neighbourhood. With a long queue on the ground floor to enter a beautifully designed restaurant filled with very cool creative people, we entered the hall to ask the young woman at the reception desk if there was availability to rent an apartment. She offered a warm welcome, the typical image of a cosmopolitan Mexican youngster. She explained how the building works, its Wi-Fi connections, the lounge rooftop terrace 'perfect to work there', the possibility to receive FedEx packages 24 hours a day. The building is owned by an Argentinian independent web platform called Nido ('nest') dedicated to short-term rentals and corporate housing for over eighteen years. The company operates in three 'Nido cities': Buenos Aires, Mexico City and Guadalajara, offering 'high speed internet with dedicated router; power sockets all across the apartment, a comfortable workspace, Smart TVs, fully equipped kitchens, comfortable bed linen and pillows, queen-sized beds, 24-hr service & top-tier on-site amenities'. On their website, Nido presents its team in a way that perfectly illustrates the interoperability between digital content and urban space:

> Our global team drives Nido's vision, bringing together expertise from across the world to deliver seamless solutions. This dynamic group ensures consistency, innovation, and unparalleled service, connecting the dots between local operations and global standards for success. . . . As one of Nido's fastest-growing markets, our Mexico team is leading the way in innovation and expansion. With their deep local knowledge and commitment to excellence, they're shaping the future of corporate housing in one of Latin America's most vibrant regions.[4]

'Connecting the dots' and tapping into 'deep local knowledge' in order to provide 'seamless solutions', buildings such as Nido could not work without constant switching between the digital and material dimensions of the present. Walking in the Roma-Condesa is something you always do with your phone at hand and attentive to notifications by Instagram influencers. These digital nodes tell you where to sleep, eat and dance. Indeed, there is a theatricality to how places like the Roma-Condesa are reassembled to receive newcomers. These bodies, buildings, objects, digital platforms, constantly shift and reconnect through the desire to inhabit. This is a conflictual process, but the affects involved go beyond the narratives of neocolonialism and gentrification (Linz, 2024). This digital-material interoperable theatricality also implies the encounter of different bodies marked by contrasting racial and class markers (dress, tattoos): bodies that operate on different rhythms (such as local school children trying to make their way among the Americans waiting in line on the sidewalk), different attunements to the environment (with regard to spices, digestion, heat, pollution, social codes on how to eat on the street), and through different 'body augmenting' prostheses (from the high-end robot-like purses and sunglasses from the Jean Paul Gaultier boutique to the most basic cell phone carried by street vendors or cafe employees). The present in the Roma-Condesa is extendable, simultaneously unfolding online and offline, in and through bodies, buildings, telephones and concrete.

Transpersonal Therapy: Traversing Bodies and the Multiverse

There were a couple of tables on the sidewalk of a quiet street in the Roma neighbourhood, outside a typical (not-yet-cosmopolitan-design) cafe. It was seven and it was already dark. I had a meeting with the mother of a child in the same class as my son. A few months back, during a relaxed gathering of fellow leftist-hippy-ish, creative class mothers from that alternative school where we send our children, she had mentioned she is a transpersonal therapist. I was hoping she could give me more context of what she does, as her explanation back then had awakened my curiosity.

She began cautiously, worried about my reaction as she opens a 'weird' world to me: 'After the birth of my son,' she commenced, 'I entered a deep crisis. I saw countless therapists who insisted on diagnosing post-partum depression. But I knew this was not what was happening to me.' She kept searching until she discovered transpersonal psychology. 'I began very cautiously,' she warned, 'you see, I am not an academic, but I am a very empirical person. I need to see proofs.' She engaged in her own process of data collection and experiments and is now offering that knowledge as a transpersonal therapist.

I interpreted her caution as based on our different levels of education, but also because I am a foreigner in this country. I suppose she was assuming my lack of Mexicanness meant that I am unfamiliar with certain ancestral practices, but also with more recent controversies related to science and magic in Mexico. She mentioned the case of Jacobo Grinberg, who founded in 1987 the National Institute for the Study of Consciousness, with funding from the National Autonomous University of Mexico (UNAM) and the national scientific funding body, where he studied the relationship between shamanism, magic and science. He worked with a healer named Pachita who conducted 'psychic surgery'. Grinberg elaborated a scientific explanation for her abilities, which were considered fraud by the scientific community. He was quickly delegitimized scientifically and disappeared suddenly in 1994. Several conspiracist and esoteric theories about his disappearance have flourished since then. She avers, 'I know this sounds very crazy, so I went to a number of events where they spoke about consciousness, ancestral mysticism. I followed workshops. And I realized this was helping me. This is when I decided to formally study to become a transpersonal therapist. I entered deep into psychology, quantum physics, and mysticism.'

Transpersonal psychology seeks to go beyond the idea that reality is external to us, and adopts a holistic vision based on our human experience of constantly transcending the biological, historical, cultural and personal limits of our being.[5] My friend put it this way: 'See, we have more than one body. We have our physical, intellectual, emotional and spiritual bodies. The spiritual body is the locus of our energy and where we feel our purpose in life. So, we have multiple selves and identities. Transpersonal therapy helps you choose what you want to be, and with which cards you want to play.'

Transpersonal therapy helps the person to 'observe, accept and love herself'. My friend uses various techniques to achieve this, according to the specific needs of each patient, ranging from traditional psychological methods to hallucinogenic mushrooms, pre-Hispanic cacao rituals and herbal medicine. This is where she began to refer to quantum physics. She explained that there are invisible worlds woven beyond us. 'Our bodies are part of a larger system. Time and space are not what we think it is.' Instead, the world is a continuous flow of consciousness. 'Have you ever experienced a déjà vu?' she asked. 'You know various timelines coexist because all of a sudden, another timeline appears to you. Everything is everywhere at the same time.' As she was speaking, I was thinking that this reminded me of a text I read from Nandor Ludvig (2022), speaking of how to access the 'Soul of Multiverse' across human and cosmic scales through religion, art, science and engineering, in other words, through a 'cosmological neuroscientific approach'.

In her studies, my friend explored various techniques with Mexican shamans who compose maps of the cosmos and use sacred plants. There is a long indigenous tradition in the use of hallucinogens in Mexico (Gruzinski, 2004), and massive events are organized where people go to a retreat to experiment with them.[6] She is very critical of these mass events, as 'we should not take the use of these substances so lightly'. Accompanying someone on such a trip is a great responsibility. The goal is to see beyond what is here right now. These sacred plants enable the patient to access 'something more that cannot be described by words, by traversing their multiple bodies'. Transpersonal therapy sometimes (not always) consists of experimenting with altered states of consciousness in order to open doors, travel between your different bodies, and see something else in yourself. In other words, transpersonal therapy is about opening various timelines, exploring the quantum multiverse, extending the urban so thin you open time–space loops.

Many of these training and therapeutic centres are located in Roma-Condesa, where creative, middle-class locals and newcomers alike are very interested in mindfulness and other alternative forms of practices. BeTranspersonal is one such centre. Founded in 2004 by Ná Áak Paola Ambrosi to 'promote education on the sovereignty of being',[7] they offer various therapeutic services, seminars, and they rent their facilities for other similar community initiatives. The use of sacred plants is not as prominent in their work. Instead, they use neuromodulation, which, according to my friend, is 'just using a scientific machine to do what shamans and men dressed in white in Asia have done for millenniums: modulating neuronal communication through meditation or the use of sacred plants'. A machine that emulates the natural stimulation or suppression of neurons by electromagnetic pulses generated by electricity is just another illustration of this tension between different knowledge legitimation strategies: science or local ancestral traditions.

Such tension between forms of knowledge is familiar to Mexico City, and arguably to most majority urban worlds. But what I wish to underscore with this example is how the present in the Roma-Condesa is extendable, not only because it simultaneously unfolds online and offline, but also because it is experienced through the simultaneously scientific and ancestral traversing of the multiverse. Traversing multiple bodies and timelines is a strategy to extend the present beyond its immediate thickness and stillness.

Living with Ghosts: Space–Time Mattering

The extendability of the present is not something visible only in the hipster corners of the city. Magic, mysticism and relationship with the dead is probably the most visible form of temporal and spatial extension in Mexico, across classes and across the urban/rural divide. This last vignette explores how the death of a human body is connected to other forms of materialized present life.

I wish to begin with a Náhuatl poem, which says that if a language dies, so does an entire world and all the worlds that could have been born from this language. In a fascinating essay on what she calls the 'presentification of the world', Natalia Ortiz Maldonado (2018) suggests that 'we no longer have the perceptional apparatus to link constellations and beings, but nevertheless, we have a place where the archaic forces of clairvoyance have been deposited, and that archive is language' (p. 334). By presentification, she refers to these moments when our perceptions are liberated from contemporary 'techno-aesthetic alienation' and we suddenly can engage in a 'sensitive co-participation in the world'. These are moments when we can relate to the potency of a sound, an image, a smell, a sensation on the skin, an intuition. Our perceptions have been atrophied by colonial modernity, something Filip De Boeck also alludes to in his chapter. But beyond the 'Colonial Library', we still have the richness of language. And this language, as De Boeck forcefully suggests, goes beyond words. This is the language of artefacts, of music, of poetry, of living bodies. The altar to the dead is an example of such language that enables presentification in Mexico.

Elsewhere, I have commented on the variety, functions and beauty of altars in Mexico (Boudreau, 2022, 2023). These altars people our sidewalks and many also install one in their home in order to feel accompanied by the saint of their choice, or connect with the cosmos, with ancestors, or the sacred feminine (De la Torre Castellanos, 2024). For our purpose here, let me describe one such altar I have seen in the house of a woman I met in the iconic working-class neighbourhood of Tepito on the Day of the Dead (1 November). It occupied half of the living room, an impressive construction of seven levels, which allude to the number of steps required to reach heaven. On the first level, she had installed a statue of the Santa Muerte[8] in the centre, surrounded by sugar skulls, an ashtray with cigarettes and a glass of tequila. Sugar skulls signify that death is always with us, and that we can taste its sweetness. The second level is dedicated to the souls still in purgatory, where the dead can be granted permission to leave in order to visit the living on the Day of the Dead. Here, it was adorned with a photo of the husband who is 'stuck there because he needs to expiate his countless sins, the bastard!' Next to the photo, there is a baseball cap and a CD, the husband's favourite objects.

On the third level, there is a small bowl of salt for the purification of all children in purgatory, along with incense meant to sanctify the home. On the fourth level is a piece of bread decorated with bone shapes, sprinkled with sugar, known as *pan de muerto*. There is also a glass of water, all of this so that the returning dead can eat and quench their thirst upon arrival. The woman also left on that level soap and a small purple towel so that 'he can clean himself before the party'. On the fifth level, she placed a bag of chips, a tamale and a plate with a piece of beef and beans. This is where she left her husband's favourite food. On the sixth step, in the centre, is a photo of her dead mother, which is turned towards the wall and reflected in a mirror placed in front of it. This way, the deceased can only see the reflection of her relatives. Finally, on the seventh level, the woman had crafted a cross out of corn and beans, which is placed under an arch decorated with lemongrass and cempasúchil flowers (marigolds). This is the portal where the deceased enters the world of the dead. In front of this impressive assemblage, candles are placed on the floor forming a path to guide the husband and the mother to reach the altar, surrounded by orange cempasúchil petals, because their scent also serves as guide for ghosts who enter the world of the living.

In order to understand this assemblage of objects, I find it useful to see the altar as an instance of 'space–time-mattering', an 'intra-action' between the dead, the living and the objects assembled (Barad, 2007). It is the relationship between the wife, her dead husband and mother, and the objects she placed on the altar that enables us to name them as such. The wife can only exist in relation to the husband, the living in relation to the dead, the objects of the altar exist as altar only because they interact with the living and the dead. In other words, these are not things and people that pre-exist their relationality. Instead, they constitute a congealing of agency entangling space and time in a very situated way. As Barad beautifully puts it, 'presence is not a matter of a thin slice of now, but rather the hauntology of inheritance, inheriting the future as well as the past' (Barad, cited in Kleinman, 2012).

This speaks directly to how pre-Hispanic cultures conceived of death as dialectically united to life. They did not have a unitary understanding of the soul like the Spaniards. Instead, the soul was distributed across the world, while a person hosted various souls, each of them with a different destiny at death. In Mexico today, many of these beliefs persist. People live with their dead, not only on the Day of the Dead when they actually come, walk and observe the altar, perceive, smell, taste, listen, and then speak, dance or eat with the living. All year long, the dead is a living presence which materializes at the altar as an instance of 'space–time-mattering' – a continuous and iterative process of rebirth. The altar condenses the past, the present and the future; it introduces another spatiotemporal dimension in the present. It extends the present into the past and the future, bridging worlds.

Switching, Traversing and Mattering: The Present and Emerging Futures

These examples of urban life in Mexico City illustrate in many ways what Simondon (2009c) calls livingness: this idea that life goes beyond the human body and that bodies, souls and machines function through distinct affective inclinations. Their perspectives are different, but they all evolve in the same web of urban connections. This is what the transpersonal therapist would call the consciousness of the multiverse. Our ability to perceive livingness has been atrophied by modern science and colonial capitalism (Simondon, 2007), and this is why transpersonal therapy makes use of hallucinogens or neuromodulation machines to recuperate such perceptive capacity. This is also the function of the objects on the altar: to make perceptible through matter the invisible presence of ghosts.

In ancient Greece perception was understood as an instrument for reaching inductive forms of knowledge, particularly with the Ionian physiologists who recognized the vital fecundity of the world and its becoming, its livingness. With the Pythagoreans and Platonists, perception began to be understood more in terms of forms and symbols than sensations. What was perceived were forms that could be compared and theorized across geographies (think of the Platonic cave). This was a first step towards the abstraction of our corporeal perception abilities. And this mathematization of the world meant a change of scale: it meant creating universal knowledge and isolating perception from the sensuality of the individual body. The leap to Descartes and Kant, who define perception as an operation useful for producing deductive knowledge, was only logical. With them, perception becomes a machine-like operation whereby information from the outside enters inside the body and is then processed abstractly by our brain. Throughout his work on the history of perception, Simondon (2012) constantly reiterates the urgency to recuperate our human capacity to perceive the living potency of the world. Working with Bergson and Merleau-Ponty, he sees perception neither as an instrument for reaching inductive knowledge, nor a machine-like operation. Instead, he positions perception as a function and an effect of life. That is, he understands perception as the subtle and immanent variations that we share with machines, rocks, smart buildings, sacred plants and seven-level altars.

Living in Mexico City, I see every day this ability to perceive and embrace livingness not only in living beings but also in objects and machines. Mexico is thick with this world of blackness, a world impossible to contain with science, scenarios and predictions. This is the surrounds (Simone, 2022), where people do not only perceive this vitality, but embrace its potency. For example, in the Roma-Condesa it is easy to perceive the digital in the urban by constantly switching between dimensions. Bumping into a queue of foreigners obstructing the sidewalk taking selfies is an obvious illustration of how the digital dimension lives in the urban dimension. It is also easy to understand how influencers produce a specific aesthetic of the Roma-Condesa in digital space. But beyond images, the extensibility of the present emerges from the simultaneity of feelings across these two dimensions (digital and urban). Living simultaneously in and between urban and digital dimensions is an intensely embodied experience that requires ability. Managing to avoid obstacles on the sidewalk in the urban material dimension, apologizing with your eyes or hand to a passerby you may have bumped into while being immersed in an audio conversation with a loved one back in Texas. . . This is the reality of the extended present, forcing the person to slow down, immerse themselves in the visual, textual and audio scapes digitally produced, while connecting themselves to the physical urban moments and spaces they need to negotiate. Tompkins (2011, p. 237) puts it beautifully: 'the disembodied voice [of the mother back in Texas] and the embodied walker [are] stitched together via the city, its map, its history, our collective histories and futures, and, perhaps most importantly, the affect that is so associated with the headphones'. This is an uneasy relationship, producing some dissonance between listening and being in the city in a specific moment and place. Yet it is fascinating to observe how people swiftly and skilfully manage the constant switching between these dimensions of the present, and by doing so, extend the potency of the surrounds.

Another example of how in the surrounds, people embrace the potency of extension is visible in the many mindfulness, yoga and transpersonal therapy centres across the Roma-Condesa. This search for expanding their consciousness through various scientific and ancestral practices indicates how people wish to connect scales, to join the body with the cosmic. More than switching, what is at stake here is traversing. It is a journey that ties dimensions of the present by consciously seeking to 'feel' their different bodies. The voyage in this continuous flow of consciousness is a search for extending the potency of the present.

While this example supports itself with various theories of the multiverse coming from the field of physics,[9] I find the example provided by Chaouche (2022) particularly revealing. In France, from the eighteenth century on, lively theoretical debates on the actor's art drew the contours of something like the multiverse. Before rehearsing a play, actors were recommended to visualize in their mind how the different scenes would unfold (a sort of inner movie screen). This inner world was thought to be entangled with the present physical moment of the performance, with memories and affects that give flesh and depth to their character, and with a-temporal images and sounds they had constructed before when visualizing the different scenes. Acting was understood as a 'transverse effect', where actors navigate diffracted inner and outer universes that interweave in the performance. This is what my transpersonal therapist friend was saying when she criticized massive events of experimentation with hallucinogens. While mushrooms enable the person to 'transverse' their different bodies in order to access past affects and reach images of what they want to be (something similar to when the actor imagines their character), in these massive events it is difficult to ensure the help of someone who can guide you back to the present embodied moment should there be an unexpected situation arising during the performance. In other words, traversing the multiverse implies negotiating the virtual and the material, articulating the bodily scale to cosmic consciousness in ways akin to what actors do while performing a play. The ability to traverse the multiverse enables people to experience the potency of the present.

The third vignette is another example of how people embrace the potency of livingness. If we consider, following Serres and Latour (1995, p. 60), that time is not linear but more akin to a handkerchief we can spread, crumple and tear, we could conceptualize the altar as a fold in the handkerchief that brings together the past and the future in the present. As a fold, or what Barad (2007) would call an 'agential cut', the altar is a place and moment of mattering, whereby the indeterminacies of livingness are temporally resolved. In the extended present, we never know what is alive, what is dead, what is machine-like. This is something strangely familiar in Latin America that has been beautifully developed in the magical realist literature. It is through the practice of mattering that we can separate the living from the dead and from the objects. In the altar, the past incarnated in the favourite objects of the dead and their photos coexists with the future embodied in the food they will eat as they come to visit the living in the present. The past, the present and the future coexist in the same point in time and space, in the universe. Multiple times and spaces are materialized in the altar. It becomes the node, the portal, that enables the wife to bring into relation the multiple dimensions of the present. Speaking to her dead husband is bringing the past and the future in the present, not in the form of memory, but through matter. The dead do not disappear, they exist in another dimension of the present. The altar enables the wife to touch them, to engage in a 'sensitive co-participation in the world'.

Conclusion and Beginning

Blackness, the surrounds, is a place where people can engage with the potency of livingness. But this is not easy to see if we remain on the surface of clearly defined time and space. As chapter 2 suggests, often 'this bitch of a city indeed becomes a witch: it unleashes, feeds off and builds on the occult and nocturnal powers of an invisible but very palpably present second world'. Here, I wanted to empirically explore where and how people access this 'second world' or what I prefer to call the extended dimensions of the present. Switching, traversing and mattering reveal a deep understanding of urban inhabitants' capacity to extend the present and generate futures.

Because in Mexico City as in most of the world, the future is not a question of hope or preparedness. In the thick fog and smog of the present, the future will not appear only through hope and preparation. Much more is needed to navigate the fog and generate the future. In these places, the future is inconceivable cognitively. Plans, utopias, educational programmes, awareness campaigns or earthquake simulations do not suffice to imagine and then generate the future. Images and promises are hopelessly shrill in this urban world stretched so thin. . .

The future, here, is a question of perception and connection with the world of the unseen. Switching, traversing and mattering the extended dimensions of the present amounts to a world-making presence. It is a generative, much more so than a responsive or adaptive practice. And this requires ability. It requires learning how to stretch our manoeuvrability through exploring various connections. It demands constantly searching for new perspectives to orient ourselves towards what is to come next. And this occurs by switching between geographies, traversing various versions of ourselves, and making the immaterial matter. Switching, traversing, mattering, these are skills that break the stillness of the present, clear the fog, make us move, oftentimes at a microscopic and often unnoticed level. These extending practices may not necessarily register attention or be performed with an intent to register attention, but their cumulation produces extending effects.

6
Time, Politics and the Incipient Urban*

> The living reduce the dead to those who have lived; yet the dead already include the living in their own great collective. . . . Until the dehumanization of society by capitalism, all the living awaited the experience of the dead. It was their ultimate future. By themselves the living were incomplete. Thus living and dead were interdependent. Always. Only a uniquely modern form of egoism has broken this interdependence. With disastrous results for the living, who now think of the dead as the eliminated. (John Berger, *Harper's*, 2008)

Introduction

In this book we have claimed that by the day it becomes difficult to think of cities as spaces of collective security and wellbeing, as their inhabitants find themselves on the front line of the climate crisis, escalating health emergencies and social inequality, and the displacements of war and violence. These threats are intensifying and generalizing old precarities of irregular work, poor housing, and inadequate service and welfare provisions, as power regroups to address them by edging out urban majorities from formal circuits of prosperity, security and wellbeing. Urban provisions of potential value, including land and territory,

* Drafted by Ash Amin.

infrastructures and institutions, markets and common assets, and plans and imaginaries of the viable future, are being reworked by coalitions of elites, corporations and developers in self-interested ways, leaving majority and minority migrants alike increasingly reliant on ecologies of self-help to negotiate the hazardous and uncertain future. The twentieth-century expectation – at least in the North – that the habitats, institutions and infrastructures of the collective urban should serve the general interest has gone into reverse, just when today's disabling circumstances most require its protection.

With little sign of such demand mounting from city makers, this book has turned to popular ecologies of future-making to look for signs of another urbanism: the vernaculars, sensoria and practices of enduring and sometimes subverting foreclosure; the ways in which time is moderated by lived experience; and the words and dispositions from which a grounded politics might grow. It has delved into the condition of urban remaindering prevalent in the South and now also affecting Northern urban majorities for detail on the embodiment of biopolitical cruelty, and for clues to address hazard and risk in communion with, rather than against, human and non-human others. It has found, and sought to name and valorize, an incipience in popular neighbourhoods of foreshadowing, improvisation and anticipation provoked by foreclosure and sometimes getting past it. The first chapter crafted a vocabulary for this fragile yet distinctive quality that upends linear and disjunctive time, while chapters on Naples, Mexico City, Lagos and Kinshasa showed how it goads the temporalities of clearance intended in power's plans, designations and rationalizations.

The book has found ample evidence of quiet response in the present anterior that bends planned and chronological time. It is a response that is consequential, in posing the contemporary as much more than a passing point between a receding past and a coming future. This present anterior has its own texture, its untimely archaeology of contemporariness, as Giorgio Agamben (2009) explains, showing no 'regress to a historical past', but only the depth of 'the unlived element in everything that is lived' (p. 51), the 'invisible light that is the darkness of the present' (p. 53) carrying the lived into the future. Agamben explains:

> It is important to realize that the appointment that is in question in contemporariness does not simply take place in chronological time. It is something that, working within chronological time, urges, presses, and transforms it. And this urgency is the untimeliness, the anachronism that permits us to grasp our time in the form of a 'too soon' that is also 'too late'; of an 'already' that is also a 'not yet'. Moreover, it allows us to recognize in the obscurity of the present the light that, without ever being able to reach us, is perpetually voyaging towards us. (p. 47)

Our material from daily struggles of urban survival speaks to Agamben's untimely contemporary where a future smoulders in the gap between the already and not yet in unanticipated ways, decentring presumed accounts of urban evolution. They expose a gap between how urban time unfolds and how it is narrated; a tension of chronicity and historiography that holds promise for finding a way into the future from the archaeology of the contemporary. This tension and its potentiality are explored in this chapter, firstly by querying, from a vantage point of urban time as a continuous present of remainders that carry the future, the political history of clearance of the unruly or inconvenient urban present in the name of the time to come as a never before. From this restitution of the contemporary, the chapter then outlines an urban politics guided by the ways of defraying foreclosure in its inhabitation, leaning into their language, amplifying their aesthetic and affective expressions, ensuring the basics of survival, and finding traction in their anarchies.

Urban Chronopolitics

How does the urban record bear down on what is to come? What lingers and what disappears, and why? What works the gap in any nick in time? These are questions of urban time, but also of temporal narrative. It is common in urban history to think of cities as overlayered pasts, a geology of stratified debris, some of it inert though not dead and some of it enrolled in ongoing urban life. Giving this genealogy a logic of succession and abandonment, of rupture and continuity, of repression and freedom, is the task of urban historiography – official, popular, scholarly and literary – seeking to place the past in connection with the present, memorializing the future, investing urban trajectories with meaning and purpose. It organizes the debris of time into fables of origin, journey and destination, casts the inconvenient out of the narrative, though not the debris of ongoing life. Placing urban chronicity and historiography side by side sharpens the analysis of legacy and futurity by putting the substrate of urban evolution in relation with epistemic or political intentions to prioritize distinct pathways. This brings the cumulative logics of urban time, and the moments of the lived with all their subversions, into the history of city making by vision and plan. It explains why these logics get suppressed but also push back. It alerts us to chronopolitics: the balance of force between tendencies of repetition, duration and evolution in the nicks of urban time (Grosz, 2004) and technicities of destiny and destination.

One aspect of this balance concerns the urban chronotype, the logic of urban remaindering. Cities are frequently understood as palimpsests, their past layers of matter, technicity and organization worked into successive presents, abandoned to make way for the new, remembered to authenticate a future direction. Urban historians liken the layering of past matter, methods and mnemonics to the ancient Greek reuse of scraped papyrus or parchment with old markings still faintly visible. In any urban present, older cartographies of ruins, reworked materials and memory lie close to the surface, in the form of strata of the old laid over the new, or as the continuous seepage of past matter. Knowing this, according to Andreas Huyssen (2003, p. 3), should make for interventions in which the 'marks of present space' incorporate 'traces of the past' in recognition of the live history of the urban present, in the way of Libeskind's Jewish Museum in Berlin commemorating the presence of Jews since the fourth century, Parque de la Memoria in Buenos Aires honouring those 'disappeared' by dictatorship, and Christo's wrapping of the unused Reichstag in Berlin to draw attention to its troubling past. Cities are 'the simultaneity of multiple material expressions, both visible as well as invisible yet formative' (Key Fowden et al., 2022, p. 5). For Nadia Bartolini (2014), observing the remains to be seen everywhere in ancient cities such as Istanbul and Rome, a more accurate geological metaphor to that of the palimpsest is 'brecciation'. She does not see city pasts as discrete strata, but as fusions of built forms and socio-technical practices from different eras, temporal amalgams that make the contemporary even if seemingly inactive, that disturb clean-slate transitions.

The history of city making is riddled with clean-slate vanities, latterly in the pretensions of artificial intelligence. The logics of algorithmic capture of the environment to plan for the urban future presume an unnecessary past, ontologically and epistemologically. Increasingly, a techne of deep computational dives into mass data to simulate world-making patterns and anticipate spot developments is driving analysis of how to organize, where to position, and what to avoid or cultivate (Amoore, 2023). Its premise on the future is synchronicity, taking diachronicity to be superseded in a world constantly remade by simultaneous time–space relations resembling the behaviour of neural networks. It presumes a hyper-technologically made 'new normal' (Bratton et al., 2020), necessitating probes into the depths of the present, no longer needing actuarial and probabilistic projections of past trends. Algorithmic planning senses a continuous present of ceaseless emergence from horizontal interactions precipitated by technological accelerations, environmental tipping-points, spreads of disease, warfare and precarity, and real-time global interactions that require a technoscience of lateral scan and anticipation (Halpern and Mitchell, 2022). Synchronicity lies at the heart of 'smart city' modelling of mass data to simulate trends and possibilities, remaindering diachronic urban time and historical discernment.

Such prognoses of urban time are consequential, whether they lean into synchronicity or diachronicity. They pretend epistemic authority. For example, the archive of Judeo-Christian and Islamic texts claiming classical Mediterranean cities for themselves is replete with authentication through select Greco-Roman, early Christian, Byzantian or Arabic ruins, while dismissing other ruins as matter out of place. It is an archive that different sides have cited in escapades of invasion, reclaim and reconstruction. Such historiographic manipulation continues, for example, in urban reconstruction tussles, as Seif (2022) shows for disputes between Shiite, Sunni, Maronite and Orthodox Christian communities seeing their own heritage laid bare in the ruins of bombed Beirut. It can be seen also in attempts to expunge inconvenient formative pasts, for example, urban renewal projects after the 1990s deleting the history of decades of communist planning in Estonia (Martínez, 2018) or China (Dreyer, 2012). With such overlaps of urban chronicity and historiography, it is appropriate to speak of chronopolitics, sometimes made explicit by future makers, as Christopher Clark (2019) shows for mid-nineteenth- to mid-twentieth-century regimes in Germany fashioning imaginaries of national time in service of power, such as Bismarck's insistence on an enduring German 'immanent force or principle' (p. 120) beneath the upheaval after the Napoleonic wars, and the Nazi projection of the new Germany as a return to the legacy of racial time from interruptive modern state-time.

The Bismarckian imaginary alludes to a durational time missing from the chronotypes of urban layering and brecciation that both recognize distinctive temporal strata. It sees a nick in time as possessing a posterior present folding into the contemporary imagined by Agamben. It echoes Henri Bergson's recognition in historical time of a chronicity of 'succession without absolute distinction', later summarized by Gilles Deleuze as the immanence of an 'eternal present' of recursions and instantiations. In urban literature this chronicity finds graphic form in

Italo Calvino's novel *Invisible Cities*, narrating Marco Polo's tales to Kublai Khan of cities he has visited during his travels. Calvino writes that in the tales, the cities visited show the past 'like the lines of a hand, written in the corners of the street, the gratings of the windows, the banisters of the steps, the antennae of the lightning rods, the poles of the flags, every segment marked with scratches, indentations, scrolls' (Calvino, 1974, p. 9). As Sambit Panigrahi (2017) argues, the tales are an allegory of the long present in real cities, in describing life in the city of Eutropia forever moving up and down like on a chessboard, bodies in Adelma incorporating the living and the dead, splendour in Clarice showing past destruction and reconstruction, debris in Leonia constantly flooding back from the outskirts, and the dead, living and unborn in Landomia appearing jammed in the pores of its stones. Calvino's exhortation is to acknowledge the remainders of durational time, to question the premise of urban time as discontinuous and asynchronous: a way of interpreting efforts by cities to visibly commemorate the past.

This sensibility is evident in Walter Benjamin's writing on the mixes of modernity and tradition in early twentieth-century Paris, Berlin, Moscow and Naples: their 'future perfect temporality' (Elliott, 2015, p. 144) is expressed in old signs of the habitual and new signs of the revolutionary in the urban fabric. In the radical innovations of the Paris Arcades, the glass towers of modernist architecture and Soviet experimental films after the October revolution, Benjamin found connections with older vernaculars inflecting the new, much like the more visible blends of tradition and modernity evident in Naples' 'inexhaustible porosity' (Benjamin and Lacis, 1986). Similarly, just a decade later, the situationists sought to foreground durational time displaced by the staccato of clock time and modernist architecture. One example is Asger Jorn and Guy Debord's collaborative film *Fin de Copenhague* diving into the city's detritus of murk and gloom, labyrinthine impenetrability, and non-utilitarian and unplanned space, while another is Constant Nieuwenhuys's plans of a New Babylon separating an elevated city of nomadic residents moving through open-webbed spaces from the automated city of traffic and production below. Situationist film, architecture and art sought out the 'temporal intensities of presence, memory, and desire' in 'subversive spatial experience' (Miller, 2017, p. 81).

To recognize durational urban time is to bring into view the designations of accreted cartographies, technical systems and governance mechanisms, the continuities of the vernacular in the shadows of power and plan, the varied speeds at which different parts and communities of a city move through time, the multiple ways in which the anterior is incorporated in the present. It is to see urban evolution as a bend in time that defies newness out of nowhere, to work the durational in social experience and perception. Writing about Naples, Paolo Macry (2018) suggests that the city's long history of continuous adaptation to disruption has produced a popular and official attitude that tends to displace a sense of loss and melancholy by a 'desire to live what the city promises, to see what might reinvent itself in response to the flux of time' (p. 15, our translation). In this claim, Macry may be overstating the conversion of durational time into cultural trait, but not the immanent force in history that has pushed back at grand designs to rework the city as blank slate and sustained in many neighbourhoods on the periphery of power a habit of continuous adjustment and adaptation to survive the future. This force is present in all cities, etched in the record of striation and smoothness generated by the overlays of vernacular, scheduled and hegemonic time, always retaining residue, even with the slow violence of when 'imposed official landscapes typically discount spiritualized vernacular landscapes severing webs of accumulated meaning' (Nixon, 2013, p. 17).

The chronicity of durational urban time is relational, an uneven balance of force between origin and destination projects to break from the past, the disfigurations of capitalist, colonial and state violence, and deauthorized life's habits of endurance and fugitivity. It produces the city of repeated imposition and cajolement but also hones 'artful practices' of survival (Boudreau, 2022). It places the untimely present in a longer history of force and counterforce yielding 'threshold' forms of urban inhabitation that blend power's subjugations and popular ways through them, as Neferti Tadiar (2022) shows in the case of colonial and extractive capitalism's remaindered spaces in Manila. It is a chronicity of embodied rhythms of anticipation with antecedents meeting pharisaical impositions without mimicry. To return to the example of Naples, already at Italy's unification, the city suffered these impositions, illustrated by the new government's response to the 1884 outbreak of cholera. The decree was to 'disembowel' (*sventrare*) the city's labyrinthine centre by building a wide boulevard, in the conviction that ample air flows would rid the miasmas of the disease. From its distance, the state saw no need to understand the social epidemiology of the disease: the contribution of poor sanitation, unsafe water, poverty and overcrowding. Instead, staying with the Northern typecast of Naples as backwardly Borbonic and Arabic, it pursued the logic of clearance in the slums, which did nothing to contain the disease (Bagnato, 2020). In 1910, cholera returned to the city, confirming long-held local opinion that the disease was connected to the health and living conditions of the poor, captured in Matilde Serao's book *Il Ventre di Napoli*, written soon after the earlier outbreak. Since then, the logic of clearance has persisted in various guises of condemnation, makeover and modernization, met equally consistently with local scepticism, popular bypasses and autonomous know-how.

Urban Foreclosure and Residual Life

Placing the untimely contemporary in a longer present is not to propose durational time as repetition, but as an antecedence of rupture and repair. It is to recognize an old fault line of lingering residue in phase shifts, an enduring crack in futurities of clearance, including contemporary moves by capital and power to reorder cities in their own interests in facing rising global risk and uncertainty. In the North, the short-lived era of urban planning for generalized wellbeing has faltered, having long eluded cities of the majority world. Universalist projects, from the utopian dreams of royals, architects and planners to the infrastructural and welfare provisions of secular and religious authorities, are giving way to developments by self-serving coalitions of city makers, big business, elites and urban developers to reappropriate urban assets. It is as though the offices of the general interest in urban planning and politics have been eviscerated, robbed of their precepts, institutions and resources. This appears as infrastructural and institutional stretch in the face of the violence of existential emergencies, capitalist profligacy and sectarian conflict combining with enduring patterns of urban inequality and division. Urban majorities and minorities are let down by urban systems unable to cope with the combined hazards of disease, climate change, resource depletion, unregulated markets, warfare and unbridled power. An old condition of urban populations having to live with disease, poverty, want and war is becoming the new norm as the urban machinery providing shelter, staples and security is undone by polycrisis.

This overexposure has its discriminations against the most vulnerable people and places because of a linked biopolitics of urban predation. The gap between those with means and those without is widening because of the power grab of space, resource, infrastructure and institutions by colluding urban (and trans-urban) economic, political and cultural elites to direct the volatile future in their own interests, to protect themselves from the insurrections of the dispossessed. To older power games of urban surveillance, control and marginalization of the poor are being added oligarchic moves to reclaim urban value through privations of land and property, pervasive commodification, centripetal technologies, redirection of public services and infrastructures, and violence against the subaltern. An urban time of power allowing majorities to share the expanding city, and marginals to make their own lives in hidden peripheries, is giving way to a time of reappropriation of the operative urban landscape, while disabling the residual surrounds, to secure the survival of the fittest. Urban risk management through technologies of anticipation and surveillance, and the repossession of territories, infrastructures and institutions are closely aligned, riding the dangerous present by instrumentalizing urban surplus for self-serving returns.

One significant encroachment is developers and planners remaking popular neighbourhoods and urban peripheries where residents have long sought to survive adversity by cobbling together their own means of habitation. In evictions, the reworking of the built environment, and increased monitoring and control, are becoming displaced, honed repertoires of place – relations with familiar others, informal arrangements, neighbourhood knowledges, interstitial opportunities, technicities of improvisation and behavioural orientations – enabling residents to make something out of little, to draw on horizontal reciprocities and connections to get by. The threats of severance from old ways of repair learnt in cohabitation are very real. Yet, they join a history of urban clearances that have failed to eliminate the residual, precisely because of the logics of chronotype discussed above. The incursions have been bent, failing to take in everything, riddled with inefficiencies and blunders, subverted or resisted, falling short of snuffing out the lifeworld. This much is clear from the copious ethnographies, past and present, of everyday urban life attesting to the forms of incipience in shadowed existence outlined in chapter 1 in this book. As one of us (Simone, 2024) observes in a preparatory note to this collaborative project:

> Places are marked by enduring traces of prolonged trauma and vitality whose residual reverberations are slow to dissipate, as well as by the faintest traces of presences that stirred things up momentarily before vacating the scene. What Ewenzor describes as 'the incontinence of memory' populates every domain with its menagerie of ghosts, demons, and spirits, all of which provide an invisible yet material backdrop to what disparate peoples might do with each other. Between the stabilizations secured through bloodshed and the curiosity driven outward movements . . .

> is an intricate architecture of both ethical and strategic decisions – i.e. how much is to be shown or said; how vulnerable is one to be in face of uncertain prospects; what responsibility does one take for the lives of others, far or near, and what are these relative distances? These are conundrums addressed every day.

In the gaps of clearance and resistance in 'placed histories' remain 'unanticipated, unprogrammed ways in which things could and might be articulated to each other', 'surfaces of contact and exploration that bring situations and actors into a generative proximity, even if still vulnerable to manipulation and threat' (Simone, 2024). The lines of sight and social familiarity and the lay lines of the built and technical environment of lived neighbourhoods, informal settlements and housing complexes become part of the landscape of orientation in conditions of foreshortened possibility. The surfaces of place 'lead residents into specific scenarios and not others, but which are also the medium through which the specificity of encounters and the domain in which they occur are both constituted. Here, the future performs in people's knowledge about what is to come: whether it will rain tomorrow, how to modify your itinerary when infrastructure fails, whether water will come out of the tap, whether an earthquake is coming' (Simone, 2024). In the intimacies of habitation form instincts of surface scanning, anticipations of environmental immersion that respond to attempts to undo the past. They form a plane of habituation in which the 'horizon of the foreclosed future . . . is pragmatically blunted, somehow domesticated' (Simone, 2024) by the demands of a near horizon of sheer survival addressed through experiential time, a history of making the future through artisanal improvisations in the moment.

The pertinent political question, then, is not whether a new age of urban foreclosure will eliminate the city of residues and its temporalities, but whether the ecology of capricious incipience can survive the onslaught of makeovers, the capture of general provisions, infrastructures and institutions by elites, and power's insistence on panoptical preparations requiring the sacrifice of the residual. Is there a point when popular neighbourhoods are so cleared, commodified, vilified, stripped of their moorings that their surfaces cease to facilitate generative associations? Are there ways in which their practices of care and repair could be made more visible, and offer alternatives to the futures of foreclosure?

Aesthetics of Surfacing

To an extent, this last question is one of political aesthetics – how the generative in shadowed urban life can find traction. Across the ages, the stock trade of city makers has been to lodge their visions and plans in the public imagination, to make them seem necessary and desirable. The history of vanity architectural projects, modernizing infrastructures, mass housing and pristine suburbs, imposing spaces and institutions, and commemorative build, is as much one of top-down urban redesign as it is one of public enrolment through the choreography of narrative, art, display and performance. Sovereigns of different stripes, whether royals and governments, planners and architects, or corporations and denominations, have made it their business to bring their far-forward projects into the present by giving them tangible form, to tantalize people into believing in them. Today's big data drives, urban clearances for tourism and consumption, financialization of the real estate, and iconic projects distracting from mounting alienation do not lack public endorsement. The futures they promise rest on popular complicity, relentlessly chased by an aesthetic machinery of data graphics, simulated scenarios and performances of the distant willing foreclosure as protective preparedness against the threatening future.

What are the chances of an aesthetics of remaindered life against the big moves of urban redesign backed by a powerful engine of sensory capture? Are neighbourhood art forms such as graffiti, popular music, rough art, youth theatre and craft enterprise – sometimes defiant, sometimes factional, sometimes celebratory – destined to become relics out of place or survive only by being exploitatively sanitized for mainstream culture? Is there a way of helping them to enunciate a less extractive and dispossessing urban future through a more deliberate aesthetics of affiliative urban inhabitation that avoids any romance of arduous and often violent life in stripped out places? And to do so without justifying the status quo of diminished rights and opportunities, failing infrastructures and institutions, embedded obstacles to security and wellbeing? One possibility – again without any sanitization and deracination – would be to make more visible popular art forms and neighbourhood practices that express resistance and care in dispossession, and which place the untimely present in an enduring tradition of lived refusal of expulsion with continuing promise against foreclosure, an explicit aesthetic counter-politics that adds form and attention to the already present.

This could begin with the charisma of what is said of residual life – the tonality of its thought-image in Benjamin's words. One of us, Filip De Boeck, has long worked with photographers such as Sami Baloji to encapsulate the ways in which a vastly exposed population in Kinshasa jostles for possibility in conditions of overwhelming adversity and lack (De Boeck and Baloji, 2025). From seamless overlays of close description, arresting imagery and keywords from the ground of survival, emerge portraits of the foraging inventions, studied collaborations and popular fabulations enabling the city's residents – mostly all somehow displaced – to look for a way forward and invest their however impossible journeys with meaning. Much more than photo-essays, the textured portraits bring to the surface existential situations, ploys and beliefs for which a new language must be invented, one urging political practice in new directions attuned to the ways and demands of the city's troubled residents. Through them we see chimeric or dispossessive projects decentred by the exhausting necessities of fabrication and fabulation to endure forced self-help. They carry many clues of black fugitivity – the duality of expulsion and generativity – for a restorative urban politics that stays with the remainders, learning from the forms of indefatigable resumption outlined in chapter 2. In this way, the portraits would travel beyond the libraries and galleries of the already convinced, into wider political campaign pressing publics, influencers and city makers to question the aesthetics of the far future.

More can be done also with neighbourhood vernaculars resisting stereotypes of abjection and degeneracy and captured in expressive art forms with potential beyond the local. One illustrative example is how youth hustle in Nairobi's large historic informal settlement of Mathare extends to art projects – facilitated by inexpensive digital technologies – to celebrate local creativity and enterprise, and place its generative waywardness in public culture. In her ethnography of the settlement, Tatiana Thieme (2025) shows how local tours organized by youth collectives, along with street-corner performances, and videos of music, economic activity and street scenes posted in the social media, are a conscious attempt to put stigmatized places on the map, challenging their caricature as outlaw spaces of violence and inactivity. These are simultaneously entrepreneurial projects in performative art and rebuttals of negative moral commentary, their sounds, stories and visuals intended to perform virtue, and present hustling as a positive and affirming way of life in a context of duress and deprivation. Undoubtedly, the art forms simplify Mathare's existential and affective variegations, yet they also add to the archive of joyful militancy in countless urban margins challenging the duplicitous aesthetics of urban foreclosure. Mathare found its political moment when William Ruto spoke of Kenya as a hustle nation during his successful bid for the presidency in 2022, but perhaps the more lasting contribution of its creative outputs lies in reinforcing the campaigns for urban recognition drawing on this archive.

This archival work includes the recovery of vanquished alternatives at historic turning points of city making that nonetheless remain close to the surface or active in collective memory. Another one of us (Boudreau, forthcoming) has revisited four moments in Mexico City's long record of Mesoamerican, colonial, revolutionary and contemporary history when people faced the end of their world. At these moments, there have been future makers written out of sovereign narratives of the city's evolution whose echoes continue to reverberate, leaving traces of residue that remain live and relevant, ready for political mobilization as part of the historical record. It is a record of fine balance between the techniques and visions of archaeologists and poets, geographers and healers, engineers and artisans, revolutionaries and community organizers, the first in each pair serving political cause to make the city and nation anew, and the second less successful in winning the city of maintenance and repair. Boudreau shows how in this record, the technologies of bold maps, hydraulic systems, revolutionary art and imagined utopia, on the one hand, and healing practices, artisanship, the poetic imagination and guerrilla art, on the other hand, operated as differentials of political aesthetic favouring state-siding projects of radical newness playing on senses of expectation, potentiality and hope, over reparative proposals appealing to senses of anticipation, destiny and speculation. But the latter never disappeared, as today, from the shadows of situated practice, steering the everyday into the future for Mexico City's populations let down by the aesthetics of radical newness.

Here are simply three examples of a political aesthetics of (re)surfacing. There are many more in the archive of everyday survival and that of anti-sovereign countermovements projecting from lived experience. The history of the labour, women's, anti-colonial, anti-racist and environmental movements is full of new forms of art, music, film, pedagogy and protest that successfully harnessed desire born in subjugation to realistic projections of liberation (Amin and Thrift, 2013). New alliances of politics and culture bringing together communities, social movements, political organizations and the arts have much to gather from the remaindered urban in exposing the duplicitous aesthetics of foreclosure. They could propose, as China Miéville (2015) suggests, 'future cities that retcon the ones we have now into worthy foundations' (p. 53) by 'reconfiguring streets and buildings ready for opposition' (p. 49), turning the alleyway once again into a barricade, by designing biomimetic and shape-shifting edifices and reviving fables and artworks that keep the city in a 'state of perpetual astonishment' (p. 50), and by upending in the way rap misuses the turntable or Situationism the map, such that it becomes standard to 'write and read meaning out of contingency, even when the intent has been to banish it' (p. 51).

The Collective Unconscious

A political aesthetics of surfacing will make tangible another urbanism, but it will not feed mouths. The clearances of contemporary urban foreclosure, from settlement evictions and makeovers to welfare and infrastructural restrictions, are forms of disablement, rupturing ecologies of attachment and proximity, sapping energies of survival, stripping out the means of subsistence. There are countless broken informal settlements, urban peripheries, makeshift camps, popular neighbourhoods, and high-rise blocks around the world, their social relations and technicities ruptured, their assets and resources threadbare, and their communities multiply deprived. In them, self-help is exhausting, opportunity is evanescent, and poverty and alienation are extensive. The social connections, improvised arrangements, intimacies with place and cultures of makeshift don't stack up, confining residents to bare existence and constraining generative incipience. The pressure on residents is to flee, if numbness from abjection does not overwhelm, to stay with the tricksters, mobsters and gangs that provide small crumbs from entrapment, to dig deep into the inner self and intimate others for fleeting comfort, to entertain ghosts, fables and substances for escape without material reward. Far too much rests on the happenchance of help from the religious and secular friends of the poor in these broken places, on the empty promises of development or relocation from vote-seeking politicians, on the illusions of wellbeing peddled in the digital media. Things are set to get worse, as the urban machinery and city assets get captured by urban elites to ward off looming polycrises.

For habitability to remain minimally generative in broken places confronting further estrangement, the burden of self-reliance must be alleviated, and there are useful clues offered by studies of long-term economic decline in the UK of how common service could play its part. These include Anne Power's (1999) work on acute deprivation in major cities, Patrick Wright's (2020) writing on memory, identity and belonging in the deindustrialized Isle of Sheppey, Madeleine Bunting's (2023) journey through England's fallen coastal towns, and Huw Beynon and Ray Hudson's (2021) study of the decline of North-East England's coal communities. Social bonds in these places are found to be tight but not open to the world or economically productive, the strong family ties, friendships and loyalties of place – laced with nostalgia for a time past of local social cohesion and economic vitality – are simply a way of managing poverty and alienation. In confronting enduring social deprivation, poor housing, failed services and economic decline, the affinities are not a source of resourceful social capital or inventiveness, but an expression of dismay at abandonment and lost worth.

The studies are instructive because of what they reveal about community senses of what has been lost. There is anger towards long-term decline, political neglect and cultural stigmatization, and it rests on memories of better times of economic prosperity and operative community (similar to the white nostalgia discussed in the Naples chapter). A common thread across the places is the frequency with which residents live in the memory of a past, however distant, of stable work and apprenticeships, improvements to housing, services and public infrastructures, and active civic organization alongside or against employers and local authorities. The reference point for desire in the dismal present is a mid-twentieth-century time when the areas were economically vibrant, courted and visited, served by functioning infrastructures and institutions, and had skills, goods and culture to offer to the wider world. The future is indexed to a past when community ties were strong but not the primary source of survival, supported by the availability of economic opportunity, public services, civic organization and external markets. What is remembered and desired is a carrying capacity of place, eroded by decades of slow decline.

The nostalgia is a signal of what must come next, its pride in the past expecting newness that is restorative, wary of interventions without organic referents. These are not the referents of social cohesion, collaboration and coproduction that have become the watchwords of community-based local regeneration today. Instead, they are about places possessing an infrastructure of seconded responsibility, a network of collective institutions negotiating with power, representing interests and providing services. In decline and social atomization, the enabling networks of labour unions, women's groups, community centres, educational ventures, church organizations, youth clubs, libraries, meeting places and public spaces have disappeared, and with this, also, place as a site of collective provisions, leaving a vacuum between improvisations of self-help and impositions of unchecked authority. This is the collective unconscious that must return to hollowed-out places, in addition to the bare necessities of water, energy, shelter, education and welfare covered by a functioning public service infrastructure. It is the lost asset that comes into view when looking back, not understood as the source of advancement, but as a social infrastructure of vitality and hope (Barbera, 2023; Klinenberg, 2019).

This is the experience of places that have lost something. Many other remaindered places do not have such a past to recall. Theirs is a history of never having had collective provisions and infrastructures, only the habits of makeshift and the technics of repurposing learnt in dwelling adversity. Yet for them too, a background of public provision and civic organization would direct incipience towards surer ends by place taking up more of the strain, protecting against chance, curbing roughshod power. The reinforcements of improved social provisions, expanded civic institutions and strengthened social power would sediment a habit of place operating less as Bergson's embodied habit-memory but rather as Bourdieu's habitus formed, as Tony Bennett (2023) writes, 'of the social mechanisms through which the interior is conditioned by the heritage that they inherit while also being conditioned by their social milieu as to how to inherit that inheritance' (p. 177). It is a habitus whose collective unconscious is 'open-ended with regard to the consequences that might follow from how it is acted on, operationalized, directed in different ways' (p. 208).

Into the Parainstitutional

To explore the character of collectives in remaindered places returns us to power relations – the balance of force between the ordained, instituted and sociated. It is to ask whether the aesthetics of surfacing and the social infrastructures proposed here can match the force and speed of the predatory coalitions of powerful city makers and their technologies hedging against existential risk by bearing down on the open-ended. How can this suffocating molar politics that inhibits popular inhabitation be resisted? Asking this same question, though not for the urban, Brian Massumi (2024) turns towards molecular politics, to the character of constitutive power able to push back at constituted power. He settles on 'parainstitutions' of anarchic organization able to harness social power alongside and against vertical power. He writes: 'the reason to introduce the term parainstitutional is to suggest that there can be sustained practices in the register of the micropolitical that build upon and enhance each other without institutionalizing themselves' (p. 12). The parainstitutional, though a disruptive force, 'paradoxically provides the occasion for organization to recompose itself around it', through a 'directionality vectoring from its impact . . . that presents more like a tendency to precipitate a tendency, or an oriented or open-ended determination to be determined, than a forecast conclusion' (p. 14). To ensure that this open-ended directionality does not dissipate, a focus on 'techniques of attunement' is integral for Massumi, so that anarchic energies are able to give 'address to transformative powers of collective existence, leveraging powers of relation' (p. 30), and bring 'a tensional field to a resolution', cutting back after each moment of activity 'to the relational field and enable a subsidence into the mute, silent, background operations of technicity bustling with quasi-chaos' (p. 31).

Efficacy in the molecular or micropolitical is imagined as the consolidation of a relational field of autonomous organization, a repetition of anarchic address and dissolution that becomes a poised technicity. With this readiness and capability to organize and connect, 'in manageable doses, the anarchic element knocks on the door, presenting itself for ingression, to reformative effect. In intenser doses, it smashes down the door, breaking through with a history-shaking revolutionary force carrying a creativity beyond the known bounds of reason' (Massumi, 2024, p. 15). The repetitions of foray and stillness, defiance and conformity, formation and rupture that characterize remaindered urban spaces not (yet) ground down by foreclosure make for parainstitutional politics. Their many horizontal relations of fabrication and association, their legacies of autonomous organization, their daily negotiations of molar violence and subjugation, make for the anarchic technicity intended by Massumi. To be brought into co-relation, supported by civic and political organizations, given improved chances of survival and advancement, availed with the resources to repeatedly come together and express, would be to build parainstitutional power in the spaces of remaindered life. It would enable generativity in dispossession to knock on the door to reformative effect, prevent the raid from time to time of latent anger in these spaces for somebody else's revolutionary games, place the quasi-chaos of makeshift and cohabitation at the centre of a new politics of repair.

But this outcome is by no means guaranteed, for remaindered places have their own molecular agitations caught up in the politics of foreclosure. For example, strong young men in remaindered places are becoming the marshals of a nativist war of hate, seduced by a far-right projection of better times delivered by the ejection of migrants, minorities, liberals and cosmopolitans. In this, they are unsettling local relations of reciprocity, reinforcing the violence of controlling criminal gangs, powerful families and political thugs. The encroachments of the BJP in the slums of India, spewing out bile against Muslims, secularity and liberal democracy, and the recurring far-right violence in Europe's left-behind cities targeting mosques, asylum centres and multiculturalism, are just two examples of enjoined molar and molecular malice. It is a war on vulnerability and difference with momentum, but it is also confronted by demand within cities and beyond for a just and inclusive future. The signs of this demand can be found in the popular protests that ousted the Hasina regime in Bangladesh, the street invasions in Nairobi and Accra against rampant inflation, welfare austerity and economic inopportunity, the mass rallies in India against discriminatory new legislation on citizenship, and the large counter-mobilizations against the far-right hate in the European towns and cities.

The potential of the parainstitutional therefore remains mixed, with the street, virtual and real, increasingly becoming the zone of popular expressions of what and whom the city and nation are for, the test bed of malign and benign anarchic tendencies – and ever more so, because the molar politics of solidarity and general wellbeing once dared by progressive parties has receded into the background, disarmed by the violent charisma of nativist nationalism. The resulting balance of power on the street is uneven, with the nastiness of nativism's shock troops propelled by the alliances of far-right parties, illiberal states, business and media oligarchs, popular influencers and negligent IT platforms, while popular protest for decency waits for the might of law, government, leadership and media culture to step in. The wait continues as appeasement keeps this might away from multiculture, the remaindered urban and the open society. For now, it seems the impetus must come from popular organization, the harnesses of technicities of co-fabrication put into relation, the clamorous gathering of anarchic cooperation forcing molar politics to turn.

It has its antecedents in the history of civil disobedience, anti-colonial and feminist refusal, self-organizing in work, housing and social economy, autonomous communities choosing the outside, liberation projects of all manner refuting power's capture. This legacy has never died. It could lean into and learn from the artisanal and relational practices of the remaindered, from the already there. Abdourahamane Seck (2023), reflecting on the postcolonial condition 'of being nothing, of always being available, of being the sucker in the farce' (p. 234), notes how '*being* is already to be in the midst of sharing, of already participating in sharing. . . . Being together is not to simply reside in a solitary crowd; it comes with a practical perimeter of sense that is the ability to sit down together, in other words, to be capable of cultivating sociality' (pp. 235–6, emphasis in original). The challenge for this condition is to 'transform everyday tools and forms of knowledge into legitimate and equitable political resources that express social ties and that are largely held by everyone' (p. 236). The urban foreshadows of foreclosure hold the same promise.

Conclusion

In the end, though, the dare posed by remaindered life is one of ethos, about the radius of feel for the future, sense of how to take and give care in turbulent times, orientation towards the trouble that comes our way, belief in what must be controlled and how. It is a dare to social disposition, in all its powerful imprecisions of sight and feel that come before the planned, the reasoned and the mapped out. This is its true force, yet one that escapes easy capture, definition, and above all, political translation.

Power's ethos – at least in its totalitarian returns today – is to clear encumbrance, to rid the city of old ways, troublesome minorities, migrants and troublesome places, to declare war on distance, dissent and difference, to sow chaos only to reap rewards from it, and to map every possible turn in the near and distant future to protect the fortress of paranoid insiders. It is a ridiculous ethos, because the dirt keeps coming back, the walls of the fortress continue to breach, the failures breed discontent, animosity and opposition, the projections and plans get caught out by new developments and untracked surplus, and – above all – the refusal of remaindered people to be strangled. The techne of clearance in all its detail and towering mastheads shows its flaws and ruptures, and is plain to spot as a conceited and genocidal attempt to rid the future of waywardness that cannot be tamed in this way. It is the ethos of clearance, with all its words and premises, sentiments and images, and injunctions and zealotries that lingers, settles as the compass of what must be done, makes the ridiculous seem sensible, rules out other ways of managing the turbulent future. Power's ethos needs no precision, only the mood of righteous necessity backed by all the weaponry of surveillant biopolitics.

The ethos in remaindered places of foregoing, connecting and exploring in anticipation to get through, temper or ward off power's foreclosures, cannot pretend such molar force. It is a personal and interpersonal, sometimes a territorial, disposition, a multitude of pragmatic orientations to simply get on, to make the unbearable bearable, to get through by communing, repairing and caring. It is an ethos of life under duress defended by gathering the means at hand, making the most of filiation, and brokering a path that includes hope through blocked prospects. Its terrain is molecular, and its force unproclaimed, rarely gathering as a societal expectation of how to meet the future. It surrounds but does not challenge totalitarian power's ethos of clearance. Yet it is far from minor, circulating as it does as a necessity of survival among billions denied urban access and who can only rely on anticipation and on the ties at hand to find a way forward. This restorative ethos is without guarantees, sometimes making headway, sometimes leading to disappointment, sometimes prolonging misery, sometimes bringing alleviation. But it is a general ethos, radiated across the large urban landscape remaindered by malign power's usurpations. It works as a way of life, and throughout this book, and more explicitly in the next chapter, we name it as a double blackness of destitution and restitution meeting foreclosure, a shadow vocabulary and temporality of incipience in the remaindered urban that refuses to be swept away. It stores a simmering thymotic rage against expulsion, but also the qualities of a restitutive urbanism.

7
The Foreshadowings of Blackness: Methods of Urbanizing Futures*

In chapter 1 we introduced the notion of foreshadowing as a way of thinking about urbanizing the future, while in the preceding chapter we outlined what an aesthetic politics of foreshadowing, of capture and sensorial amplification of shadow contemporariness in spaces of duress and remaindering might look like. But such a politics is not straightforward, for at the heart of anticipatory shadow work in response to urban foreclosure lie questions of how the nascent, the incipient, the occluded claiming light, is to be expressed. These are questions of method: how the unknown is to be known, both by people on the ground making forays into the future, and by research (and politics) seeking to express this work. Foreshadowing breaks definitional boundaries, the dualisms of darkness and light, with another way of understanding by those who are making their way through being remaindered. There is another epistemics – practical and interpretive – that requires articulation.

In this final chapter we consider certain dimensions of what we call black urbanism as a way of thinking about a specific practice of foreshadowing. Here the impossible simultaneity of blackness as both nothing and everything, both the object of seemingly interminable derision and envy, the thing which is depended upon to constitute

* Drafted by AbdouMaliq Simone.

the difference of the modern urban subject might offer some clues as to how to implement a foreshadowing of an incipient future. Much of this chapter will, as such, be informed by black study but often not deal explicitly with blackness per se, as it is, by definition, something always overrunning definitional boundaries, something beyond the histories of it being the burden of specific types of persons.

Still, black people, across different geographies and political histories, have inhabited urban spaces and contributed to urbanization processes in ways that remain unprecedented and unparalleled. Equipped with vernaculars, socialities, temporal orientations and techniques, they attempt to insert themselves into what passes as the normative ethos and demeanours of urban life – whose affordances have been largely foreclosed or distributed unevenly – while simultaneously refusing to 'normalize' themselves according to the structures of power and codes that have subjugated them. In these volatile, often ephemeral middle spaces, emerges the materialization of distinctive ways of being urban that are constantly recalibrated, yet constitute a living archive whose sensibilities are constantly being ignored, repressed or coopted.

While there is much that needs to be said about the structures of racial capital and dispossession that shapes the terrain of black urbanities, and while it is impossible to extricate notions of *blackness* from the histories of bodies that were and are compelled to bear it, we want to emphasize not so much the dispositions of black persons, but how blackness might bring new understandings of and practices of urbanizing the future: where blackness is not a racial identity per se, not a categorical equivalent or alternative to whiteness, not exclusively territorialized within a specific status or even body. Far from being a defining characteristic of a particular population, blackness is everywhere, not as a transcendental ontology or rubric, but as a specific material existence, that of extended flesh beyond the conceits of an individualized subjectivity. Blackness has since its inception operated as the foundation for the sovereign enactment of the 'self' and the basis for the self to enact a sovereign decision – which constitutes the 'truth' of any situation. It underpins the sovereign decision: '*I* determine this to be so.'

Blackness functions in the world as both the *lesser* and the *beyond* – a simultaneity of subtraction and infinity without limits. If blackness simultaneously has existed through history as simultaneously *both* the 'not quite' and the 'beyond' of conceptualization – that which is insufficient and exorbitant of the formation of entities and processes through which the world is normally known – how might this positionality be mobilized to engage the tremulousness of the 'city' and the settlement and unsettlement of the urban?

Blackness and Incipience

As Stuart Hall (2006) often reminded us, the dismantling of a situation, the opening of a context to a new conjecture, always entails the incipience of a new dispensation – a process that is marked either as a disjuncture, a continuity in new guise, a fulfilment of an aspiration, or the next increment in a long road of unyielding progress. In other words, situations rarely simply end without efforts to posit and concretize a future. This takes place either with the sense that a present is coming to an end to make way for a future that is to rectify all the limitations of that present or that this future emanates from the present as its logical or expected outgrowth. Of course, what is also at work are the various efforts to preclude future dispositions that otherwise would seem not only possible and viable, but also even preferable in terms of expanding the scope of opportunities on the part of a larger number of people to derive their own possible futures from their labours in the present.

Here, in familiar examples, revolutionary actions on the part of collective forces can be abrupted, diverted, quelled and compromised, ushering in protracted periods where reactionary apparatuses do whatever they can to ensure that any such future possibilities are foreclosed.

Developmentalism, as a progressive unfolding of capacities and progress, can chart its upward paths largely on the back of obdurate violence or repression, especially if such paths depend on maximizing accumulation as its evidentiary underpinning. Here, widened and heightened claims to share the benefits of such progress engender a sense of loss of a future on the part of those who experienced privileged access based on identity: an identity that is usually white. There is an affective dimension that views the crises of the present as rectifiable in a revalorization of a (white) past: a past that always promises a better future, and as such an irony. If the past was so great, then why bother to promise something else, and then how can such a promise be predicated on something that did not do such a good job in the first place?

In this case, the present is seen as a deviant future, a future that has got out of hand, that has lost its way in the lack of diligence applied to maintaining cherished values and ways of life. Whatever ensued from that past was thus an abnegation of a 'real' future, a mark of overconfidence or lassitude, a lack of appreciation for the need to defend specific forms and meanings. Occluded are the ways in which specific attachments to practices, orientations and relationships that are seen as the appropriate resources for navigating the uncertainties of what is to come end up limiting, even debilitating, the capacities of persons to deal with such uncertainties. An aspect of such an affective economy entails the vilification of those who would seem to render familiar ways of life expendable, or depreciable. And therefore, one is forced to limit the reach of those vilified (the black particularly), to deter their impact and participation; to assign them to a place removed. This move becomes self-defeating in that such removal or deferral of reckoning consigns them to possessing a 'remote' power, amplifying the uncertainty supposedly being defended against.

There is also a more overarching theoretical matter here as well. For the material instantiation of the 'real' remains indifferent to perfection or progress. Whereas whiteness in its imperial and colonial projects staked its legitimacy on bringing development to the world, the world itself is indifferent to this claim and process. Philosophy, long complicit with these projects, transposes the 'real' into automatons simulating the real. As such it reifies the real by submitting the simulations to philosophy's own interminable logic. This entails a further making of a self-sufficient language, relegating all experiences of a 'remainder' – those instantiations of the real which are not entirely subsumed into philosophy's axiomatics – to a play of absence and loss underpinning a continuous game of compensations to be consumed. Though traumatic, loss is also rendered exciting because it allows compensations, exceptions and excuses. Remainders are incitements to explanation, as one's 'real' situation, no matter how seemingly trivial, must be explained. Note the extent to which people are always explaining themselves, where the explanations become substitutes for the experiencing of the real. As such, viewing or understanding something becomes more real than that something – or even makes that something real. As Timothy Morton (2014, p. 4) points out, 'in a sense, philosophies of access – which are now commonly called correlationism – are saying that you must open the refrigerator door of a thing to find out whether its light is on or not. In other words, the opening, the accessing, is what makes a thing real.'

But there is a fundamental asymmetry in a relation between the material contexts in which humanity exists and the transpositions of their material positions into language – as a multiplicity of formalized logics. Here, the relation of everyday language – often nonsensical, frivolous, playful – to the 'language' of capital attempts to totalize everything under the ambit of a 'truth' (becoming more real than real itself). This is a manoeuvre that leaves a decimated, suffering prelingual body in its wake. Witness the ways in which the complex intonations, syntactic improvisation, polyrhythmic vocalizations of African oralities were usually demeaned for the lack of systematicity, their lack of writing.

The promise of developmental progress underpins the axioms of capital as a form of promising without end.

As Kolozova (2020, p. 42) argues, 'the capitalist treats the body as philosophy treats the real – inferior to its valorization as exchange value'. Bodies become not only the source for extraction, but the argument for extraction as well – their sheer physicality persisting in the weakness of cultural capacity makes them legitimately available for the material productions necessary to construct the imagination of progress. For the real presents the problem of immanence, the incessant process of something becoming something else. This is a plane of experience not confined to the ontology of the subject but rather to the apprehension of a larger power (such as the divine), something that both refuses mediation but also instigates the particular use of language as carrying the unsayable into the sayable. Whiteness as salvation. This not only takes place through philosophical representation but also rites, invocations, music – a performative language of self-abnegation accompanying immanence itself.

Yet there are possibilities aside from representation and performance, sometimes entailing silence, sometimes invented vernaculars that may not be phonetic or graphic, but which appear as the arrangements of bodies and built environments, of haptic and aural ecologies. Just as in the previous chapter where we talked about the surfaces of the built environment acting as a platform for varied and unanticipated circulations (all the chase movies), there is a way of 'speaking' that refuses the locations above and beyond: a speaking that entertains a future that is not about an appeal to a superlative power or to something out there on the horizon, but always already present apertures moving in all directions. Sometimes these are only available in a rare instant, as in Ghosh's (2016) view that recognition 'occurs when a prior awareness flashes before us, effecting an instant change in our understanding of that which is beheld' (p. 52); there is a drive to establish some kind of shared language, even if the actualization of such a language remains impossible.

So, if the future as the demarcation of progress largely exists as a ruse, a process that never arrives, then the language of blackness becomes the predominant vernacular of a process of non-arrival. For we don't know how it starts out, beyond multiple narratives of what its *purported* existence accomplished, nor do we know where it is going since it doesn't appear as a coherent subject affording it any specific trajectory of development. As David Marriott (2019) propounds:

> Not only is blackness considered fallen, but even the concept of its existence has no meaning prior to this fall, since it posits a fallenness that, even before it happens, has always already fallen and so knows itself to be an event that never as such happens but is always awaited. This is the case (casus) of blackness – meaning its fall or lapsus – whose occurrence has been historically determined as a void haunting spirit, concept, or representation, and that has come to signify its own absence, or absence itself. No salvation is expected for this fallenness, no redemption for its advent, no recognition for its nothingness. (p. 180)

Such fundamental ambiguity has not obviated a multiplicity of political struggles undertaken in the name of blackness, as well as all the manifestations of black power, black beauty, black critique and black study. While invocations of blackness may largely be shaped by the living conditions faced by blacks at a particular time and place, they are also undertaken as a matter of 'conversion' – i.e. to take a situation which has been experienced as deleterious and convert it into a new way of being in the world, one that in practice seeks to eradicate any need for blackness, either as excuse or identity, deconstruction or difference. In this way black politics brings a version of the future to an end rather than positing a specific imagination of it. For black politics is excessive of both the present and the future – where the future is nothing but an excessive present, and the present nothing but an unrecognized and heavily policed future. Again, Marriott (2019):

> I have said that this excess (this X) is what, in racist ideology, pertains to an absence that can neither be nor conceived without blackness, and vice versa, a blackness that can neither be nor conceived without that of a void

> that falls without end. That is to say, to seek to know this X, to embrace it, is to confront the experience of meaninglessness itself. (p. 186)

So, black reality is real in a way that compels its transposition into an eternal insufficiency; it cannot speak in any other terms than that of approximation, leaving the subsequent gap as a condemnation to elision. Political claims made in the name of blackness cannot avoid attributions of a nagging falseness; yet blackness is nothing else but a political claim, a decision about who counts in what way. As a generalizable arbitrariness, blackness connotes the parameters of meaningless meaning; yet every time it attempts to 'speak for itself' it compels the invocation of other more seemingly superseding tropes which invalidate its innocence, targeting it as a deviation, an inadequate metaphorization of any significant difference. After all, 'we are all human in this bus'. 'It is what a person makes of themselves that is the real difference, not race.' Yet, the difference referred to here, that there is something other than race, could not exist without that (blackness) of which it attempts to make rapid disposal.

For example, with all the attention to the radical media insurgencies of black comics and filmmakers – presenting various tropes of usually male, daring authenticity – what is amplified are not new forms of truth but fictional capacity, i.e. all that veracity is manoeuvred by the continuities of a minstrel sensibility that must be assumed but reconfigured into something more uncertain, a destiny impossible to either abandon or fulfil. For a person is always an error, which simultaneously lends credence to the legitimacy of an order that depends on that accordance of error and demeans it as something incomplete. In a speech that owes everything to an always present absence, blackness will mean whatever anyone decides it will mean on any given occasion.

Blackness also owes nothing because it never seeks to consolidate its position in the world according to its own terms because it has no terms proper to it. Its language is a disclaimer and thus an opportunity to speak for all of that which it is not, but which in those aspects of Western modernity and rationality that slip from its grasp could well be. Thus, its vernaculars are neither nonsensical nor derivative but affirmative of what exists on the other side of an essential derision. It is as Chandler (2014) says, 'an exorbitance for thought' (p. 607). These are complex processes of storytelling, and attention to them seems critical to our attempts to engage a future always able to parade around as something else. So how to 'let it go'; how not to be overly preoccupied with identifying it; how to live in constant *error* as generative possibility?

In Simondon's notion of transduction, things have no proper mode of existence that could determine their function, properties or impact, neither as prognostic nor a diagnostic applied retrospectively. Transduction rather thinks in terms of *absolute contingencies* (Meillassoux, 2012) where things don't exist in possible states but are what they are, precisely because they also could be otherwise. Yet this *otherwise* is not a function of the passage of time, but a fundamental principle of the inner constitution of things, a function of their *ontogenesis*. This point mirrors the dual dimensions of the fundamental fungibility of blackness. Black bodies could be converted into anything, any type of labour because they had no self-essence. But at the same time blackness could 'discover' and enunciate itself through any form – always capable of being a simulation of a simulation. As such, black sociality and the technical practices overlap. This happens in such a way that the black body, largely foreclosed of the possibility of individuated subjectivity – something that displaces the body's recognition as fundamentally black – is cohered through a continuous political history of unsettlement through practices of technicity. This entails all the gestures, coordination, protocols of mutual and implicit recognition, the tacit understandings and micro-rituals of living as black. Here again we have a form of 'knowing before knowing'.

Technical Blackness? Enlivening the Surfaces

What kind of technicities are these that appear critical to the formation of black bodies? Even though technical operations may 'bring something forth into presence', as Heidegger indicates in his essay 'The Question Concerning Technology', it is not necessarily as the revelation of a previously unforeseen truth. Technical operations instantiate activations of that which the components it brings together are potentially capable of producing. At the same time, these activations 're-write' these virtual possibilities, setting in motion new forms of the un-thought, the unprecedented. Because technical operations act as a hinge of these simultaneous yet different manoeuvres, they don't belong to a specific line of historical development; they are not embedded in a specific story line.

They do not exist to uncover or reveal an essential crystallization of the coming together of critical forces – whether these are political, geological or molecular. They do not 'speak' in the name of a specific collective. Within this interval between activation and potentiation are the possibilities of assembled matters not having to reach any potential and things not having to connect. Agamben (1999) calls this a kind of impotentiality that need not render itself as the destination or outcome of action.

There are urban environments, then, whose potentials, implications and trajectories are not so much suspended in mid-air but continuously altered or renewed in ways that not only could be experienced and interpreted in terms of many different probable futures, depending on the 'supplemental tools' available to read them more clearly, but which simultaneously exist within the improbability of any definitive outcome. While statements about a district's salubriousness or economic productivity certainly can be made, they fail to register any traction on the ground and thus are experienced as irrelevant, presumptive or manipulative. Where the unintelligibility of the terrain may prompt political decisions to 'make things clear', the realities of this improbable existence push back to make the politics of deciding things-as-certain more uncertain. Of course, urban environments such as these can be bulldozed out of existence, but, in most cases, they engender a certain wariness in those inclined to move too definitively against them or to control them.

So, the importance of technical operations for this discussion lies in how they contribute to producing spaces of prolonged immunity. In other words, it is in the way they contribute to the elaboration of an urban environment whose reverberations of diverse, intersecting matters – agendas, concerns, activities, calculations, affective intensities and compositions – make it difficult for any single set of actors to unilaterally restructure the textures and uses of that environment. Whether property developers, municipal governments, finance capital or mafias, the illegibility of such environments makes it difficult for any single actor to confidently assess the implications of their 'moves' in relationship to it.

Rather than highly textured, differentiated genealogies applied to circumscribed geographies, black people have endured across a vast surface replete with gradations, ruptures, holes and granularities along which heterogeneous and provisional constellations of matter – and mattering – take place. This has been the case in self-produced black neighbourhoods in Brazil, maroon communities in the dense underbrush of the Caribbean, and in the assemblages of black twitter. These surfaces are not identifiable entities with discernible functions or lifespans, but rather, as Massumi (2019) puts it, 'events' that emerge from intensifications of the relationalities among things brought into proximity. It is a matter of things 'jumping out of their skins', of settings no longer capable of holding things together as they all stumble over each other rushing towards either the 'exits' or a feigned 'middle'.

Of course, there are different kinds and scales of surfaces – not just those of the chase movie or parkour enthusiasts or the builder of auto-constructed neighbourhoods that attempt to maximize (not value) but every inch of available space. Then there are the surfaces of the planetary that conjoin the places that were, in part, never really places to begin with, but rather 'basins of attraction' (to use a term from cybernetics) whose representations perhaps connoted some overarching stability, but the appearance of which depended on circulations of expulsion, importation, incarceration or exhumation. What exists, for example, as a city – as an identifiable, administered entity – depends less on a consolidation of forces than it does on intensifying the ramifications of its existence along these planetary surfaces. It is true that aspects and territories of some cities may have limited reach, may be cut off from the affordances necessary to viably reproduce themselves, or be forced to extend the bulk of their energies fulfilling the contingencies of precarious labour. Yet even here, elaborating the terms of a detachment – not only as an inheritance but an object of their own composition – engenders a kind of incipient universalism, an endless work in progress. This is manifested sometimes in a steady incrementalism of improvements to a built environment and a remaking of solidarities. In some instances, these territories become platforms of dispersal and pluralized affiliations with an outside world.

In the now heavily policed working-class bastion of Imbaba, Cairo – one of the densest urban districts on earth – a faith in the possibility of an extended reachability has not waned. Once the centre of Egypt's Islamic movement and the site of prefiguration and rehearsal for the country's 2011 revolution, the physical coherence of the district is being altered through large investments in infrastructural projects whose partial objective is to interrupt everyday circulations. The political capacities of Imbaba had largely been in its extensive network of *zawiyah* – highly localized Islamic centres that combined pedagogy, neighbourhood socialization, information exchange, entrepreneurial collaboration and social welfare. Linked to each other, they managed to exert substantial political impact. Given the intensity of the state's present surveillance of daily life, much of this has subsided. Even though inhabitants of a neighbourhood may spend much of their lives within a very narrow spatial circumference, interacting with the same people day in and day out, there remains a conviction that through the *zawiyah* they can reach a wider world, a near infinite series of possible connections and opportunities. Even if none of this materializes, they conceptualize their lives as situated on a vast surface of potential articulations: that, if need be, it is possible to reach out across a vast distance and be recognized as someone worthy of being considered.

The Surfaces of Memory

Part of Imbaba's capacity to consider itself in terms of an extended surface relies upon the specific material surfaces of its own construction: all of the ways in which things passing through exerted an impact, all of the small adaptations to accommodate new residents and visitors, all the ways that the neighbourhood's sightlines are kept open onto vast corridors heading north and south, and all the ways that rooms are chock full of the remainders of past visits. Here, memory plays the role of a wild card – but memory as a temporal surface of navigation, rather than a repository. For memory can serve as a reminder to double down on a commitment to specific practices because one remembers how difficult and dangerous pasts could become; or it can be invoked as a form of critique of the present – remembering how 'good' the past was in comparison to a problematic present. As all memory is selective, these are amplifications of the partial, something reified to represent an entire situation undoubtedly more ambiguous than it is made to appear.

There is also a memory of what could have been, if only circumstances or personal behaviour had been different. In some instances, the window of opportunity to actualize this 'could have been' is definitively closed, leaving only feelings of regret or fondness. But in other instances, this 'might have been' remains in play, with persons scouring both the present and future for possible apertures to realize some parts of what is imagined. Or, alternatively, it might be to discover unforeseen opportunities through which such imaginations could be materialized. Rather than memory as a retrospective instrument, it actively reads the horizon for signals of possibility allowing in certain circumstances for what might be experienced as definitive 'cuts' from the present. This constitutes a wholesale jettisoning of a way of life for what is seen as 'already there', if only one peels back the veneer of conventional assessment and normative action.

While contemporary everyday life is replete with platitudes about how anyone can be whatever they want as long as they work hard or desire enough, memory is often mobilized to amplify discontinuities, accidents and fortuitous encounters. As William James had indicated, the accidental, indeed, was the incorporeal backbone of evolutionary processes (Savransky, 2024). These culminate in a multiplicity of divergences, as expressed in individual lives, which can incite each other, and aggregate into a 'zone of formative processes . . . the line where past and future meet' (James, 1956, p. 259).

Whatever one does to prepare for a future, to carve out specific path dependencies, to set objectives to be fulfilled, to adhere to disciplinary regimes purportedly guaranteeing specific outcomes, it is not sufficient for engaging a future. There are always other contingencies at work which are indifferent to any planning or discipline. People are recipients of 'lucky breaks', make impulsive decisions, refuse expected trajectories, or gamble on chancy endeavours – emphasizing that futures might be subject to 'odds' or proportions but that there are no obligations, as chance and determinisms may be seen as equally well positioned.

Memories themselves are inventions and serve to recalibrate cognitive excesses – i.e. when things appear to be radically similar in their progression, memory is incited to pay attention to more granular differences within that which appears similar. Equally, when things appear overly divergent, memory is occasioned to pay attention to a field of similarities. Thus, a temporal politics is informed by attentional economies, a play of what is construed as similar or different – where these terms are incessantly unstable and can be made to mirror each other.

I remember accompanying a fifteen-year-old boy to visit a grandmother he had not seen for years in a black self-constructed neighbourhood in Salvador. Inexplicably, as we walked through the streets, he pointed out places where important ceremonies were conducted decades ago, places which once housed samba schools, and streets where there were once slave insurrections. He was able to do so not because he remembers these sites as the scenes of these specific stories; they were never directly pointed out to him. Rather he intuited them from his grandmother's stories to him as a child. He is not only reading the surfaces but also intuiting how a *longue durée* of black history – depleted, recovered, forgotten, revised – generates continuities for black sensibility despite the passing of time. It is the sense of shifting proportions among sameness and difference.

Not only is memory instrumental in elaborating the experiences of continuities and discontinuities but in forgetting as well. For the imperative to forget also becomes a critical narrative device in constituting a future; where what is to come is relieved of the burden of saying something about the past, of marking a particular relationship. Instead, it becomes a difference that makes a difference – rather than existing as a modality that sneaks certain stabilities into a new situation or time. Deleuze pushes this line of thought to think of reality consisting primarily of difference, not between pre-existing things but difference before identities. Deleuze called this difference-in-itself, 'pure difference' (Deleuze, 1994, p. 20), 'without reference to a transcendent essence or concept or to human consciousness' (St. Pierre, 2019, p. 6). Deleuze emphasizes that it is important to identify the immanent processes and relations that produce the world, i.e. 'the movement, forces, speeds and intensities' (Deleuze and Parnet, 1987, p. 11).

If there is to be a story of the future it rests in the invention of new concepts that enable a momentary, provisionally pragmatic engagement with such immanent processes. This is the 'might be' of the world, something indeterminate that is thoroughly intertwined in the present, sufficiently experienced to exceed fabulation, but also taking from fabulation the freedom to circumvent empirical certainties. It is a capacity for inventiveness that need not arrive at a specific destination, that may never arrive yet incites 'behind the scenes', leaving open 'what could be done'. It is the unruly 'event and intense feeling of bare activity at the edge of things' (Savransky, 2024, p. 8) insinuating itself into the dynamic inter-flows of everyday transaction. This is a matter of the outside breaking in, of the way in which strange affinities are crafted between the forces of unpredictable incursions – storms, invasions, precarities and the wayward practices of experimenting communities, and which are especially salient in an era of acceleration that tends to flatten the distinctiveness of spatial arrangements.

In relation to the exigencies of climate change, this 'what could be done' often takes the form of a multiplicity of small projects, usually 'off the grid' from normative policy prescriptions and large-scale infrastructural interventions. This largely entails a restitution of the technical capacities to peoples and contexts that have been deemed as technically deficient or backward, in need of development – especially the transfer of technical instruments and knowledge. But in lieu of access to these purportedly necessary affordances, such contexts rediscover technicities that have long been dormant or viewed as residues of heritage. They are usually articulated and deployed in unprecedented forms that are actively linked to those past inheritances as continuities.

Those whose futures were largely seen as determined elsewhere or at least dependent upon the importation of foreign epistemologies, take the future into their own hands, knowing full well that the scope of the problem and its rectification exceed whatever they can do. But this recognition of the enormity of the challenge does not deter them from affirming a capacity largely thought to be absent. In their multiplicity and coverage across a wider terrain, these 'projects' not only point to a willingness to tackle a situation that is largely being deferred by nations who disproportionately contribute to the crisis but also signal a way of enjoining a universal effort by operating off the grid of what has passed as the form of such universality.

While the future may remain foreboding to the participants of these projects, it also acts as a way of nurturing a life in general by detaching from the normative modalities for assessing efficacy to affect micro-climates and renewed ecological relationalities that do not so much resist contemporary planetary trajectories but pluralize possible futures within them. Even if the forces of climate significantly reduce the time horizons of viable life, the response of these projects is to materialize a different story – that no matter how long 'we might have', within this period we will create the world in a different way – one that might stir a process of imitation and contagion, or, at the very least, constitute rehearsals for how collective life might endure generatively in conditions of intense heat, scarcity or flooding.

What we learn from blackness is a specific technical orientation. For often this 'what could be done' keeps itself away from bold announcements or major manoeuvres. Édouard Glissant (1997) warned against the ways in which differences of all kinds are bracketed within specific kinds of formats, such as the urbanized forms of interlocution – the platform of the city where residents are expected to announce themselves, exchange their views, and deliberate on their antagonisms. In the intensely social-mediated form of solidarity, the compulsion to talk, to reveal who one is, to share one's excitement to be present in particular ways, to express one's likes and dislikes, is an omnipresent lure to enumerate difference only to reaffirm the extent to which it is bracketed, that any difference can belong to an 'inside'.

In distinction, Glissant affirms a 'right to opacity', to forms of solidarity within spaces which no communicative regime can recognize. Stiegler (1998) argues that only a diversity of local knowledge, engaged in a genuine contention of standpoints, possesses the wealth and the strength to produce genuine leaps. Here, differences generated are *different*, in that there is no ready language to account for and incorporate them, and so they are marked initially by intensities and thresholds rather than conceptual categories. They act as sources of illumination that enable a visualization of the space in which distinct enactments are seen and felt as having a relationship with each other. That which comes from the inside, the indeterminacy generated by the operations of the apparently familiar, is extruded, projected onto an outside, so that it may be either disattended to or defended against.

In the vast black peripheries of Brazil, hampered by multiple and competing regimes of authority – the police, the criminal syndicates, the state, the evangelicals, to name a few – everyday navigation becomes increasingly precarious. Yet from the beginning the built environments of these peripheries were intensely heterogeneous, and few generalizations could be made. The territories were replete with varied capacities, histories, shared practices and contestations. Even as life is now intensely precarious for most, embedded in the very constitution of these territories was a capacity for collective action – not based on conventional solidarities, but a gathering of sympathetic differences, differences that kept each other in view and that are hardwired into the very surfaces of the territory. It is something that is readable perhaps only across the surfaces; something that is not common or even specialized knowledge but a manifestation of a 'knowing before knowing'. A non-actualized existent that cannot so much be mobilized as a collective resource in a present of complex political navigations and enduring racial subjugation exists nevertheless as a tacit resource potentially activated 'someday'.

Instead of the unfolding of urban life being subjected to measures of development (or underdevelopment), it is important to engage political transformations that on the surface seem to veer in many different directions and that are not clear evidence of any theorization or historical stage. The challenge is how to think through the transformation of a particular place in its own terms, of how it creates the conditions and possibilities to actualize itself as both rupture and continuity. Here, past work undertaken by Gilbert Simondon (2009a, 2009b) and Michel Foucault on notions of political technologies – as *inventive methods* for looking at the *intersections* of differentially materialized environments – provides an important conceptual foundation, as does Catherine Malabou's (2009) work on the neuro-philosophy of trauma. This rendering of political technologies would then be the inverse of their conventional connotations as instruments to 'naturalize' specific norms, devices and presumptions to lessen the chance that they will be contested (Glynos et al., 2012). Rather, the use here entails the putting of things into relationship to make contingent the use to which they have been put in the past, to open spaces of contestation and experimentation.

What is missing in the deliberations of global (dis)order then is a sense of *refusal.* A refusal that is blackness. Not as something refused a normative ontological status or even the refusal of racial oppression, but as Fred Moten indicates, a refusal to be *one thing or another.* A refusal to be recognized, to be integrated into the vernaculars of citizenship and freedom. A refusal to be a captive audience, to be extracted from. A refusal to be a part of a society; to make one's desires known. An indifference even to the capture; to find within every *hold* scenarios and dispositions that cannot be understood in any language. For example, the significant enlivening of feminism in Latin America during the past decade, expressed through the continuous feminist general strike, asserts the importance of 'destituent desire', i.e. the capacity to say 'no', no to every dimension of state violence, to every hegemonic form of managing social reproduction and precarity. This 'no' is the predication of the capacity to bring new things to life, not simply as an abstract negation, but as the active enunciation of a collective in the making. The general strike is an active withdrawal of implicit confirmation, a refusal to go along with the programme, even with the prolongation of life taken as a value that outweighs the end of patriarchy or state terror. For urban inhabitants have long relied upon everyday antagonisms in situated encounters with powers whose seemingly arbitrary distribution made it difficult to generate the most elemental plans for a tomorrow, narratives without conflict.

This destituent desire, far from representing any ideological purity or cultural programming, is the only mechanism for inhabitants to insert themselves in the middle of things. To design from the middle, as blackness has always had to do, must then incessantly be on the lookout, and indeed supportive, of these manoeuvres to upend capitalist geographies, and how hands might be lent across the shifting, interplaying grounds of revolt, dissimulation, interplay and opacity. After all, there are no final moves here, just an open invitation to keep on moving.

Foreshadowing, Fugitivity and the Edge

The characteristics of black life have often centred on its ungovernability and waywardness. Black sociality points to the fundamental emptiness of social life, not as a void, but as interminable open-ended possibility without prescription. It wavers in its situatedness between being anything it wants and being almost nothing at all, an oscillation between the abyssal and some unfathomable plenitude. For blackness came into the world so as to cast a shadow, to demarcate an earthly existence removed from the light of enlightenment, and to enable light to constitute its very difference. 'Just how ironically central to all that we might wish to name as modern is that which appears to lie at its periphery, that which seems to flow along marginal passageways' (Chandler, 2011, in Wagner, 2011, p. 392). Rational man then was always something removed no matter how much he came to dominate the earth; there was a separable difference.

If blackness is a world of shadows, such are not simply the configurations created by the angles of enlightenment, but their own substrate, a stratum which stretches across the earth, making available the innumerable irruptions and insurgencies occasioned by various forms of extraction and control. While the light illuminates the abstractions of entities, all the details that are subtractions from a larger gestalt, shadows are slippery streams of fuzzy boundaries and shape-shifting agencies. As Harney and Moten (2013, p. 94, as cited in Houdek, 2023, p. 362) put it,

> And as Descartes re-articulated Plato to spread his dualist visions across the ontic-epistemic plane, planting seeds of suffocating enclosures, the shadow followed along, beneath and in excess of the modern episteme, bearing within it all the stories, sights, smells, visions, pain, languages, struggles, love and radical potentials the cave dreamers witnessed/felt in their space-time together. And that shadow follows us still – in/as breath in the embers of the abolitionist undercommons – waiting for you to enter and breathe in the kaleidoscopic fumes through a radical art of refusal and conspiratorial study with others.

The movement from a captive position to one of emancipation could never be a linear journey, as what was purportedly free was inextricably linked to capture, and what constituted a position of capture was perversely a sign of respect; the way in which the 'master' so feared the undefinable capacities of the black body that its relegation to servitude was compulsory. It was unimaginable to live amongst blackness as something 'free', as if it outpaced the 'speed of light' and proffered its own modality of dazzlement. Fugitivity then is a mission never accomplished but also never deterred. It is a means of engaging the certainty of death but in a way that keeps death off guard, and that even ambiguates whether it has transpired or not, for the agent of fugitivity need not assume the corporeal. As Bradley (2021) contends, the 'black body' is a fiction to begin with, as it always already existed as a kind of surrounds, the architectural edifice of white interior life, the distribution of physicality always 'neurologically diverse'. Just as soon as you think you have pinned it down, locked it up, killed it off, it reappears in a different guise, as it sets its 'eyes on the prize', towards a future that remains simply that, a potential, and instantiation of liveliness not bound to any specific subjective or temporal form. As Cristina Sharpe (2016) puts it:

> the track left on the water's surface by a ship; the disturbance caused by a body swimming or moved in water; . . . the air currents behind a body in flight; a region of disturbed flow; . . . the state of wakefulness; consciousness; . . . in the

> line of recoil of (a gun); . . . a watch or vigil held beside the body of someone who has died, sometimes accompanied by ritual observances including eating and drinking; . . . grief, celebration, memory, and those among the living who, through ritual, mourn their passing and celebrate their life. (p. 74)

So, there is something about blackness that connotes a fugitivity essential for the foreshadowing of the incipience headed towards a future. For what we suggest is that fugitivity constitutes and navigates an *edge*. This is an edge between appearance and disappearance, between continuity and discontinuity, between capture and freedom. Under slavery, the fugitive always sought to traverse the edges – the edges of property, of swamp, of jurisdiction and state lines. The task was to flee along the edges: to, as Moten puts it, 'improvise through horror'.

Here, in our notion of foreshadowing, the edge is an always negotiable and unsettled interface between visibility and invisibility; it is about how much to make incipience known and available, and how to keep it away from prying surveillant eyes and debilitating violence. It is an insurgency intensely futuristic as it is a movement intent upon undermining the present or identifying a destination. As Moten (2018) emphasizes, it is also never an individual act, as it engenders and lives through various forms of *accompaniment*, those whose active or silent complicities bear witness to the extended spatial productions etched out in fugitive trajectories; those left behind that vociferously pray for the fugitive's safety, the native Americans in the bush that provide both shelter and long-term belonging, the occasional passer-by that offers food and water, those that practised the arts of 'stealing away' that provided essential knowledge for the subsequent flight, and a host of unknown others waiting in the wings.

Foreshadowing also in many instances depended on the homiletics (sermon delivery) that Hortense Spillers (1988) indicated were a critical part of fabulating a history for the enslaved beyond the predominant structures of recognition and thus emphasizes that what is at stake is a future, the process of becoming. 'Fabulation and world-making intersect with each other: community itself unfolds through fabulation within fugitive living socialities that engage in futural world-making otherwise' (Odysseos, 2019, pp. 363–4). When Spillers talks about the refused permission for blacks to be part of this world, it is the ushering in of an 'apprenticeship' to black projects of liberations and to futurity in general, both as a modernist construct and something more unfathomable.

The edge is also that interplay between a vast extended surface of multiple irruptions, experiments, queer manifestations and mutations that make up a plane of fugitive navigation – all the ways in which the 'flight' can blend in, take rest, learn new tricks, forge friendships, lay low and rehearse acquired knowledge – and the disappearance of the surface, all the vacancies, voids and abysses whose densities are so overwhelming that all distinctions and textures are obliterated. Here is the nearly invisible line between conjunction and disjunction. Sometimes the edge is felt and not seen or seen as an unreachable horizon. It is not one thing; it pretends to be definitive, but it is not, although despite our empirical engagements with this uncertainty, we continue to believe that it is.

These notions of the edge are further elaborated in the lyrics that Moor Mother wrote for the 50th anniversary album of the Art Ensemble of Chicago, entitled *We Are on the Edge*:

> We are on the edge, we are on the edge of victory, after all that dope, and dancing and drunkenness, we are on the edge, you hear that Tinky, Swamp Thing, Bozzy and Cinderella, we are on the edge of victory, edge of the Bug, Peewie, Tweetie Bird, Cissy, Ella May, Constance. After all those church dinners and church trips, women's days and men's days; all those choirs singing in the background, yeah, we are on the edge of victory. All those sit-ins and daughters graduating from black colleges, only to return to the projects to gather the family. . . out. We on the edge, all of us; all that hope overcome a lie, dripping in blood from

> the rat race, from doin' time, doin' plantation time, for the blue-black blood stain of flag of liberty, or is it democracy. We are on the edge of existence, in slave chains, in prison gangs; from the edge of Mamie's head festering from all the sweating, sweating from escaping the advances of Mr. and his master's clock; escaping from shutting down and closing up, and protecting the displacement between her legs and hearts. No longer creating a new slave force. A new work force under a god, under a sun, under a god, under a sun. We are on the edge of open fire, a new line, a funeral line, a new line, broken with her-story, his history. A map of ritual brought us here to the edge of ourselves, to the edge of what is to come brand new. A name not spoken. We are on the edge, the edge of victory, and a choir is singing in the background. We are on the edge; we are on the edge of victory.

Here, the edge is redemption for a 'people of sorrow' long chained to subservience, fungibility or premature death; the material underpinnings of an indifference to the racialized apparatuses of rule; and the brink of abolition. While the edge may be all these things, pointing to 'the edge of victory' perhaps signals something more diffuse; where victory has an 'edge', a sharp border able to 'cut away' from the hegemonic scenarios, to leave them behind to create a new scenography upending valuation based on extraction and exchange. To the edge is as far as genealogy and history will take you. But the edge is where everything eventually ends up – every interpretation, every deal and disposition. This coming to the 'end' thus signals what Judy (2020) would call the end of the human as a means to an end, where human existence is an end in itself and the edge simply a marker of a 'being-with-one another in-flight apart from. . .' (p. 116).

The edge is certainly not some linear geography, but wavers across multiple registers of referentiality, from cartoon characters, to stereotypes, to shifting dispositions for what might be just beyond that edge, as well as a refusal of whatever might be under a god or under a sun. Perhaps the edge is as far as one can go. Perhaps all maps only bring us to the edge of ourselves, something that will remain unknown, unoccupied. And is this perhaps the notion of victory, that one never goes over the edge, or if one does cross the edge into a kind of abyss, then nothing is lost or gained? Is it an escape from shutting down or closing what (black) life might really look like, as Moor Mother seems not to leave any edge unturned?

No matter what side you might be on, the lines are broken in advance, and this appears to be the responsibility of all sides, as there is no straightforward path to the victory signalled – something to which choirs have testified for a very long time. In popular terminology, *edging* is a practice of entering sexual climax but then pulling back and beginning again. One experiences the 'taste' of climax without it taking place: displacing it as a possible disposition for something yet to come, a different approach and time, in a blur of linearity, and even difference. Yet *edging* also points to a way of enduring, exposed to everything, the violence and generosity of the world, where one is always something else besides that which is singled out or targeted, but at the same time never nothing or everything. Edging is the blur that does not erase or cancel, nor is it a way of hiding, for we know whatever is there, is there. It is just that we do not know for sure *how* it is present or just how much force or significance it exerts.

So, the edge may simply be this alignment of now inseparable differences, not so much facing a common fate but the necessity to invent a trajectory. Everything at the edge must be prepared, not for salvation or an inevitable demise, but rather, as Hortense Spillers in many of her writings says, as 'surprise'. Surprise that everything that seems over and done with is not. Not in the persistence of past dispensations but in the seeming absence of a death that so long was associated with the edge. That if things did not continue the way they did as an 'order of things', then the human, and especially what was considered the 'sub-human', would be lost, finished. And so, the edge is ironic in its intensive proximity to victory: 'We don't have to be what we thought we had to be any more', even if the shape of this is not knowable at the edge. Whatever the action, replete with tragedy and mistakes, the choir (the chorus) keeps on singing.

At the edge, it really doesn't matter what any of the differences lined up are as specific entities. For what they are does not matter in terms of what 'they' will do with each other. Rather, the edge is not the disappearance of identities who then will interact, but rather, at a moment when there is nowhere and everywhere to go, there is a bringing-into-relation a virtual matrix of possible relations that will give rise to specific entities. As such matter does not stabilize as much as it is incessantly mutable through variegated relationalities, a constant work in progress contributed to by the rearrangements of intention, figuring, deciding, enacting and dissimulating. Blackness then perhaps is always at the edge, or at least in the sense that J. Kameron Carter (2023) renders:

> Blackness, its nonreduction to racial category, and thus as a flash point for raising cosmological, mythological, and philosophical questions about the universe (which itself, as contemporary physics makes clear, is unfinished) and indeed about matter, what is called black religion involves practices of the ongoing unveiling or revelation of the im/possible as rooted in an alternative imagination of matter as the material generativity of kinetic uncertainty or indeterminacy. . . . Blackness reveals this alternative imagination of matter, this in-finite naturalism, we might say. Matter's wandering, its gathered escape, its constant ongoingness, its uncapturable migrancy, its moving-on-ness, expresses itself in and as the blackness of black religion. In this sense, as noted earlier, blackness is apocalypse. It uncovers or discloses a haptic, a materially sensual understanding of matter in which matter constantly, differentially touches itself, affects itself, in and as and through sentient flesh and nonsentient nature. (p. 81)

Why are Carter's words important? Because they work their way out of the dilemma that blackness has historically faced in relationship to whiteness. But what Carter describes is an edging that frees blackness from the demands of habitability – of what kinds of bodies, attitudes, orientations will enable blacks to survive the conundrums they face – without necessarily forgetting whiteness. Rather it is to turn away from it, by turning away from what offers itself as the climax of liberation and instead move along an edge that is not a straight line or border or precipice onto an abyss, but something that goes somewhere else not defined as a destination, a waywardness. It is a way to ward off having to be this or that. It is where victory might always already be at hand, but elusive, avoiding any empirical proof.

Perhaps such waywardness is the only way to get blackness out of always being in the thick of things. Always in a thicket of conundrums that keep reproducing an untoward resilience. In a poem by Andre Codrescu, there is a line, 'We are a voice from elsewhere free to say exactly what they want.' Is this not a strange kind of freedom? One that is unable to 'own' itself; a dissociation of subject and body, a *n'est pas* (Marriott, 2023) long characterizing the conundrums of blackness. For the question of habitability – what and who inhabits – cannot be addressed through methods that render a truth to the identities of inhabitants or an overarching frame of their relations. The uninhabitable is the default condition of any settlement in that for any specific inhabitant a *non-relation* to other entities and worlds remains permanent, without reconciliation or redemption. Who we are to each other remains undecidable, unsettled – an ongoing dilemma to which all kinds of politics and technics are thrown, from property relations to fantasies of justice. But what Carter suggests is that we, whatever we are, can still do things with each other, at the edge, where everything ends up, without coming to an end.

Otherwise, to be an 'inhabitant' is to be sequestered in an experience of interiority based on the demands of rational deliberation. This deliberation requires an individual that both must speak for themselves and be spoken for (capable of being addressed) in alignment. But it is an alignment dependent upon a form of speech, a form of being present that speaks a language that is not its own in order for it to be recognized as an inhabitant, a subject. Here we reiterate what was said at the beginning of this chapter about a speech that is brought into a developmental logic – the imposition of whiteness as the captive power of truth. It is dependent upon the materialization of non-being necessary for that alignment of a self-reflexive inhabitant and its recognition as such to take place, and necessary for an environment to be habitable by something known as a constituent component who knows that environment as something indeed knowable.

But then what is the 'free' entailed in speaking something which is entirely 'not yours' in a 'speaking' that is otherwise judged to be permanently deficient or inauthentic? For whatever apparently belongs to it – all we could say about its character and possibilities – does not belong to it. The notions of inhabitation have required an inhabitant aware of their relations each-to-each other, capable of assessing both self-interest and responsibility as well as the proportionality of value. Each-to-each other. If this form of being is one to each other, what can possibly be this 'one' – which is utterly transparent and devoid of content since it is seemingly set off from the entirety of the world.

Whatever interior is curated in the context of an individual self depends on an occluded flesh, a corporeal platform whose boundaries are limitless and extend across an infinite field of actual and potential differentiations without the necessity of genealogy or depth. Otherwise, how would such an interiority exist as more than phantasm? This process of enfleshment is symbolized in a black body that blackness is not, a body always aware of the impossibility of their situation. Here, a refusal to be captured by this situation is cited as evidence of an embrace of non-being. At the same time, appeals to be recognized like everyone else is to mark an infinite dependency on the salience of an authority that has consigned this body to a non-being in the first place (Bradley, 2021). Before any deliberation on what that body 'is' is the issue of where that body should put itself. This position always oscillates between nowhere and everywhere. It entails an inevitable loss of geography and the possibility to speak as a subject in one's own right; but as unlocatable in any specific instance, it is a speech intrinsically deceptive and undecidable – a fugitive speech.

In this process of speaking, where attainment of any subject position produces a kind of self-effacement, any assertion of being in hope of affirming the importance of that which never can aspire to subjecthood – i.e. an indecipherable flesh whose dissimulated body is the constant object of excoriation – is considered out of place. Or it confirms the exclusivity of the right of whiteness to define the proper place of the subject. For black peoples faced with the choice of confirming a subject which is the source of interminable hatred or refusing the salience of being a subject altogether in an ironic embrace of non-being, Fanon will argue the importance of throwing into doubt all representation, of getting rid of the counting of entities and their respective qualities and needs.

For as Daniel Barber (2016) points out, 'captivity is not a space within the world, but the world itself; as the world is the very inheritance of being, the line of flight is less a matter of escape than a matter of knowing – without inheritance – to antagonize being as such. Escape, then, is not the (ultimately inextinguishable) appearance of a freedom of being' (p. 14). It is instead the (intrinsic) experience of vertigo in non-being. The operations of the force immanent to this vertiginous non-being are indexed at an epistemic (rather than ontological) register: it is the refusal of *conversion* – into value or translation.

Conversion is indeed the problem, or, more precisely, the capacity for seamless convertibility or interoperability – where everything is relatable to something else. In conversion, everything can become something else, to the point of a total invagination of life and death. Today money, more than ever, is a photographic device for producing negatives of the contemporary dead called the developed. Using Mbembe's (2020) term, 'the becoming black of the world', we are all then the bodying, the materialization of the dreams of capital – anything can be anything, the conceit of endless fungibility, transparency and extraction. Nevertheless, whiteness remains the pre-eminent means to keep 'reality' out of view – the reality that human life cannot be consolidated in terms of any definitive trajectory of 'human' development, as development is the very production of the living dead (Geschiere, 2021).

Today we face the automatization of the collective self that is incapable of imagining, even dreaming, of a life beyond value, one that doesn't contemplate its worth: a life that is extended across various materializations of technicity, unsettling the possibility of memory, extended in the infinite running of algorithmic relations, but unable to extend itself into the creation of new modalities of being beyond the 'more-or-less'. Living through extensionality is both a device of constant in-forming and converting rather than knowing – constant announcements, displays of, 'this is who I am, period', rather than the reciprocal working out of something unanticipated in any gathering as an act of knowing. For *real* knowing would entail: 'You' may act like me, but I must learn about the 'you' that is nothing like 'me', for me to give back to 'you' the 'me' that is not 'you', nor 'me'.

Here, we might consider then Fanon's wretched, which need no mirrors for their collective efficacy. They need no image of a conjoined body, for it is invented in their very trembling, tentative, half-baked extending towards each other – all the incipient gatherings that shatter and scatter coherent viewpoints. If the evolutionary processes of recalibrating the organicity of the body to enhance its survivability in changing contexts are a matter of coming up with the right form, then the edge releases the adherence of that body to this sense of appropriateness, allowing all the other potential mutations, all of that which the body could have become, to now inform the enlivening of collections of disparate materials. Yet somehow the binary of the living dead or the dead who are living, the included excluded or the excluded included, remains a captive even if captivating mirror.

So how might we think of what Denise Ferreira da Silva (2016) calls the 'all, together' in the terms Carter provides for us. This may be simply another vain abstraction, but it does point out something inherent to habitability today: that any settlement cannot pick and choose its own exemplary definitions, that it cannot be in one place to the exclusion of others. It cannot manifest itself as something 'more or less', as all the old 'trademarks' of density, locational advantage and proximity are no longer the arbiters of what is settled or not. The lines of implication, of circulation, logistics, inputs and outputs continuously establish and erase makeshift boundaries, and depreciate any privileged linkage between the techniques of differentiation – of the 'here' and the 'there' – with some natural history of place or origin.

In a time of quantum physics where locality does not entail physical proximity, the human congregation is necessarily diffuse and shape-shifting. It is at the edge. Power differentials of course remain, certain lives can be wasted at will, yet the 'all, together', far from connoting a human nature in the last instance, reflects the fundamental indeterminacy of what counts and what doesn't, even amid an unprecedented machinery of accounting. For there is nothing *not* there. Despite all of the histories of getting rid of things, of eliminating dangers, of expelling the apparently useless, of deciding what lives, what dies and what simply is lifeless form, any habitat's lines of implications, its extensions across time and space and enfolding of diverse logics and practices of making, posit a world where nothing can be counted out. For, the 'out there' becomes something more intimate, as compensation, possibility and remainder. So, the 'all, together' is not an advocacy of universality, it is not one big happy family, but urbanization's very horizon as a positing of gatherings among the disparate, as the eventual coupling of that which does not belong, as in the Islamic notion of *tawhid*, where everything that exists as different has something fundamental and unique to say about everything else, so that the completion of any event or existence is only possible in a gathering 'all, together'.

At the same time, every place that is inhabited is always troubled by the hints and spectres of that which is not contained in that place, of worlds that have nothing in common, that exist only for themselves, and not for us. As Calum Hazell (2022) points out, 'For it is not the case that different animals – which is to say different humans – see the same things and the same world in different ways, but that *different species of human see in the same way as we do different things and different worlds altogether*' (p. 16). As such, any integrity of the selves of inhabitants is ruptured at and through the edges of worlds that are not ours. Yet we also become counter-parts in ways that are not for us to define or represent. Our habitat thus becomes the uninhabitable. 'We do not renounce our humanity in our encounter with the other, but we are renounced and stripped of the attributes that make us human for ourselves in the encounter by the other, and every encounter is grounded by a non-encounter or a non-relation' (Hazell, 2022, p. 24). Something beyond inhabitation. Something at the edge.

So, what happens if we go over the 'edge'? Are we like Wile E. Coyote, who in chasing Roadrunner finds themselves suspended in time, caught in a strange time warp 'before/after the fall'? We might think of edging as an interfacing already amid an abyss, where grounding might take place in any form at any time, creating the experience of anchorage in even the most seemingly ephemeral geographies. Did we 'come' or not becomes irrelevant. For the edge of victory is not oriented towards 'suspension' but what the Five Percenters in East Brooklyn used to call 'the firmament' – a surface of movement elaborated through the murky flesh of ties, ties that do not so much 'bind' as register a renewal of touch.

This is touch not done as a representation or medium of solidarity or consolidation. It is touch as the collective choreographing of indeterminacy, where that which is touched goes its own way, while keeping each other in view. For in touch, as Manning (2020) emphasizes, the surface of the other's body remains impenetrable; there is no getting to the heart of the matter but rather a gesture born out of a desire of accompaniment, of the difference the other might provide to a standpoint that must be treated as inevitable, stalwart, provisional – even as that difference is always 'moving on', becoming something else altogether. The touch of the fugitive in flight.

In Raven Jackson's resplendent film *All Dirt Roads Taste of Salt*, touching is a predominant feature. In this poetic meditation on fifty years in the life of a Mississippi black woman, MacKenzie, the haptic is not so much a force of consolidation or the binding of bodies to a superseding solidarity. Instead, it is a medium through which the prophetic, the sacred or mystical dimensions of life are reiterated across generations. It is the medium of recognition that all that which is experienced now has also come before, not as an ineluctable and immutable force or destiny, but the reiteration of the ongoing responsibility to bear witness to all that which has been learned so far: that one's body is not one's own, in the sense of an individuated, singular inscription on flesh. Rather, the body is an extension of the trials, tribulations and joys of kin, loosely defined, that have long 'negotiated' relations with the larger surrounds.

These surrounds are not only the violent and turbulent archives of racial oppression, but an interweaving of the body with dirt and water. MacKenzie tells her daughter, upon her birth, that dirt and water are inside her. Perhaps this is because she comes from a family of dirt eaters, always exposing their bodies to rain. But there is something more than this, something more that they *touch upon*. Touch is not only that excessive gesture imbued with tenderness, sorrow and mercy, not simply an act of reconfirmation, but the materialization of an opening out of relation, a propulsive yet unhurried longing to become with the world, something impossible without the breadth of others.

Even beyond this, touch becomes the modality through which a temporality beyond time is experienced. For the film is rendered as a series of vignettes that engage critical moments in the life of its character, neither as linear progression nor as flashbacks from a predominant 'presentist' standpoint. Rather, time is a polyrhythmic oscillation of multiple pasts, presents and futures all in touch with each other and recuperable for the moment at hand, a hand extended to a mother's toes, an infant's mouth, a sister's hands, a lover's waist.

Touch is a way into a world unable to reconcile completion with comprehension. Touch is not the modality of suturing or conjunction but as Simondon (2009b) would indicate for 'technical objects', the *preparation of availability*. It is not the confirmation of consolidation but the possibility of detachment and rearrangement. Just because things are next to each other does not mean that they are capable of being enjoined in a generative relationship. Proximity does not equal connection, nor does distance equate with disjunction. What the edge indicates is the requirement for *gathering* without preconditions, proportions or functions.

At times, such gatherings face 'rough terrain', and adaptations must be made to facilitate the interrelationships among those things that are gathered. This is particularly evident in the case of social robotics, where interfacing always must concern itself with continuous adjustments in the nature of the milieu of interaction, establishing corridors of interaction that are not apparent beforehand (Lipp and Dickel, 2023). At the same time, there are affordances, in terms of the relationships among things, in terms of what they can do with each other, that rely upon intricate infrastructures of mediation, of reducing complexity, so that conveyances across distinctive modes of being in the world can take place – as in the example of communicative bots.

So, in Moor Mother's 'flight' to the edge, there is an entire assemblage of the flotsam, critical moments and cadences of black life whose gathering is facilitated by an orientation of both jarring and seamless contiguities. Each element reaches far beyond this invocation across a vast expanse of black liveability – without rendering judgement. Cartoon characters, blatant stereotypes, emblems of struggle and familiar tropes all simultaneously are implicated in whatever victory the edge has in store. But more importantly, they are marshalled as facets of a milieu that will enable communication between the overwhelming weight of black forbearance, the abyss and nation-time. Moor Mother seems to imply that there is no need at the edge to know the full story, or even the truth of the story; no need to know all of the ins and outs of an enormous and bleak history in order for us to do something at that edge, to forge a gathering that institutes a rupture in what we otherwise might be condemned to be. In the gathering up of lives, something must be left behind, withdrawn; not everything needs to connect.

Less prosaically, this interval between what is given and what is held back is not only a matter of *delay*. On the one hand, when we perceive something, we tend to be conscious of quantity, degree, magnitude, breaking things down into parts, or considering the thing to be part of something, a category to have an overview – in relations of what something is next to, similar to, contained by, adhered with. But we also sense things, as lures with their own inexplicable force, which provokes an affiliation that does not exert control, projection or judgement. So, this is an interval where everything is not given all at once. Rather it is an indeterminate, *inventive* moment. It is the condition of being otherwise than what something is now. There is no guaranteed 'we'. Yet 'we' endure, perhaps not as 'we' think we are. For we exist as a 'we' only on the edge.

Blackness thus is a method for navigating this edge, an edge upon which incipience is always positioned, both daring and vulnerable. And sometimes incipience must endure on such an edge, refuse to go one way or another, perhaps content to destabilize what sits on either side of it. And sometimes it will take Fanon's 'leap' into unprecedented inventiveness with no guarantees. More than simply position, the edge that is blackness is an engine for urbanizing the future that must risk the impossibility of both the urban and the future.

As Marriott (2018) argues, with respect to decolonization and sovereignty, the absence of any 'we' that could give a ground to revolutionary and world-ending violence cannot be an unfolding of the human but rather must be a negation of the 'petrification' that occupies consciousness: 'The masses have to both perform and invent themselves in the event of indecision. The fact that this is what the wretched show should not be lost sight of; invention is the stage on which "the people" can be both resuscitated and shattered, and precisely because it is not easy to be freed from the contagion of petrification' (p. 26). If saving the world has always required saving an 'us' from a 'them' and if the end of the world has been depicted by using the landscapes and conditions that we have demanded of them, then the end of the world might be thought affirmatively as the end of us, the end of an absolute right to life and the beginning of the thought of what other lives might matter. So, in what sense, might the edge be the end of the world and the beginning of the future?

Notes

Chapter 2. To Resume Reprendre*: Urban Futures in the Era of the Congolese Anthropocene*

1 In Lingala: *Nakati rouge, libanda chocolat, penepene zamba, okiti moke libulu, okiti lisusu libulu, okiti lisusu libulu*. For the video clip of this song see: https://www.youtube.com/watch?v=Q9lxmONaovc

2 Reportedly, the expression *mougou* was initially invented and used in Abidjan.

3 The Malebo Pool, formerly Stanley Pool, was also known as Mpumbu, Lake Nkunda or Lake Nkuna by local indigenous people in pre-colonial times. It is an expansive, lake-like widening in the lower reaches of the Congo River.

4 For a more detailed description of the *lukasa* object and its uses, see e.g. Nooter Roberts and Roberts (1999).

5 From an interview with Mudimbe on the occasion of his honorary doctorate in Leuven in 2006 in *Veto*, 32(16), p. 4.

6 See also the ongoing doctoral research by Pietro Manaresi at the *Université catholique de Louvain* (UCL), on strategies for new community-based alliances against hydrogeological threats in the valley of the Bumbu River, in the municipality of Selembao, Kinshasa (DRC).

7 Even though the fishing hook and net, for example, are commonly evoked as metaphors for the capturing and trapping technologies that the authoritarian Congolese state deploys to subjugate its population. For example,

Kinshasa's police recently (winter 2024) launched Operation Ndobo (lit. 'fishing hook' in Lingala) to 'capture' members of Kinshasa's street gangs in its nets in order to clean the streets of the capital. See also Pype (2022) on the fishing net imagery used to describe the mechanisms of state corruption during Joseph Kabila's rule.

8 With thanks to my student Priya Krishnamoorthy for suggesting this term.

Chapter 4. To be Suspended: The 'Black Heart' of Naples

1 When the Black and White association organized a football tournament in Castel Volturno and invited the Napoli player of Senegalese origin Kalidou Koulibaly to meet the children as a positive role model, Napoli football club refused permission, considering the place too dangerous.

2 Research in Castel Volturno started in autumn 2024, involving site visits and interviews with many migrants and social actors, facilitated by Sabrina Efionayi, Matar Coura, Luca Oliviero and Erica Ciccarelli, writer-activists in their own right with strong connections to the settlement, and whose guidance has proved invaluable.

3 The Regi Lagni is a historic feat of engineering, a unique example of rural architecture which, in its conception and size, remains significant testimony to Bourbon rule in the Kingdom of the Two Sicilies.

4 The official resident population of Castel Volturno is nearly 30,000 inhabitants, of whom 18 per cent are foreign residents, with 70.7 per cent from African countries.

5 A different type of illegal housing can be found in Bagnara, where many small houses resulting from self-construction without building permission are gradually sinking due to coastal erosion.

6 There has been a surfeit of output, including *Pummarò* (1990) by Michele Placido, *The Embalmer* (2002), *Gomorrah* (2008) based on the best-seller book by Roberto Saviano, the grim *Dogman* (2018) by Matteo Garrone, *Fortapàsc* (2009) by Marco Risi, the detective

series *La squadra, L'uomo in più* (2001) by Paolo Sorrentino and *Là-bas: Educazione criminale* (2011) by Guido Lombardi, inspired by the killing of six innocent migrants in September 2008.

7 The main character of the film is Maria, a young woman forcibly embroiled in the trafficking of infants born to immigrant sex workers, who helps the women escape by ferrying them across the Volturno River under cover of darkness. In the film the bodies of women are 'vessels for trade', as Maria's boss tells her reproachfully, but Maria decides to free the women.

8 'Nigerian mafia' is a loaded term; its criminality frequently used in the rallies of the far-right parties of Fratelli d'Italia and The League as a form of negative propaganda against migrants.

9 The unmarried white Italian woman took in Sabrina on an agreement of mutual trust, without formalizing custody, typical of the tradition of informal bonds of care between neighbours in Naples.

10 Graphically exemplified by the looks of white men in a bar at a young Nigerian we met there because of the lack of other meeting spaces. In their gaze Mary (pseudonym) was a hooker, not the discomfited girl speaking of her arrival three years ago, of not knowing anyone, of giving up on university to work in the fields to supplement her father's meagre earnings, of attending Italian classes in the hope of better days.

11 A Ghanaian activist who started the Miriam Makeba Association to promote black cultural activity, after the singer's sudden death in Castel Volturno during a solidarity concert she gave in 2008. There are other examples of political solidarity in those years, for example Ifi's recordings of her activities as a photographer and activist in Castel Volturno (commemorated after her death by Andrea Segre in a 2017 docufilm for Rai Cinema).

12 Figli del Bronx Production, Rai Cinema.

13 Trans: 'My place. An encounter in Parco Saraceno', Radio Tre. Tre soldi, 2019. https://www.raiplaysound.it/audio/2019/01/TRE-SOLDI---IL-MIO-POSTO-P01-803c089b-b042-4d38-85d9-9389ad3b1428.html

14 Paola Russo, who works at the association as a volunteer, says 'I was wrong believing that I was empowering these women: it ended up that they have enriched me. I have had the opportunity of entering a community of women who come from a culture very different from mine, which I presumed to know but did not know at all. I thought I had all the answers, and I didn't even understand the questions.'

15 Aptly illustrated by making us wait hours for an appointment and then cancelling it.

Chapter 5. Extendable Present: Making the Future through Smart Buildings, Sacred Mushrooms and Ghosts in Mexico City

1 See for instance the following groups: Mexico Remote Workers and Digital Nomads; Nomads Giving Back! Mexico City Community; International Travelers in Mexico City; Make Friends and BlaBla Language Exchange Mexico City; Digital Nomads & Expats in CDMX; or Mexico City (CDMX) Remote Workers & Digital Nomads. Or the following reels: https://www.instagram.com/reel/DFlAwhsxigb/?igsh=cGZ5YjhscmZpZHJ4, https://www.instagram.com/reel/DG3Z1eINLiA/?igsh=MWx4bnV3MWl0Z295bw%3D%3D, to give but two examples.

2 According to the American Citizens Abroad (ACA), one out of five Americans living abroad live in Mexico. According to Google Trends, on 22 December 2024, just after the election of Donald Trump, the phrase 'move to Mexico' reached maximum popularity (https://elpais.com/mexico/2025-02-24/estadounidenses-los-migrantes-con-mayor-presencia-en-mexico-una-radiografia-en-ocho-graficos.html).

3 https://www.jefaturadegobierno.cdmx.gob.mx/comunicacion/nota/unen-esfuerzos-gobierno-capitalino-unesco-y-airbnb-para-convertir-la-ciudad-de-mexico-en-capital-del-turismo-creativo

4 https://www.staynido.com/

5 https://centrotranspersonal.com.mx/nosotros.html

6 For an excellent contextualization of these practices, please refer to De la Torre Castellanos (2024).

7 https://www.betranspersonal.com/

8 The Santa Muerte's origins are unknown. Some religious experts trace the cult back to pre-Hispanic beliefs. Some believe it may be related to colonial religious sodalities that became secret sects in the eighteenth century. Others trace it back to the transformation of Spanish Catholic saints during colonization. Yet another explanation ties it to the arrival of Afro-Cuban Santeria practices in Mexico.

9 There are four main theories of the multiverse proposed by the current state of research in physics: (1) the 'Big Bang' could have produced many parallel universes; (2) the constant expansion of the universe can produce copies; (3) timelines can branch out through specific events; and (4) each parallel universe is based on a different mathematical structure and laws of physics (Fairchild, 2023).

References

Addie, J-P.D. (2024) 'Rhythmic infrastructure', in Addie, J-P.D., Glass, M.R. and Nelles, J. (eds.) *Infrastructural Times*. Bristol: Bristol University Press, pp. 25–46.

Adeniyi-Ogunyankin, G. (2024) 'Empowered, almost: Luxury consumption and the crooked urban life', *Urban Geography*, 45(9), pp. 1536–55. https://doi.org/10.1080/02723638.2024.2336849

Adichie, C.N. (2019) 'Still becoming: At home in Lagos with Chimamanda Ngozi Adichie', *Esquire*, 29 April.

Agamben, G. (1999) *The Man without Content*. Stanford, CA: Stanford University Press.

Agamben, G. (2009) *What is an Apparatus? And Other Essays*. Stanford, CA: Stanford University Press.

Agbiboa, D.E. (2018) 'Conflict analysis in "world-class" cities: Urban renewal, informal transport workers, and legal disputes in Lagos', *Urban Forum*, 29, pp. 1–18.

Agbiboa, D.E. (2022) *They Eat Our Sweat: Transport Labour, Corruption, and Everyday Survival in Urban Nigeria*. Oxford: Oxford University Press.

Ahmed, S. (2000) *Strange Encounters: Embodied Others in Post-Coloniality*. London: Routledge.

Akinwotu, E. and Bright, J. (2025) 'A Lagos community, destroyed in one day', *NPR*, 7 March.

Amin, A. and Thrift, N. (2013) *Arts of the Political*. Durham, NC: Duke University Press.

Amin, A. and Thrift, N. (2017) *Seeing Like a City*. Oxford: Wiley.

Amoore, L. (2023) 'Machine learning political orders', CRASSH seminar, Selwyn College, 7 March.

Bagnato, A. (2020) '"We must disembowel Naples!"', *AA Files*, 77, pp. 39–43.

Baldascino, M. and Casale, A. (eds.) (2005) *Donna tratta . . . ta*. Castel Volturno: Centro Fernandes.

Barad, K. (2007) *Meeting the Universe Halfway: Quantum Physics and the Entanglement of Matter and Meaning*. Durham, NC: Duke University Press.

Barad, K. (2012) 'On touching – The inhuman that therefore I am', *differences*, 23(3), pp. 206–23.

Barad, K. (2018) 'Troubling time/s and ecologies of nothingness: Re-turning, re-membering, and facing the incalculable', *New Formations*, 92, pp. 56–86.

Barber, D.C. (2016) 'The creation of non-being', *Rhizomes: Cultural Studies in Emerging Knowledge*, 29. https://doi.org/10.20415/rhiz/029.e10

Barbera, F. (2023) *Le piazza vuote: Riprendiamoci gli spazi della politica*. Rome: Laterza.

Barry, A. and Thrift, N. (2007) 'Gabriel Tarde: Imitation, invention and economy', *Economy and Society*, 36(4), pp. 509–25.

Bartolini, N. (2014) 'Critical urban heritage: From palimpsest to brecciation', *International Journal of Heritage Studies*, 20(5), pp. 519–33.

Benjamin, W. and Lacis, A. (1986) 'Naples', in Benjamin, W. (ed.) *Reflections: Essays, Aphorisms, Autobiographical Writings*. New York: Schocken, pp. 163–73.

Bennett, T. (2023) *Habit's Pathways*. Durham, NC: Duke University Press.

Beynon, H. and Hudson, R. (2021) *The Shadow of the Mine: Coal and the End of Industrial Britain*. London: Verso.

Biehl, J. and Adams, V. (2023) *Interference: Medical Anthropology for Worlds on Edge*. Durham, NC: Duke University Press.

Bola, G.B., Tshimanga, R.M., Neal, J., Trigg, M.A., Hawker, L., Lukanda, V.M. and Bates, P. (2022) 'Understanding flood seasonality and flood regime shift in the Congo river basin', *Hydrological Sciences Journal*, 67(10), pp. 1496–515.

Boudreau, J.A. (2022) 'City of repair: practicing the future in Mexico City', *International Journal of Urban and Regional Research*, 46(5), pp. 851–64.

Boudreau, J.A. (2023) 'Materializar la protección en su cuerpo y su entorno', in Zamorano Villareal, C., Capron, G. and Díaz Cruz, A. (eds.) *Dispositivos de seguridad*. Mexico City: CIESAS-Casa Chata, pp. 73–90.

Boudreau, J.A. (forthcoming) *City of Repair: A Street Epistemology of the Future City*. Berkeley, CA: University of California Press.

Bradley, R. (2021) 'On Black aesthesis', *Diacritics*, 49(4), pp. 21–53.

Bratton, B., Boyadjiev, N. and Axel, N. (eds.) (2020) *The New Normal*. Moscow: Strelka Press.

Breytenbach, B. (2009 [1984]) *Mouroir*. New York: Archipelago.

Bunting, M. (2023) *The Seaside: England's Love Affair*. London: Granta.

Calvino, I. (1974) *Invisible Cities* (1st edn). London: Secker & Warburg.

Calvino, I. (1977) *Invisible Cities* (2nd edn). London: Vintage.

Campbell, J. (2012) 'Lagos a success story?', Council on Foreign Relations, 9 July.

Carter, J.K. (2023) *The Anarchy of Black Religion: A Mystic Song*. Durham, NC: Duke University Press.

Castoriadis, C. (1997) *World in Fragments: Writings on Politics, Society, Psychoanalysis and the Imagination*. Stanford, CA: Stanford University Press.

Chandler, N. (2014) *X – The Problem of the Negro as a Problem for Thought*. New York: Fordham University Press.

Chaouche, S. (2022) 'Live performance as a multiverse: from the present moment to the transverse effect', *Junctures*. https://doi.org/10.34074/JUNC.22091

Clark, C. (2019) *Time and Power*. Princeton, NJ: Princeton University Press.

Colebrook, C. (2017) 'We have always been post-Anthropocene: The Anthropocene counterfactual', in Grusin, R. (ed.) *Anthropocene Feminism*. Minneapolis, MN: University of Minnesota Press, pp. 1–20.

De Boeck, F. (1998) 'Beyond the grave: History, memory and death in postcolonial Congo/Zaire', in Werbner, R. (ed.) *Memory and the Postcolony*. London: Zed Books, pp. 21–57.

De Boeck, F. (2005) 'The apocalyptic interlude: Revealing death in Kinshasa', *African Studies Review*, 48(2), pp. 11–32.

De Boeck, F. (2011) 'Inhabiting ocular ground: Kinshasa's future in the light of Congo's spectral urban politics', *Cultural Anthropology*, 26(2), pp. 263–86.

De Boeck, F. (2012) 'City on the move: How urban dwellers in Central Africa manage the siren's call of migration', in Schielke, S. and Graw, K. (eds.) *The Global Horizon*. Leuven: Leuven University Press, pp. 59–86.

De Boeck, F. (2015) '"Divining" the city: Rhythm, amalgamation and knotting as forms of urbanity', *Social Dynamics*, 41(1), pp. 47–58.

De Boeck, F. (2016) 'Corpus vile: Death and expendable youth in urban Congo', in Das, V. and Han, C. (eds.) *Living and Dying in the Contemporary World*. Berkeley, CA: University of California Press, pp. 743–69.

De Boeck, F. (2021) 'Death and the city: Necrological notes from Kinshasa', in Lancione, M. and McFarlane, C. (eds.) *Global Urbanism*. Abingdon: Routledge, pp. 166–75.

De Boeck, F. and Baloji, S. (2025) *Suturing the City: Living Together in Congo's Urban Worlds*. Leuven: Leuven University Press.

De Boeck, F. and Devisch, R. (1994) 'Ndembu, Luunda and Yaka divination compared', *Journal of Religion in Africa*, 24(2), pp. 98–133.

De Boeck, F. and Plissart, M-F. (2004) *Kinshasa: Tales of the Invisible City*. Ghent: Ludion/Royal Museum of Central Africa.

De Filippo, E. and Strozza, S. (eds.) (2012) *Vivere da immigrati nel casertano*. Milan: Franco Angeli.

De Groof, M. (2020) 'Congocene: The Anthropocene through Congolese cinema', in Gržinić, M. and Uitz, S. (eds.) *Rethinking the Past for a New Future of Conviviality*. Newcastle upon Tyne: Cambridge Scholars, pp. 88–109.

De la Torre Castellanos, A.R. (2024) 'Neo-Mexican home altars: Daily reconnections with the spirit of nature', *Journal of Beliefs & Values*, pp. 1–20. https://doi.org/10.1080/13617672.2024.2429950

Deleuze, G. (1994) *Difference and Repetition*. New York: Columbia University Press.

Deleuze, G. and Parnet, C. (1987) *Dialogues*. London: Athlone.

Devisch, R. (1990) 'The Mbwoolu cosmogony and healing cult among the Northern Yaka', in Jacobson-Widding, A. and van Beek, W. (eds.) *The Creative Communion*. Stockholm: Almqvist & Wiksell, pp. 111–28.

Devisch, R. (1993) *Weaving the Threads of Life*. Chicago, IL: University of Chicago Press.

Doe, B. (2023) *The Giant in Me*. Croydon: Sophos.

Dreyer, J. (2012) 'Shanghai and the 2010 Expo: Staging the city', in Bracken, G. (ed.) *Aspects of Urbanization in China*. Amsterdam: Amsterdam University Press, pp. 19–38.

Efionayi, S. (2022) *Addio, a domani: La mia incredibile storia vera*. Turin: Einaudi.

Elden, S. (2010) 'Land, terrain, territory', *Progress in Human Geography*, 34(6), pp. 799–817.

Elliott, B. (2015) 'Ground Zero: Walter Benjamin's urban politics', *Architecture and Culture*, 3(2), pp. 141–57.

Emezi, Y. (2018) 'Forced out', *The Weather Channel*, 27 December.

Fairchild, N. (2023) 'Multiverse, feminist materialist relational time, and multiple future(s)', *Qualitative Inquiry*, 30(6), pp. 493–501. https://doi.org/10.1177/10778004231176753

Felder, M., Stavo-Debauge, J., Pattaroni, L., Trossat, M. and Drevon, G. (2020) 'Between hospitality and inhospitality', *Urban Planning*, 5(3), pp. 55–66.

Ferreira da Silva, D.F. (2016) 'On difference without separability', in *32ª Bienal de São Paulo – Incerteza Viva* (exhibition catalogue), pp. 57–65.

Foster, J.G. (2023) 'From thin to thick: Toward a politics of human-compatible AI', *Public Culture*, 35(3), pp. 417–30.

Foucault, M. (2005) *The Order of Things*. Abingdon: Routledge.

Freud, S. (1957 [1915]) 'Thoughts for the times on war and death', in Strachey, J. (ed.) *Standard Edition of the Complete Psychological Works of Sigmund Freud, Volume XIV*. London: Hogarth, pp. 275–300.

Galloway, A.R. (2014) *Laruelle: Against the Digital*. Minneapolis, MN: University of Minnesota Press.

Ganic, E. (2023) 'Dredging, land reclamation and poverty in Makoko', *Dredging Today*, 20 February.

Gerdes, P. (2007) *Lunda Geometry: Mirror Curves, Designs, Knots, Polyominoes, Patterns, Symmetries*. Maputo: Universidade Pedagógica.

Geschiere, P. (2021) 'Dazzled by new media', *African Studies Review*, 64(1), pp. 71–85.

Ghosh, A. (2016) 'Writing the unimaginable', *The American Scholar*, 85(4), pp. 42–53.

Gilmore, R.W. (2007) *Golden Gulag: Prisons, Surplus, Crisis, and Opposition in Globalizing California*. Berkeley, CA: University of California Press.

Glissant, É. (1997) *Poetics of Relation*. Ann Arbor, MI: University of Michigan Press.

Glynos, J., Klimecki, R. and Willmott, H. (2012) 'Cooling out the marks', *Journal of Cultural Economy*, 5(3), pp. 297–320.

González de la Rocha, M. (1994) *The Resources of Poverty*. Oxford: Blackwell.

Gordon, A.F. (2008) *Ghostly Matters: Haunting and the Sociological Imagination*. Minneapolis: University of Minnesota Press.

Grosz, E. (2004) *The Nick of Time*. Durham, NC: Duke University Press.

Gruzinski, S. (2004) *La ciudad de México: Una historia*. Mexico City: Fondo de Cultura Económica.

Guma, P.K., Akallah, J.A. and Odeo, J.O. (2023) 'Plug-in urbanism', *Urban Studies*, 60(13), pp. 2550–63.

Guyer, J.I. (2007) 'Prophecy and the near future', *American Ethnologist*, 34(3), pp. 409–21.

Hall, S. (2006) 'Cultural studies and its theoretical legacies', in Chen, K-H. and Morley, D. (eds.) *Stuart Hall: Critical Dialogues in Cultural Studies*. Abingdon: Routledge, pp. 272–85.

Halpern, O. and Mitchell, R. (2022) *The Smartness Mandate*. Cambridge, MA: MIT Press.

Hansen, M.B. (2015) *Feed-Forward: On the Future of Twenty-First-Century Media*. Chicago, IL: University of Chicago Press.

Happe, K.E. (2024) 'Rethinking utopia as form', *Theory & Event*, 27(2), pp. 172–98.

Harney, S. and Moten, F. (2013) *The Undercommons: Fugitive Planning and Black Study*. Brooklyn, NY: Autonomedia.

Harrison, R. (2016) 'Archaeologies of emergent presents and futures', *Historical Archaeology*, 50(3), pp. 165–80.

Hayles, N.K. (2014) 'Cognition everywhere', *New Literary History*, 45(2), pp. 199–220.

Hayles, N.K. (2021) 'Three species challenges', in Lindberg, S. and Roine, H-R. (eds.) *The Ethos of Digital Environments*. Abingdon: Routledge, pp. 25–45.

Hazell, C. (2022) 'Thinking-with the human that we are', *Oscillations: Non-Standard Experiments in Anthropology, the Social Sciences, and Cosmology*, 1(1).

Hoffmann, D. (2017) 'Toxicity', *Somatosphere. Science, Medicine, and Anthropology*. Available at: https://somatosphere.net/2017/toxicity.html/

Hong, K.H. (2015) *Death Beyond Disavowal: The Impossible Politics of Difference*. Minneapolis, MN: University of Minnesota Press.

hooks, b. (2000) *Where We Stand: Class Matters*. London: Routledge.

Hopkins, A.G. (2024) *Capitalism in the Colonies: African Merchants in Lagos, 1851–1931*. Princeton, NJ: Princeton University Press.

Houdek, M. (2023) '(An) allegory of the undercommons: A rhetorical slipstream into the fugitive temporal horizon', *Rhetoric Society Quarterly*, 53(3), pp. 353–65.

Hughes, R. (2013 [1981]) *The Shock of the New: Art and the Century of Change*. New York: Alfred A. Knopf.

Hui, Y. (2016) *On the Existence of Digital Objects*. Minneapolis, MN: University of Minnesota Press.

Hunt, N.R. (2016) *A Nervous State: Violence, Remedies, and Reverie in Colonial Congo*. Durham, NC: Duke University Press.

Huyssen, A. (2003) *Present Pasts: Urban Palimpsests and the Politics of Memory*. Stanford, CA: Stanford University Press.

ICIR (2015) 'Group demand halt of Eko Atlantic City project', International Center for Investigative Reporting, 22 July.

James, W. (1956) *The Will to Believe and Other Essays*. Mineola, NY: Dover.

Judy, R.A. (2020) *Sentient Flesh: Thinking in Disorder, Poesis in Black*. Durham, NC: Duke University Press.

Kaplan, S. (2014) 'What makes Lagos a model city', *The New York Times*, 7 January.

Key Fowden, E., Çağaptay, S., Zychowicz-Coghill, E. and Blanke, L. (2022) 'Historical distance, physical presence and the living past', in Key Fowden, E., Çağaptay, S., Zychowicz-Coghill, E. and Blanke, L. (eds.) *Cities as Palimpsests?* Oxford: Oxbow, pp. 1–20.

Kienge-Kienge Intudi, R. and Liwerant, S. (2017) *Violence urbaine et réaction policière à Kinshasa*. Louvain-la-Neuve: Academia-L'Harmattan.

Kisukidi, N.Y. (2021) *IDS Lecture Series* (video). Available at: https://www.youtube.com/watch?v=BdhlbfAM3Q8

Kleinman, A. (2012) 'Intra-actions', *Mousse*, 34, pp. 76–81.

Klinenberg, E. (2019) *Palaces for the People*. London: Penguin.

Kolozova, K. (2020) *Capitalism's Holocaust of Animals*. London: Bloomsbury.

Lambertz, P. (2024) 'Underwater architecture: Scoop fishing (kopepa) & the psychology of fish'. Available at: https://banturivers.eu/en/underwater-architecture-scoop-fishing-kopepa-and-the-psychology-of-fish-written-by-peter-lambertz/

Lee, D. (2015) 'Absolute traffic: Infrastructural aptitude in urban Indonesia', *International Journal of Urban and Regional Research*, 39(2), pp. 234–50.

Lewis, O. (1961) *The Children of Sánchez*. New York: Vintage.

Linz, J. (2024) 'Imagining home in the ambivalent borderlands of Mexico City', paper presented at *Imag(in)ing the Urban Future*, CIFAR workshop, Mexico City, 29 October.

Linz, J. and Secor, A. (2021) 'Politics for the impasse', in Kingsbury, P.T. and Secor, A. (eds.) *A Place More Void*. Omaha, NE: University of Nebraska Press, pp. 199–212.

Lipp, B. and Dickel, S. (2023) 'Interfacing the human/machine', *Distinktion: Journal of Social Theory*, 24(3), pp. 425–43.

Livingston, J. (2019) *Self-Devouring Growth: A Planetary Parable as Told from Southern Africa*. Durham, NC: Duke University Press.

Liwerant, S. and Kienge-Kienge Intudi, R. (2019) *Puzzle de sorties de violence urbaine à Kinshasa (RD Congo)*. Louvain-la-Neuve: Academia-L'Harmattan.

Lucht, H. (2012) *Darkness before Daybreak*. Berkeley, CA: University of California Press.

Lucht, H. (2024) 'Distressed: Migrant underworlds and travels in hyporeality', *Anthropological Theory*, 25(3), pp. 268–88.

Ludvig, N. (2022) 'A cosmological neuroscientific approach to the soul of multiverse', *Open Journal of Philosophy*, 12, pp. 460–73.

Lynch, K. (1960) *The Image of the City*. Cambridge, MA: MIT Press.

Macry, P. (2018) *Napoli: Nostalgia di domani*. Bologna: Il Mulino.

Makengo, N. (2024) *Tongo Saa* [Documentary film]. Brussels: Twenty Nine Studio & Production.

Malabou, C. (2009) *What Should We Do with Our Brain?* New York: Fordham University Press.

Manning, E. (2020) *For a Pragmatics of the Useless*. Durham, NC: Duke University Press.

Marijsse, S. (2023) *Ambient technologies: An ethnography of extractive pathways in eastern DR Congo*. Unpublished PhD thesis, Universities of Antwerp & Leuven.

Marriott, D. (2018) *Whither Fanon? Studies in the Blackness of Being*. Stanford, CA: Stanford University Press.

Marriott, D. (2019) 'The X of representation', *New Formations*, 96, pp. 177–228.

Marriott, D. (2023) *On Effacement*. Stanford, CA: Stanford University Press.

Marshall, R. (2009) *Political Spiritualities: The Pentecostal Revolution in Nigeria*. Chicago, IL: University of Chicago Press.

Martínez, F. (2018) *Remains of the Soviet Past in Estonia*. London: UCL Press.

Massumi, B. (2019) *Architectures of the Unforeseen*. Minneapolis, MN: University of Minnesota Press.

Massumi, B. (2021) *Parables for the Virtual* (20th anniversary edn). Durham, NC: Duke University Press.

Massumi, B. (2024) 'The parainstitutional imperative: Towards an anarchism of value', unpublished manuscript, SenseLab, University of Montreal.

Mbembe, A. (2002) 'African modes of self-writing', *Public Culture*, 14(1), pp. 239–73.

Mbembe, A. (2020) *Critique of Black Reason*. Durham, NC: Duke University Press.

Mbembe, A. (2024) 'The earthly community', Holberg Prize Lecture. Available at: https://holbergprize.org/events-and-productions/holberguken-2024/holberglecture-2024-the-earthly-community/

Meillassoux, Q. (2012) 'The contingency of the laws of nature', *Environment and Planning D*, 30(2), pp. 322–34.

Miéville, C. (2015) 'Future city', in Folkerts, H., Lindner, C. and Schavemaker, M. (eds.) *Facing Forward: Art and Theory from a Future Perspective*. Amsterdam: Amsterdam University Press, pp. 43–53.

Miller, T. (2017) 'Utopian interiors', in Gandesha, S. and Hartle, J.F. (eds.) *The Spell of Capital: Reification and Spectacle*. Amsterdam: Amsterdam University Press, pp. 67–88.

Monaville, P. (2022) *Students of the World: Global 1968 and Decolonization in the Congo*. Durham, NC: Duke University Press.

Morton, T. (2014) 'Weird matters', in Arns, A. (ed.) *World of Matter*. Dortmund: HMKV, pp. 1–14.

Moten, F. (2018) *Stolen Life*. Durham, NC: Duke University Press.

Mpiana, A. (2025) *Parcours de l'eau*. Kinshasa: African Photography Initiatives.

Mudimbe, V.Y. (1973) *Entre les eaux*. Paris: Présence Africaine.

Mudimbe, V.Y. (1982) *L'Odeur du père*. Paris: Présence Africaine.

Mudimbe, V.Y. (1991) 'Reprendre', in Vogel, S. (ed.) *Africa Explores*. New York: Center for African Art, pp. 277–89.

Mudimbe, V.Y. (1994) *Le Corps glorieux des mots et des êtres*. Paris: Humanitas / Présence Africaine.
Mudimbe, V.Y. (2008) 'What is a line? On paradoxes about allegories of identity and alterity', *QUEST: An African Journal of Philosophy / Revue Africaine de Philosophie* 21, pp. 23–62.
Murray, M.J. (2015) 'City doubles: Re-urbanism in Africa', in Miraftab, F., Wilson, D. and Salo, K. (eds.) *Cities and Inequalities in a Global and Neoliberal World*. Abingdon: Routledge, pp. 106–23.
Musa Obadia, P., Milambo Kapia, P., Bonneure, A., Duca, R.C., Creta, M., Kayembe-Kitenge, T., Tytgat, J., Okitundu, D., Banza Lubaba Nkulu, C. and Nemery, B. (2023) 'Bombé: An undetermined substance', *Clinical Toxicology*, 61(12), pp. 1055–8.
Nail, T. (2018) *Being and Motion*. Oxford: Oxford University Press.
Nixon, R. (2013) *Slow Violence and the Environmentalism of the Poor*. Princeton, NJ: Princeton University Press.
Nooter Roberts, M. and Roberts, A.F. (eds.) (1999) *Memory: Luba Art and the Making of History*. Munich: Prestel.
November, V., Camacho-Hübner, E. and Latour, B. (2010) 'Entering a risky territory', *Environment and Planning D*, 28(4), pp. 581–99.
Nugent, P. and Locatelli, F. (eds.) (2009) *African Cities: Competing Claims on Urban Spaces*. Leiden: Brill.
Odysseos, L. (2019) 'Stolen life's poetic revolt', *Millennium*, 47(3), pp. 341–72.
Olaoluwa, J. (2022) 'Makoko residents reject planned demolition of their community', International Center for Investigative Reporting, 18 May.
Ortiz Maldonado, N. (2018) 'Presentificación del mundo', *Pensamiento de los Confines*, 31–32, pp. 329–34.
Packer, G. (2006) 'The megacity', *The New Yorker*, 13 November.
Panigrahi, S. (2017) 'Postmodern temporality in Italo Calvino's "Invisible Cities"', *Italica*, 94(1), pp. 82–100.
Perry, A. (2011) 'Making over Lagos', *TIME*, 26 May.
Petrarca, V. (ed.) (2016) 'Migranti africani di Castel Volturno', *Meridione. Sud e Nord nel Mondo*, XVI, pp. 31–240.

Porcaro, S. (2019) 'Microstoria di una periferia', in *Atti della XXI Conferenza Nazionale SIU*. Rome and Milan: Planum, pp. 84–92.

Porcaro, S. (2021) *L'estate è finita: Racconto corale del litorale domizio*. Naples: Monitor.

Povinelli, E.A. (2016) *Geontologies: A Requiem to Late Capitalism*. Durham, NC: Duke University Press.

Power, A. (1999) *Estates on the Edge*. London: Macmillan.

Pype, K. (2022) 'Fishing nets, Kabila's eyes and voter's card', in Adebanwi, W. (ed.) *Everyday State and Democracy in Africa*. Athens, OH: Ohio University Press, pp. 259–80.

Rancière, J. (1999) *Disagreement: Politics and Philosophy*. Minneapolis, MN: University of Minnesota Press.

Renaissance Capital (2011) 'A survey of the Nigerian middle class', 26 September.

Roy, A. (2022) 'Grammars of dispossession', in Amin, A. and Lancione, M. (eds.) *Grammars of the Urban Underground*. Durham, NC: Duke University Press, pp. 41–57.

Roy, A. and Ong, A. (2011) *Worlding Cities: Asian Experiments and the Art of Being Global*. Oxford: Wiley-Blackwell.

Savransky, M. (2024) 'In the fourth person singular', *Subjectivity*, 31, pp. 1–15.

Seck, A. (2023) 'Healing commonality', in Mbembe, A. and Sarr, F. (eds.) *To Write the Africa World*. Cambridge: Polity, pp. 216–39.

Segre, A. (2017) *Ibi* [film]. Rome: ZaLab.

Seif, A. (2022) 'Beirut as a palimpsest', in Key Fowden, E., Çağaptay, S., Zychowicz-Coghill, E. and Blanke, L. (eds.) *Cities as Palimpsests?* Oxford: Oxbow, pp. 387–410.

Serres, M. (1982) *The Parasite*. Baltimore, MD: Johns Hopkins University Press.

Serres, M. and Latour, B. (1995) *Conversations on Science, Culture and Time*. Ann Arbor, MI: University of Michigan Press.

Sharpe, C. (2016) *In the Wake: On Blackness and Being*. Durham, NC: Duke University Press.

Silva, S. (2011) *Along an African Border: Angolan Refugees and their Divination Basket*. Philadelphia, PA: University of Pennsylvania Press.

Simondon, G. (2007) *El modo de existencia de los objetos técnicos*. Buenos Aires: Prometeo.

Simondon, G. (2009a) 'The position of the problem of ontogenesis', *Parrhesia*, 7(1), pp. 4–16.

Simondon, G. (2009b) 'Technical mentality', *Parrhesia*, 7(1), pp. 17–27.

Simondon, G. (2009c) *La individuación a la luz de las nociones de forma e información*. Buenos Aires: Cactus-La Cebra.

Simondon, G. (2011) 'On the mode of existence of technical objects', *Deleuze Studies*, 5(3), pp. 407–24.

Simondon, G. (2012) *Curso sobre la percepción*. Buenos Aires: Cactus.

Simone, A. (2018) 'Precarious detachments: Circulating futures in urban Southeast Asia', in Low, S. (ed.) *Routledge Handbook on the Anthropology of the City*. Abingdon: Routledge, pp. 27–40.

Simone, A. (2020) 'O Vangelo, Africa', in Besteman, C., Cabot, H. and Kalir, B. (eds.) *Post-Covid Fantasies* [online]. *American Ethnologist* website. Available at: https://americanethnologist.org/features/pandemic-diaries/post-covid-fantasies/o-vangelo-africa

Simone, A. (2022) *The Surrounds: Urban Life within and Beyond Capture*. Durham, NC: Duke University Press.

Simone, A. (2024) 'Sub-group work programme note' [internal document]. Canadian Institute for Advanced Research's programme on Humanity's Urban Future.

Simone, A., Somda, D., Torino, G., Irawati, M., Ramesh, N., Bathla, N., Castriota, R., Vegliò, S. and Chandra, T. (2023) 'Inhabiting the extensions', *Dialogues in Human Geography*, 15(1), pp. 5–27. https://doi.org/10.1177/20438206231168896

Sluga, H. (2005) 'Foucault's encounter with Heidegger and Nietsche', in Gutting, G. (ed.) *The Cambridge Companion to Foucault* (2nd edn). Cambridge: Cambridge University Press, pp. 210–38.

Somotan, T. (2025) 'Popular planners: Newspaper writers, neighborhood activists, and the struggles against housing demolition in Lagos, Nigeria, 1951–1956', *Journal of Urban History*, 51, pp. 243–67.

Soyinka, W. (2020) 'Unsinkable city: Reflections on a lifetime in Lagos', in *Stranger's Guide. The Past and Future City: Lagos, Nigeria*. Austen, TX: Strangers' Guide.

Spillers, H.J. (1988) 'Moving on down the line', *American Quarterly*, 40(1), pp. 83–109.

Spurling, N. and Kuijer, L. (eds.) (2016) *Everyday Futures*. Lancaster: Institute for Social Futures.

St. Pierre, E.A. (2019) 'Post-qualitative inquiry in an ontology of immanence', *Qualitative Inquiry*, 25(1), pp. 3–16.

Stiegler, B. (1998) *Technics and Time, 2: Disorientation*. Stanford, CA: Stanford University Press.

Tadiar, N.X.M. (2022) *Remaindered Lives*. Durham, NC: Duke University Press.

The Economist (2015) 'Learning from Lagos', 2 July.

The Economist (2018) 'Redemption city is the anti-Lagos', 20 October.

The Guardian (2022) 'Supreme Court directs settlement in Lagos, Magodo conflict', 20 December.

Thieme, T. (2025) *Hustle Urbanism: Making Life Work in Nairobi*. Minneapolis, MN: University of Minnesota Press.

Tomás, A. (2022) *In the Skin of the City: Spatial Transformation in Luanda*. Durham, NC: Duke University Press.

Tompkins, J. (2011) 'Site-specific theatre and political engagement', *Theatre Journal*, 63(2), pp. 225–43.

Tsing, A. (1994) 'From the margins', *Critical Anthropology*, 9(3), pp. 279–97.

Tsing, A. (2013) *The Mushroom at the End of the World*. Princeton, NJ: Princeton University Press.

Veithen, C. (2024) 'After eviction, before emergence', *Environment and Planning D*, 43(1), pp. 115–37.

Virno, P. (2009) 'Natural-historical diagrams', *Cosmos & History*, 5(1), pp. 92–104.

Wagner, B. (2011) 'Global souths', *American Quarterly*, 63(2), pp. 391–7.

Watson, V. (2013) 'African urban fantasies', *Environment & Urbanization*, 26(1), pp. 215–31.

Wilhelm-Solomon, M. (2024) 'Uncommon rhythms: Rupture and retreat in inner-city Johannesburg', *Cidades*. Available at: http://journals.openedition.org/cidades/9366

Wright, P. (2020) *The Sea View Has Me Again: Uwe Johnson in Sheerness*. London: Repeater.
Xiang, B. (2021) 'Suspended: Seeking agency for change in the hypemobile world', *Pacific Affairs*, 94(2), pp. 233–50.
Zeiderman, A. and Dawson, K. (2022) 'Urban futures', *City*, 26(2–3), pp. 261–80.

Index